BEYOND ALL REASON

Moving Out of Logic

Into the Supernatural

REV. MARJORIE KUMMROW

Sweet Manna Ministries
www.sweetmanna.org

SWEET MANNA PUBLISHING

BEYOND ALL REASON Moving Out of Logic Into the Supernatural
Copyright © 2019 by Rev. Marjorie Kummrow. All Rights Reserved.

All rights reserved. No part of this book may be reproduced in any form or by any electronic or mechanical means including information storage and retrieval systems, without permission in writing from the author. The only exception is by a reviewer, who may quote short excerpts in a review.

This book and cover, was designed and prepared to be published by Tracey Kummrow at TNT Xpressions. tntxpressions@cox.net

Rev. Marjorie Kummrow

Printed in the United States of America

ISBN: 978-0-578-61912-5

info@sweetmanna.org
Scripture taken from the New King James Version® Copyright © 1982 by Thomas Nelson. Used by permission. All rights reserved.

DEDICATION

First and foremost, I dedicate this book to God who initiated the writing of it a decade ago, and confirmed His word to me, through various prophetic utterances from time to time, that encouraged me to write it. It would never be completed without the Lord's encouragement and motivation. I am eternally grateful to my Heavenly Father for revealing Himself to me and loving me unconditionally. I am thankful for the priceless gift of salvation obtained through the shed blood of Jesus, whose death, burial and resurrection reconciled me to the Father, and, for the precious gift of the Holy Spirit, who leads me into all truth, and guides me daily. This writing is His story; much more than my story. Therefore, I dedicate *"Beyond All Reason"* to the Lord as a First Fruit offering.

In addition, I dedicate this book to my three children, Billy, Kelly and Tracey, who were sent from heaven in bundles of love. They were tools in the hand of a wise Father, teaching me incredible lessons throughout my life. Each of them has loved Jesus since childhood. They all imitate a character of their Heavenly Father. They are three of the most generous people I know. Life without them would have been so dull and boring, for they brought such joy and laughter to our home. I love each of them more than they will ever know, this side of Heaven. I thank God that He chose me to be their mother. It has been a great honor to fulfill that role in their lives.

ACKNOWLEDGEMENT

I also want to acknowledge my daughter Tracey for her selfless sacrifice of countless hours spent in the editing of a book that could never be published without her permission. Without her input, editing, and graphic design skills for the cover, this book would have remained an unfinished manuscript. I want to thank Tracey for being patient with me for the numerous re-writes and additions made in the process. Words are not adequate to express my grateful heart for Tracey's contribution to the completion of *"Beyond All Reason."* I pray the Lord will reward her for her efforts in ways that will "bless her socks off."

FOREWORD

"Take the dare!" That's the adventurous challenge Marjorie Kummrow gives as she not only shares some of her life's adventures of walking with Jesus, she communicates her desire to see others live this kind of lifestyle of divine destinations. In *"Beyond All Reason — Moving Out of Logic into the Supernatural,"* Marjorie thoughtfully intertwines her story with an awakening that it's His-Story. Her testimony reveals the very present Testimony of Yeshua HaMashiach who miraculously empowers Believers by His Holy Spirit.

Take this book into your hands and you will sense the thrill of sitting with the author and enjoying her stories, testimony, and the fantastic applications she associates from the Biblical Text. Marjorie also places golden nuggets of scriptural foundations with theological substance for readers to build upon. Not only that, but you will find her research and practical knowledge will bring liberty *"Beyond All Reason."*

Dare to embark with this author into God's unknown destinations that reveal His destiny at every turn of the page. You'll discover the Biblical Text is brought to life for salvation, healing, the Gifts of the Holy Spirit, and so on. Take leaps of faith with Marjorie that will activate God's greater mindset and catapult you into living the Word *"Beyond All Reason."*

Dr. Pamala Denise Smith, GateView Ministries
Author, Apostolic-Prophetic Speaker, Trainer, and Teacher

I have known Rev. Marjorie Kummrow founder of Sweet Manna Ministries for 16 years now, and I know how committed she is concerning her Jewish Roots and the people of Israel and their salvation. She has been a part of my ministry (Mayim Hayim) for about 12 years. Marjorie graduated from CFTN (Christ for the Nations) a great school and has a degree from them as well as Mayim Hayim Ministries in Phoenix, AZ. Her book needs to be read by everyone who loves to SEE how God works in the life of a person who is "fully committed" to Him. Miracles upon miracles that would seem to be "Beyond All Reason" take place in these pages, full of wonder and awe in what God does. This is not commonplace either, but are "extraordinary miracles" in a vessel willing to follow the leading of the "Holy Spirit of God, and Gods Holy "Shekinah Glory" no matter what the cost. In Hebrew Gematria, the title of this book "Beyond All Reason" = 808, and so does "Gods Holy Shekinah," telling you who helped write this story. What a witness to discover that. Everyone reading this book will be blessed by Marjorie's honesty in it. I highly recommend it to you. You'll want to buy more copies after you read this to give away like I am doing. I feel richer for reading it, and I know it's been years in the making.

Rev. Barbara A. Di Gilio, founder of Mayim Hayim Ministries, Phoenix, AZ. Author, and Teacher of Hebrew Roots

TABLE OF CONTENTS

BEYOND ALL REASON

INTRODUCTION 1
CHAPTER 1   His Ways Are Beyond All Reason.................. 7
CHAPTER 2   Choose This Day.. 19
CHAPTER 3   Jesus Took the Wheel 39
CHAPTER 4   Washing of the Word 73
CHAPTER 5   Positive Obsession... 93
CHAPTER 6   He Is Alive... 111
CHAPTER 7   Divine Appointment... 119
CHAPTER 8   Go Tell Jesse 145
CHAPTER 9   Everything Hidden Will Be Uncovered......... 161
CHAPTER 10 The Suddenlies of God..................................... 175
CHAPTER 11 Discerning the Voice of God 193
CHAPTER 12 The Power of Forgiveness............................... 211
CHAPTER 13 He Came to Set the Captives Free.................. 223
CHAPTER 14 The Power of a Vow 247
CHAPTER 15 Code Blue.. 253
CHAPTER 16 My People Die From Lack of Knowledge... 259
CHAPTER 17 God Works in Mysterious Ways.................... 267
CHAPTER 18 Provision For the Vision 279
CHAPTER 19 Heaven's Connections...................................... 297
CHAPTER 20 More Adventures With the Lord.................... 307
CHAPTER 21 A Taste of Glory.. 319
CHAPTER 22 The Cost of Glory 341

INTRODUCTION

The book you hold in your hand has several decades of my experiences. It's hard to believe so many years have passed since the God of all creation invaded my space and changed the very fabric of my life. I was introduced to the supernatural realm of the Almighty, and I am walking in that realm ever since. Previous to that time, His realm had been hidden from me. Just as it still remains hidden from millions of Americans and the masses of foreign lands. I believe the "Realm of the Supernatural" is about to be unveiled in measures the world has not yet seen.

It is clear to me that we are living in a period called "the last days." I don't even hesitate to say that we are probably in the final days of "the last days." According to scripture, this world is going to grow darker and darker as we approach the return of the Lord Jesus. There is about to be a grand unveiling of the supernatural, and this also means Satan's supernatural powers will be released to deceive the people. However, Jesus will be demonstrating a power much more supreme than Satan's as we wind down six thousand years of history.

When I was in darkness, I had no idea that a supernatural invisible Kingdom of God was operating right alongside the system of the world familiar to me. I was a member of a congregation and rarely missed a Sunday morning service. However, I never saw anything supernatural take place from the pew where I sat. Perhaps it did, but at that time, I was spiritually blind and deaf. Unfortunately, I believe this is the same state most pew-sitters find themselves in today across America.

The world's system is ruled and operated by the fallen angels, with Lucifer, otherwise known as Satan, as their leader. They also move about in the supernatural, although it's the dark evil side of the supernatural. Most who are in darkness do not know that they are in darkness. They are Spiritually blind and cannot see into this Supernatural realm of light. Satan is a master of deception and the father of lies. We have all been programmed to believe the lies of propaganda that have entered our brains since childhood. Only when Jesus, the "light of the world," sheds His light upon us, do we recognize the extent of darkness we have been walking in. Even Satan worshipers believe they are walking in the light of Lucifer.

It is not until Jesus sets them free they realize just how dark their darkness was. We can only walk in the light shed in our hearts by the Holy Spirit. Everyone will walk at a different pace in this Kingdom of light. It depends on how much light is shed on the path they are on. I believe the amount of light the Holy Spirit shines upon each of us is in direct correlation with the desires of our hearts. Those that are on a quest for truth no matter what it will cost them are bound to receive more revelation than those that are indifferent to spiritual enlightenment.

I am writing this book out of obedience to the King of this invisible Kingdom of truth and light, Jesus the Messiah. I hope the Lord will somehow use my story to shed His light. There are areas where false concepts may be keeping His people in bondage and robbing them of all that they were meant to experience. I hope my experiences will propel your faith to believe that you too can climb higher and encounter elevated heights of His Glory.

I will be sharing a lifetime of my experiences with the Lord and His invisible Supernatural Kingdom as well as some experiences of others in my ministry. This book is about my life adventures with God. It is impossible to share the marvelous things the Lord has done without sharing the interaction I have had with others on this miraculous journey.

The emphasis of these stories is not about the people involved, although their occurrence is important. The focus is to glorify our God because He is alive and well on planet earth. He continually intervenes in the life of His Children, revealing His Love, His mercy, and His compassion. I hope my glory events will motivate you to press into the glory realm and experience a dominion hidden for those who desire to know God in a deeper and more fulfilling way. His glorious Kingdom of the supernatural is often called the Upside-down Kingdom, which will become apparent as we search the scriptures. His heart is to reveal Himself to you and to take you deeper into His presence. He will then lift you higher in His glory, and ground you to be effective while you are earthbound.

Upon entering this upside-down-Kingdom, we soon discover the ways of the world are in opposition to the principles of this supernatural Kingdom of God. All our lives, we have been taught to reason, to figure things out. We are challenged daily to solve problems and to come to reasonable and logical conclusions. In this world of ours, when things do not make sense, we become very frustrated and begin to search for common sense answers until it satisfies our sense of reason. Our ability to reason and solve problems is a gift from God, and we should be forever grateful for a sound mind that functions in such a manner. However, it may be a shock to you to discover that "reason" under the right circumstances can be an enemy to the supernatural way of the Lord. Walking in His Glory and the Supernatural realm is beyond all reason. Therefore, it is essential to learn to discern when to put reason on the shelf so that we can flow with the Holy Spirit. Before we embark on the following chapters of this book, I want to lay a foundation from the scripture reference that says:

Isaiah 55:8-9 8 For my thoughts are not your thoughts, neither are your ways my ways, saith the LORD. 9 For as the heavens are higher than the earth, so are my ways higher than your ways, and my thoughts than your thoughts.

The Lord spoke the above scripture to the Israelites through the prophet Isaiah to encourage Israel to repent and to enjoy an abundant life with Him. Within the contents, the Lord is encouraging His people to rely upon Him for all their needs. Even though they were spending their money on the necessities of life, they were unsatisfied. So then, what we can glean from this chapter is this truth — only when God's people do things His way will they find real satisfaction in life. The challenge is to trust His thoughts and His ways even when they are contrary to the natural mind.

God's ways are a mystery to us, and more often than not, His ways defy reason and logic. Hopefully, by the time we finish, you will have had a paradigm shift in your thinking. This process should make it easier to submit in obedience to the "Voice," beyond all reason. Our God, our King, and our Redeemer.

We have been programmed to believe that our world system is the only reality. When we cross over into the Kingdom of God, we are confronted with a new and seemingly outrageous way to navigate through life. For we soon learn the Kingdom of God is an upside-down Kingdom in so many ways, and we also discover the wisdom of this world no longer applies. To navigate in this invisible Kingdom of God, we must learn to put reason aside. Logic can hinder our ability to step out in faith. Too often we will miss the supernatural provision because we are stuck in the realm of reason. We must learn to trust the Almighty and His mysterious ways, which are truly beyond all reason. You are about to discover supernatural experiences that defy all reason.

The chapters that follow are true stories of how the God of creation has revealed Himself and asked things of me that are "beyond all reason." Therefore, it seems a very fitting title for this book. I hope you enjoy reading about God and His Kingdom reign in my life. My goal in sharing the things that I have learned in these years of walking with the King is that you will be encouraged to step out in faith and dare to trust the Lord when He asks something unreasonable. May the Lord of Glory be glorified in your life as you strive to be obedient to those things that are Beyond All Reason!

BEYOND ALL REASON: Moving Out of Logic Into the Supernatural

Chapter 1

HIS WAYS ARE BEYOND ALL REASON

I have so many awesome and glorious encounters with the God of creation that I want to share with you. Before I begin, let's have a short Bible Study together.

My motivational gift is of a teacher. Therefore, I find it nearly impossible to write this testimonial book without interjecting the study of the most incredible book ever written. I want to make you aware of some marvelous examples in the Bible, where the people of God obeyed the Lord by putting reason aside.

As we open the pages of the New Testament, we are confronted with one of many seemingly unreasonable facts. We are told a Virgin has conceived a child by the power of the Holy Spirit. Reason says, how can this be? How can child development within the womb of a woman be without the seed of a man? Even Mary questioned, how can this be? She confessed she had never known a man in this way, yet Mary had the faith to believe and willingly, she submitted to the will of God. She put all reason aside as she stepped into the supernatural realm of faith. Perhaps Mary remembered Sarah, whose pregnancy in her old age made no sense to the natural mind. Sarah, like Mary, had set aside reason and trusted the word of the Lord, who had spoken Sarah would have a child even though she was way past childbearing age. Sarah did not believe at first. She laughed at the ridiculous idea that she could bear a child at her age. The word of the Lord proved to be accurate, and she delivered Isaac at the age of ninety.

What about Abraham? He heard the Word of the Lord, left his country with his family to travel without knowing where he was going. Reason would insist on knowing where, how far, how long, and are there enough provisions to get there? Likewise, Noah chose to be obedient and built a ship in the middle of a desert, which would appear unreasonable, but Noah trusted the word of the Lord, not reason.

What about when Jesus healed the blind man by spitting in mud and applying the saliva clay mixture to his eyes? This is a bizarre action and beyond all reason.

John 9:6, When He had said these things, He spat on the ground and made clay with the saliva; and He anointed the eyes of the blind man with the clay. 7 And He said to him, "Go, wash in the pool of Siloam" (which is translated, Sent). So he went and washed, and came back seeing.

As we will see, the Bible is full of examples of faith that are beyond all reason. Like reading the story about Jonah getting swallowed up by a whale and remained alive, then vomited upon the seashore. The intellectual mind reasons this is some fairy tale and is unbelievable. Reason becomes such a great enemy to the intelligent person; it often keeps them from the gift of salvation. They have a hard time believing that a Savior was born of a virgin. Those intellectuals that think the Bible is full of fairy tales mock those of us that believe them to be true.

I think my favorite story beyond all reason is the story of Gideon and how his faith carried him to victory. Now, the Bible says God called Gideon to conquer the Midianites, whose numbers were as the sand on the seashore. Gideon had thirty-two thousand men, and still, the Midianites outnumbered Gideon's men by far.

Just imagine for a minute you are Gideon, and you are the Captain or the General of a military campaign, and you know that the enemy outnumbers you and your soldiers by thousands and thousands. You receive your order informing you to reduce the number of men. Then you are told to tell your soldiers, "Anyone fearful may go home." You now have ten-thousand men instead of thirty-two thousand against a horde of soldiers too vast to count, and you still have too many men.

Obediently, to test for the most observant and aware, you take them to a river and test them as to how they drink from the water. Those that bend the knee and drink from the water, you are to send home. The men that gather water in their hand and lap the water like a dog are to remain. They have not let their guard down. To your surprise, only three hundred men are left to fight the vast number of men that you have seen with your own eyes. What type of military strategy is this? You would think this is totally unreasonable. How in the world will three hundred men get out of here alive? If that's not enough, you are now instructed to tell your men to put their weapons down and pick up a trumpet, a pitcher, and a torch. The strategy for this battle is to surround the camp of the Midianites, then blow the trumpets, smash the pitchers, and wave the torches. No man of reason would submit his men to such a plan. Gideon was not a man of reason. He was a man of faith and trust and did set reason aside when the Lord spoke. He heard the word of the Lord, obeyed His orders, and won a great victory. Gideon won because the battle was the Lord's, and he chose to move into the realm of the supernatural.

The Lord brought confusion into the enemy's camp and won this battle for Gideon and his men. For the Midianites drew their swords against one another and fled in fear. Gideon won the war because he was obedient to the Word of the Lord. He did exactly what was commanded of him to do. I love this story because it shows us how the Lord will confound the mind of the wise with what may seem like foolish behavior for HIM to get all the glory. There was no question in the camp that night as to who won the victory in that battle.

Now let's take a look at that famous battle at Jericho. The Lord tells Joshua that He is going to give the city of Jericho into the hands of the Israelites, but not by conventional strategy. No, instead, they are to march around the city. They are to march once each day for six days in silence. The priests were an exception because they were instructed to blow their trumpets. We are told the city was small and about 7 acres. It was a walled city and was closed off to the Israelites due to the inhabitant's fear of the Israelites and their God. On the seventh day, they were to march around the city seven times. The priests were to blow their trumpets, then at the signal Joshua gave them — everyone was to shout. Well, as history records, the walls came tumbling down, and they took the city and the treasures within. It was their faith to believe the word of the Lord, and faith caused them to be obedient to a strategy that defied all reason. It was their obedience that caused the hand of God to bring down those walls.

Have you ever heard of an army going out to battle the enemy with the singers in front of the foot soldiers singing praises to the Lord? It doesn't sound like a very good military maneuver, yet this thing is recorded in the Bible. During the reign of Jehoshaphat, a great multitude of Moabites, Ammonites, and Syrians were plotting to annihilate Judah. Jehoshaphat, Judah's King at the time, humbled himself in prayer and sought the Lord for help, and all Judah stood with him.

Then through a prophet, the Lord spoke. "Listen, all you of Judah and you inhabitants of Jerusalem, and you King Jehoshaphat, thus says the Lord to you. Do not be afraid nor dismayed because of this great multitude, for the battle is not yours, but God's." The prophet told them that the next day, they were to go down against them and that they would not have to fight in this battle. They were to position themselves, to stand down, and watch the salvation of the Lord, for this was His battle. So, in the morning, Jehoshaphat appointed those who should sing to the Lord, and who should praise the beauty of His holiness, as they went out before the army saying: "Praise the Lord, for His mercy endures forever." The Bible goes on to tell us that when they began to sing, the Lord set ambushes against the enemies of Judah, and Judah's enemies were defeated.

These examples from the Old Testament are my favorites because they make the point that God's ways are not our ways. There are many more stories in the text that would drive this point home, but I am sure no more examples are necessary.

It is apparent that when the Lord speaks and gives us instructions on what to do to be victorious, our job is to be obedient and do whatever He instructs us to do, even when it does not seem rational to us. Had Gideon, Joshua, or Jehoshaphat, begun to reason and use their human logic, I dare say it certainly would have been an entirely different outcome for Israel and Judah. Perhaps they remembered what happened in the wilderness when reason overwhelmed the spies sent to spy out Canaan. When their eyes saw giants in the land of Canaan so vast that they felt like grasshoppers comparatively, reason took over and deceived them into believing it would be impossible to take the land, even though God said they could.

Faith would have said they could take the land no matter how many or how large the giants were because God said so. Only Joshua and Caleb had the faith to believe what God had said. They were able to see that God's ways defy all reason. Sadly, because reason deceived the tribes of Israel, they wandered in the wilderness for forty years. The lesson learned in the wilderness was likely on Gideon's, Jehoshaphat's, and indeed on Joshua's mind. Therefore, they were determined not to be defeated by reason again. Reasoning in each case would have cost them their lives.

Now can you see how reason can be an enemy of the Lord? As previously noted, "reason" can develop such a stronghold in the mind of an unbeliever or intellectual it becomes an enemy to their salvation. They cannot accept the truth that the Lord's ways are "beyond all reason."

Notice how each situation was handled differently by the Lord. There is no formula that one can use again and expect the same outcome. Jehoshaphat would have committed "the sin of assumption" during his military crisis, had he said, "I know what I will do. I will do what Gideon did." When you assume what the Lord will or will not do, it is very grievous to the Lord, and the outcome could be hazardous. When we, as the body of the Messiah, apply these principles to our own lives, we need to remember that we must never assume that what worked last time will work again. It is so important to understand that we must hear from God for every situation and then be obedient to what He has said to us to do for that circumstance, even when it seems ridiculous to our way of thinking. Obedience is the key to having God move on our behalf, in the supernatural realm.

I learned to put reason aside when I perceive I have heard the voice of the Lord. Doing so is not always easy. Often there is a battle that takes place in the mind. The chapters ahead are full of supernatural experiences that I have had where I put reason on the shelf and made a choice to walk by faith. Not one experience drives this point home as much as the next brief encounter with the God who defies all reason.

My daughter Tracey and I were watching TV in her living room. I was under the weather, with a very bad cold and feeling miserable. I mentioned to her how sick I was feeling. She immediately began praying for me, and then she said, "The Lord just said, stand up, turn around three times, blow your nose, and your cold will go away." I sat there thinking to myself that my daughter was just a babe in the Lord, and she could not have heard the voice of God. I was thinking, this is ridiculous, the Lord would not say something like that. There is no way that I am going to make a fool of myself and do what she just said.

I sat there, mulling these words over in my mind for some time. Then I arose from where I sat and left the room for the bathroom. While I was in there, I said to myself, "Oh, what the heck, what do I have to lose?" I turned around three times and blew my nose. To my great delight, my sinuses cleared up instantly, and every cold symptom disappeared immediately. I returned to the living room, apologizing to my daughter for what I had been thinking. It was my obedience to the word of the Lord that brought the healing. My reasoning almost cost me a blessing. This lesson has remained as a standard throughout my walk with the Lord. His ways are beyond reason.

After obeying Tracey's bazaar instructions, and discussing with her the many unreasonable acts spoken of in the Bible, I recalled the story of Naaman. This mighty man of valor was the Captain of the Syrian Army, and he had leprosy. The instructions from Elisha the Prophet, for his healing was to dip himself seven times in the river. Sounds crazy, doesn't it? Yet, Naaman was healed when he obeyed.

2 Kings 5:9-10 9 Then Naaman went with his horses and chariot, and he stood at the door of Elisha's house. 10 And Elisha sent a messenger to him, saying, "Go and wash in the Jordan seven times, and your flesh shall be restored to you, and you shall be clean."

Naaman like myself did not believe or obey and had wrong thoughts about it. It seemed beyond reason for a messenger of God to tell me to turn around and blow my nose or for Naaman to dip into a muddy river like the Jordan when he could dip into a clean river where he came from. Especially in Naaman's case with his skin condition and the bacteria from the water.

2 Kings 5:12-14 12 Are not the Abanah and the Pharpar, the rivers of Damascus, better than all the waters of Israel? Could I not wash in them and be clean?" So he turned and went away in a rage. 13 And his servants came near and spoke to him, and said, "My father, if the prophet had told you to do something great, would you not have done it? How much more then, when he says to you, 'Wash, and be clean'?" 14 So he went down and dipped seven times in the Jordan, according to the saying of the man of God; and his flesh was restored like the flesh of a little child, and he was clean.

It was a lesson on obedience. Both of us were healed when we obeyed the voice of the Lord that was beyond reason.

Let me interject something important right here before we move on any further. Learning to hear the voice of the Lord is a process that takes time to develop. Not everyone is able to listen to the Lord with the same degree of accuracy. I realize each of us matures in the Lord at different levels, and likewise, as we grow, so does our spiritual hearing.

The Lord speaks in various ways. First and foremost, His voice is recorded in the Bible. The Bible is our instruction book, and the truth contained within it is our guide for Godly living. Even when the Lord speaks to us in that small still voice within us, He will never say anything contrary to His written word. At the same time, the Holy

Spirit's job is to lead us into all truth. He leads each of us, and He will never require something of us contrary to the written word. It is imperative to know our Bible. It is the standard to judge whether we are listening to His voice or another. Secondly, when it comes to personal guidance, I always ask Him to confirm His word to me in some way or through someone, for the Lord does use other people to speak to us.

Even Gideon did not set reason aside to obey the Lord until he was sure as to whose voice he had heard. Gideon asked for confirmation so that he could be positive that he heard the voice of God Almighty. He asked the Lord to confirm His word to him by giving him a sign.

Judges 6:17, Then he said to Him, "If now I have found favor in Your sight, then show me a sign that it is You who talk with me.

Judges 6:36-40 So Gideon said to God, "If You will save Israel by my hand as You have said— "look, I shall put a fleece of wool on the threshing floor; if there is dew on the fleece only, and it is dry on all the ground, then I shall know that You will save Israel by my hand, as You have said." And it was so. When he rose early the next morning and squeezed the fleece together, he wrung the dew out of the fleece, a bowlful of water. Then Gideon said to God, "Do not be angry with me, but let me speak just once more: Let me test, I pray, just once more with the fleece; let it now be dry only on the fleece, but on all the ground let there be dew." And God did so that night. It was dry on the fleece only, but there was dew on all the ground.

The Bible is clear that two or three witnesses should establish every word. So, this is my guideline, and it will serve you well if it becomes your guideline as well.

There is another way to judge the leading of the Lord in your circumstances. Pray for peace within your heart and mind whenever you are struggling with a decision. If you do not have peace about something, it may indicate it is not the right time, or it is not the right thing to do. Sometimes the timing may be off, and waiting on the Lord for a while may bring the calmness needed to proceed. Sometimes peace never comes, which may mean the Lord is going to move you in another direction.

These guidelines are helpful to me, and I have learned to rely on them through the years of learning to discern the Lord's guidance in my life. I hope they will be helpful to you as well.

BEYOND ALL REASON: Moving Out of Logic Into the Supernatural

Chapter 2

CHOOSE THIS DAY

Now I want to take you on an incredible journey in time when I had my first encounter with the Creator of the Universe, your Father, and mine.

My day started just like any ordinary day in my hometown. I had driven my car into town and was sitting in it, waiting for a friend when Heaven opened up. God came calling, making His grand entrance on the stage of my life. God spoke, and that was the day that opened the door to the supernatural. The memory of the first time the Lord spoke to me is indelibly engraved in the crevasses of my brain stored in my memory bank forever. Thinking about the day that God made His grand entrance on the stage of my life conjures up emotions that words are inadequate to describe, yet I will try. The memory of the day that changed my life for the better is as fresh today as if it just happened yesterday. The reality, though, is it happened decades ago.

I was thirty-eight years old at the time. At the age of thirty-eight, I was living a life that most women only dream about. I was married and had three children, two boys and a girl. My firstborn son William Jr; known as Billy, and my younger son, Kelvin or Kelly, and then my daughter Tracey. At the time of my encounter with God, all three of our children were in a private school. Together, my husband and I owed a successful Construction, Real Estate, and Interior Design business. Our success allowed us to travel to several countries. Some of these trips were paid for by the manufacturers that we represented. We won several vacations abroad due to the high sales volume that we did together. My husband had built me the home of my dreams, a beautiful Country French Chateau; that had taken me years to design. I had everything this materialistic world could provide. Our social life was very active as we had many friends, neighbors, business associates, and relatives that shared our experiences. If you were on the outside looking in, it would have looked like a fairy tale come true. However, what was happening behind closed doors was an entirely different matter.

Our marriage can best be described as a roller coaster ride. We either were experiencing the highest of highs or the lowest of lows. I do, however, have precious memories of our life together with our rambunctious creative and funny kids. I remember telling our pastor at one time we loved each other only 50% of the time and hated one another 50% of the time. We had our demons to deal with and the emptiness within, we were expecting the other one to fulfill. So, consequently, we went looking for something or someone to fill and satisfy that empty void. I did not understand at the time, the undeniable truth. Every human ever created by our Creator has a vacuum shaped emptiness reserved for God alone. Only God Himself can fill and satisfy the empty vacuum within the human soul. Without God, each of us in our own way, tries to fill that void with all sorts of things, a new car, a bigger house, a pool, a trip, another child, a change in career, an affair, more education, a different spouse, another drink, a drug, a new boat, a dog, more money, a summer home, more food, a different drug, or different friends, change of furniture, you name it, and we will try to stuff some impostor, into that God-shaped vacuum and try to make it fit. Oh, these things may bring a sense of satisfaction for a little while, but that sense of well-being fades because it is the wrong component to fit into that unseen vacuum waiting for God. The Lord allowed me to try to fill my vacuum shaped space up with just about everything this world has to offer. I didn't know what was missing; I just knew that something was missing. Thankfully, God knew the dimension that would fit my empty void was Himself!

I was sitting alone in my car when the God of the Universe arrested me! Just imagine for a minute what it might be like to be sitting alone in your vehicle, and a thundering voice invades your car...yet you see no one. It's just you and a "VOICE," a voice larger than life. Well, this is what happened to me on that day many years ago. I heard that voice say, "CHOOSE THIS DAY WHO YOU WILL SERVE — HIM OR ME?" I froze and was completely undone, not knowing how long I sat there stunned by the words echoing over and over in my ears. They pierced my heart like a two-edged sword. HIS words left me breathless as they invaded my car and my mind. They were decision-making words of correction, yet the overwhelming feeling was not of condemnation, but instead, they were words that conveyed complete acceptance, beckoning me to make the right decision. I instinctively knew I had just heard the VOICE OF GOD, only it did not compute with anything stored within my thinking process. God did not speak to people today, or, so I thought.

However, He just did! I knew He was asking me to make the most critical decision of my lifetime. He was asking me to choose Him above everything and everyone else. Intuitively, I knew that I might not have another opportunity to make this choice again. This moment in time could very well decide my eternal state, and I knew it. This was my Kairos moment.[1] I knew I would never walk this same way again. It was now or never! The same voice that spoke the world into existence had invaded my car and spoke volumes to me in these few words, "CHOOSE THIS DAY WHO YOU WILL SERVE — HIM OR ME?"

The voice I heard that day was not just a thundering sound that exhibited strength and authority; it was a voice that penetrated profound truth within my heart. At this moment, I was naked before my Creator. I was like Adam and Eve in the garden, naked and ashamed. Without another word, my sin exposed for me to see who I was, and I did not like what I saw. Although He did not say it, His words were conveying another message as well; they were saying, stop it, turn around, and follow me.

My mind was racing because it was trying to compute and make sense of this supernatural divine intrusion into my life. I was gathering information from the knowledge stored in my brain, trying to make

---

[1] A Kairos moment is an opportune time when a decision must be made, because this exact circumstance may never repeat itself again.

some logical sense of what was taking place. But there was nothing stored in the compartment of my brain called "reason" that could explain what had just happened. This Kairos moment was beyond all reason. I began to analyze that something supernatural had just happened to me. The Holy One, The One who has all authority in Heaven and on Earth, The One who had created all Universes had just spoken to me. The One who had placed every star in the heavens and called them by name had just called out to me. The One who set the boundaries of the sea, telling the waves, this far, no further, had just called me to set new boundaries in my life. An awestruck wonder, type of fear filled my soul. Somehow, I understood the moment I heard these words, "CHOOSE THIS DAY WHO YOU WILL SERVE — HIM OR ME?" I knew what choice I would make. There was no contest I knew I would walk away from the sin in my life. More importantly, I was choosing HIM and not him. Yes, I wanted to walk away from intentional sin, for I knew that I would never again find myself in the arms of the man with whom I was having an affair. For the moment I heard THAT VOICE, I had decided to choose HIM above him.

The awesomeness of God Himself visiting me and asking me to choose to serve HIM was not lost on me. He came looking for me; I was not consciously looking for HIM. HE knew the exact moment that I would be willing to give it all up for HIM. My life had been a quest to fill that vacuum shaped hole in my heart, unaware that the search I had been on was a pursuit for God Himself. At that moment, I knew deep within my soul; He was what I had been looking for all along. I don't know how long I sat there. It seemed as if I was frozen in a time capsule. So much had happened; so much had changed during that moment in time. My plans for the day had been changed in an instant. I had parked the car, waiting for the man with whom I was having an affair. When HIS VOICE changed my course for the day, and the plan for the rest of my life. Finally, I could focus on where I was and what had just happened to me. I, without the slightest hesitation, found my car keys, turned on the ignition and drove away knowing that I would be traveling on a far different road from then on, a route much too narrow to include my partner in sin. With the Thundering Words of Authority echoing over and over in my ears, I headed for home.

I drove away in disbelief that the God of the Universe had just spoken to me, yet I knew that He had. There was no doubt in my mind that this was indeed the Voice of God. I just could not come to grips with the fact that God had spoken to me. I mistakenly believed He only spoke to the prophets of old. That Voice had not only called me to repentance, but it also apprehended me and set me free from the sin that had enslaved me, and set me on fire for Him. I left with such a burning desire to know the One whose Voice had just reached into the depth of my soul. This Kairos moment in time was so sacred to me that I never shared it with anyone until many years later. That awesome day began a gloriously beautiful and sometimes sorrowful journey with my Savior, and Restorer of my soul. That same Voice that called me to repentance has been guiding and directing me ever since. These days, if several days happen to go by without that Voice, I am saddened because His Voice is my lifeline. I love the intimacy I have had throughout the years listening to and being guided by "That Voice."

This book is filled with my amazing experiences with the God of creation. He introduced Himself to me with His thundering Voice so many years ago. It was, in fact, His Voice who instructed me to write this book in the first place. I have made many attempts to share my story, but truthfully, I find it very difficult because it is not my story, it is His story, and I want to tell it well. It is His story of how He came looking for me and how He has been interacting in my life ever since. I do not want to fail in my effort to convey the awesomeness of God, His Love, and His desire to make Himself known to each of us. I hope and pray the words in this book will end up in a finished manuscript, bound into a published book that has found its way into your hand to read. I desire everyone reading this book will come away with a quest for God, unlike anything they have ever encountered. Not because of my life experiences, but because of the One who orchestrated those life experiences. He wants to orchestrate your life experiences, as well. Jesus is alive, He is no respecter of persons, and what He has done for me He wants to do for you. He wants to be known as alive and well on planet earth today, not some historical figure of yesteryear.

When I first heard the voice of our Lord, I did not know of one other person who had experienced anything as I had. I guarded my experience because I did not want anyone to think that I was having a mental breakdown. For, this is what the world thinks when people confess to hearing voices. I did not know at the time the Lord had many more like me all over the world. There were people that He had spoken to, right in my hometown. As time went on, the Lord saw to it that I was introduced to many other Christians that have heard the voice of the Lord. What I was soon to discover was the Lord's Kingdom is operating and advancing in another dimension. A supernatural sphere hidden from me was opening for my discovery. Choosing to follow after the One whose voice thundered in my car was the doorway to this unseen supernatural realm.

God is Speaking. Are you listening?

We have been lied to over and over again, even from the pulpits of America. I am not saying that all these lies are intentional; they are not. I was told God stopped speaking to His people after John received the revelation of Jesus on the island of Patmos around 70-95 A. D. Also, I heard the revelation of Jesus is the final book in the Bible, and is supposedly the last word heard from God to the Jews, Christians, and mankind. Even though pastors are merely repeating what they were taught, this teaching is in error. My own experience and others that I have met or have read about are in direct opposition to this teaching. God has always communicated with a remnant of people around the world. Guess what? He wants to communicate with you!

There are several ways that the Lord communicates with us. First and foremost, He communicates with us through the written word, the Bible. The Lord spoke audibly to the prophets of old for four thousand years, recorded in the Old Testament. God came to earth in the form of the man Jesus, and He spoke volumes to us. He also has spoken to us through the authors of the New Testament who were trained by Jesus. The Lord continues to talk to us today through many people that have a prophetic function and through various anointed vessels that He chooses to use. I pray that HE is speaking to you through this book.

Sometimes to the intellect mind, the Bible is ridiculed and thought of as a book of fabricated stories. I want to interject some facts about the Bible at this point that should silence even the most intellectual and solidify the accuracy of the Bible. The Bible has stood the test of time. It is the only book that has accurately foretold the future. In total, the Bible is twenty-seven percent prophecy predicting many things, including the rise and fall of nations and kings throughout history. Since the Bible's emphasis is on the King of Kings, Jesus, I did some research on the fulfillment of the prophecies concerning just Jesus' first and second coming. There are many discrepancies in the actual number of prophecies about our Lord in the Old Testament because of repetitive predictions by authors at different times in history. Many of them have recorded the same events predicted to occur. In total, we have around seven hundred references in the Hebrew text about the coming of the Messiah.

First, let's look at the astonishing fulfillment of the prophecies that Jesus fulfilled in His first coming. From Genesis to Malachi, prophecies foretell the exact events of Jesus' life. You can find a prediction in the Old Testament speaking of His place of birth and the tossing of lots for his garments. These predictions span four thousand years, written by different prophets at various times in history. All these prophecies were written long before the man Jesus was ever born. The accuracy in which Jesus fulfilled them is astounding!

Mathematicians have figured the odds of one single person fulfilling all seven hundred of these prophecies is so astronomical, our minds could not possibly comprehend it. History confirms Jesus did fulfill every single prophecy written of his first coming. For instance, Dr. Peter Stoner has estimated the odds. With only forty-eight of approximately three hundred Old Testament prophecies about the Messiah to be fulfilled in one person, it is truly amazing. He calculated the odds at 1 in 10 to the 157th power.[2]

What it means for these prophecies to be fulfilled by just one person is 1 in:

1,000,000,000,000,000,000,000,000,000,000,000,000,000,000,000,000,000,000,000,000,000,000,000000,000,000,000,000,000,000,000,000,000,000,000,000,000,000,000,000,000,000,000,000.

This number continues on and on, and the zeros would fill up several pages. Jesus, however, fulfilled more than forty-eight prophecies. He fulfilled around seven hundred. If you calculate the odds, those calculations will fill an entire book full of zeros. These odds are so beyond reason, to what our natural minds can comprehend. One must conclude none of these predictions or their fulfillment has happened by chance. It is only possible through the supernatural hand of God Almighty, who has written history in advance of it happening through the prophets of old. History, after all, is His story.

There are two hundred sixty chapters in the New Testament. Dr. Mark Hitchcock has a book on prophecy in which he mentions there are more than three hundred references to the Lord's coming in the New

---

[2] *"Science Speaks"* by Dr. Peter Stoner 1958

Testament. Prophecy makes up twenty-eight and one-half percent of the New Testament. There are over three hundred prophecies concerning Christ's Second Coming in the New Testament, making one out of every thirty verses, prophetic. He also states there are one hundred nine prophecies of His first coming, which the Lord completely fulfilled. There are two hundred twenty-four that forecast His Second Coming yet to be fulfilled. Twenty-six books of the New Testament refer to the promise of His coming, and three of those were personal letters to individuals.[3] The rest highlighted this important doctrine preached in the earliest days of the Church. It would do the Church well if these truths were taught fervently today.

This statistical data are facts, not just someone's opinion. An honest intellectual must come to terms that their opinion is contrary to the mathematical facts of history and the prophecies of the Bible. I believe this type of information is so important because of all the negative input in our culture today concerning the Bible. Those who continue to think it's a book full of fairy tales and old wives' tales have not yet considered the astronomical odds presented here. They have not yet come in contact with the risen Lord, Jesus, personally. Jesus is the volume of the book we call the Bible. All you have to do is ask God to prove His existence to you. He will if your heart is sincere. He wants to be intimately acquainted with you. Jesus has shown us that the Word of God is true and trustworthy. We have great hope Jesus will indeed fulfill the remaining prophecies about Himself. He fulfilled each

---

[3] *"The End"* by Dr. Mark Hitchcock, page 4

prophecy concerning his first coming, even though some of those prophecies were written about him long before He was ever born. The Bible is the only book with a voice that speaks accurately about events before they happen.

It is a thrill and wonderment to hear the voice of the Lord when you are "born again" and baptized in the Holy Spirit. You may hear His voice either audibly or by a still small voice from deep within where the Holy Spirit resides. The truth is, however, that if the Lord would choose to never speak again to anyone, we have in the written text enough information to last us a lifetime. The Bible is the greatest book ever written. From the beginning of time, God's creation heard the voice of the Lord. The Lord walked with and communicated with Adam and Eve in the Garden of Eden. The first words that are recorded of God speaking to Adam and Eve were words of blessing.

Genesis 1:28-30 28 Then God blessed them, and God said to them, "Be fruitful and multiply; fill the earth and subdue it; have dominion over the fish of the sea, over the birds of the air, and over every living thing that moves on the earth." 29 And God said, "See, I have given you every herb that yields seed which is on the face of all the earth, and every tree whose fruit yields seed; to you it shall be for food. 30 Also, to every beast of the earth, to every bird of the air, and to everything that creeps on the earth, in which there is life, I have given every green herb for food"; and it was so.

After the Lord God put the man Adam in the garden, He told him that he could eat from every tree in the garden except one.

Genesis 2:16-17 16 And the LORD God commanded the man, saying, "Of every tree of the garden you may freely eat; 17 but of the tree of the knowledge of good and evil you shall not eat, for in the day that you eat of it you shall surely die."

Moving on within the text we find the Voice of the Lord as He continues,

> *Genesis 3:1-13 1 Now the serpent was more cunning than any beast of the field which the LORD God had made. And he said to the woman, "Has God indeed said, 'You shall not eat of every tree of the garden'?" 2 And the woman said to the serpent, "We may eat the fruit of the trees of the garden; 3 but of the fruit of the tree which is in the midst of the garden, God has said, 'You shall not eat it, nor shall you touch it, lest you die.'" 4 Then the serpent said to the woman, "You will not surely die. 5 For God knows that in the day you eat of it your eyes will be opened, and you will be like God, knowing good and evil." 6 So when the woman saw that the tree was good for food, that it was pleasant to the eyes, and a tree desirable to make one wise, she took of its fruit and ate. She also gave to her husband with her, and he ate. 7 Then the eyes of both of them were opened, and they knew that they were naked; and they sewed fig leaves together and made themselves coverings. 8 And they heard the sound of the LORD God walking in the garden in the cool of the day, and Adam and his wife hid themselves from the presence of the LORD God among the trees of the garden. 9 Then the LORD God called to Adam and said to him, "Where are you?" 10 So he said, "I heard Your voice in the garden, and I was afraid because I was naked; and I hid myself." 11 And He said, "Who told you that you were naked? Have you eaten from the tree of which I commanded you that you should not eat?" 12 Then the man said, "The woman whom You gave to be with me, she gave me of the tree, and I ate." 13 And the LORD God said to the woman, "What is this you have done?" The woman said, "The serpent deceived me, and I ate."*

We are not privileged to know the amount of time that elapsed between the time of the Lord's commandment to Adam and the disobedient act of Adam and Eve to disregard the Lord's instructions and to believe the lie of the serpent. Eve, believing the lie of the serpent, ate the forbidden fruit and giving it to her husband, he ate it as well. Death to their innocence came immediately, for they hid from God, and they became ashamed. [4]

When asked by God why they were hiding, Adam replied he hid because he heard the voice of the Lord in the garden and was naked and afraid.[5] This verse indicates to us that even after their act of disobedience, they were still able to hear the voice of God. Death came to them spiritually, for they had to leave the Garden of God and live in a world cursed because of their sin. Physical death would eventually come to them even though their bodies were created to live forever. The Bible records that Adam lived for nine hundred thirty years.[6] It is interesting to note that elsewhere in the Bible it is recorded that a thousand years is like one day to the Lord.[7]

---

[4] The implication is that they were ashamed because they hid from God. Genesis 3:7 And the eyes of both of them were opened, and they knew they were naked; and they sewed fig leaves together and made themselves coverings. Earlier when they were naked, they were not ashamed. Genesis 2:25 And they were both naked, the man and his wife, and they were not ashamed.

[5] Genesis 3:10 So he said, "I heard Your voice in the garden, and I was afraid because I was naked; and I was afraid.

[6] Genesis 5:5 And all the days that Adam lived were nine hundred and thirty years: and he died.

[7] 2 Peter 3:8 But beloved do not forget this one thing, that with the Lord one day is as a thousand years, and a thousand years as one day.

That being the case, Adam, due to his sin, did not live to fulfill one entire day from the Lord's perspective. The fallen nature of Adam and Eve would affect all their offspring throughout the history of mankind. The curse of death came because of their inability to say "no" to the serpent. The devil was tempting them by appealing to their fleshly desires. Things are no different today. Satan continues to tempt us to sin and lie to us, which shortens our lives.

We see from the account of Adam and Eve that the Lord desired to communicate with His creation from the very beginning. From cover to cover of the Bible, there are recorded messages to us from the Lord God. He spoke in ages past through the prophets who were called to record His Words. Compiled into the books of the Old Testament, these ancient documents have stood the test of time for all generations. The voice of God instructs us in the books of the Old Testament, and the New Testament writers recorded precious words of Jesus and an account of his brief time with them. An example of this is when His voice was heard from Heaven when Jesus was baptized by John. Also, the thundering voice on the mountain of transfiguration.

The Baptism of Jesus

Matthew 3:13-17, 13 Then Jesus came from Galilee to John at the Jordan to be baptized by him. 14 And John tried to prevent Him, saying, "I need to be baptized by You, and are You coming to me?" 15 But Jesus answered and said to him, "Permit it to be so now, for thus it is fitting for us to fulfill all righteousness." Then he allowed Him. 16 When He had been baptized, Jesus came up immediately from the water; and behold, the heavens were opened to Him, and He saw the Spirit of God descending like a dove and alighting upon Him. 17 And suddenly a voice came from heaven, saying, "This is My beloved Son, in whom I am well pleased."

The Transfiguration

Luke 9:28-36, 28 Now it came to pass, about eight days after these sayings, that He took Peter, John, and James and went up on the mountain to pray. 29 As He prayed, the appearance of His face was altered, and His robe became white and glistening. 30 And behold, two men talked with Him, who were Moses and Elijah, 31 who appeared in glory and spoke of His decease which He was about to accomplish at Jerusalem. 32 But Peter and those with him were heavy with sleep; and when they were fully awake, they saw His glory and the two men who stood with Him. 33 Then it happened, as they were parting from Him, that Peter said to Jesus, "Master, it is good for us to be here; and let us make three tabernacles: one for You, one for Moses, and one for Elijah"—not knowing what he said. 34 While he was saying this, a cloud came and overshadowed them; and they were fearful as they entered the cloud. 35 And a voice came out of the cloud, saying, "This is My beloved Son. Hear Him!" 36 When the voice had ceased, Jesus was found alone. But they kept quiet, and told no one in those days any of the things they had seen.

These two accounts tell us that during the time Jesus walked on this earth, the same voice Adam and Eve heard four thousand years earlier was heard by those that had ears to hear. Both of these accounts record the voice they heard was the "Father's" voice thundering from Heaven. Having had this same experience in my car, I can relate with their Holy moment of wonderment. We notice in both of these accounts the Father was announcing His pleasure with His Son.

We have been told God was silent during the four hundred years between the death of the Old Testament prophets and the life of Jesus. I am sorry, but I do not believe this to be true, and I intend to discredit this statement by looking at historical documentation during this period. It is true that nothing new is recorded in the Bible, but I believe, God has always had a remnant that He has spoken with to accomplish His will in history.

Probably the most famous person living during this four-hundred-year period was the conquering king, Alexander the Great. Alexander did not live very long. His life ended at the young age of thirty-three. However, in his short career, he nearly conquered the known world of his day. He had a charismatic personality and was either loved or feared. Historians tell us Alexander was arrogant and ruthless and was thought of as a god. Although he was not mentioned by name, Daniel the prophet prophesied about Alexander and his kingdom, saying that he would be a willful king, of great strength, and wealth, and will stir up all against the kingdom of the Greeks,[8] which indeed he did.

Josephus, the historian, records a fascinating story for us about Alexander and the Jerusalem high priest Jaddua, which makes the point that God was indeed communicating during this period. After Alexander conquered Syria and took Damascus, his campaign took him into Phoenicia, known as Lebanon today, to conquer Sidon and Tyre; port cities on the Mediterranean Sea. Conquering Sidon, his armies moved south to Tyre, and during the time the city of Tyre was being

---

[8] Daniel 11:2-3 "And now I will tell you the truth: Behold, three more kings will arise in Persia, and the fourth shall be far richer than *them* all; by his strength, through his riches, he shall stir up all against the realm of Greece."Then a mighty king shall arise, who shall rule with great dominion, and do according to his will.

besieged, he sent a letter by messenger to the high priest Jaddua. He requested that Jaddua should supply Alexander's army with provisions. All supplies formerly sent to Darius, King of Persia, should now be sent to him and his army. Jaddua refused, stating that he had made an oath not to bear arms against Darius, and he could not break his oath while Darius was alive.

This action angered Alexander, and he prepared to head south, to make an expedition against the high priest, and to teach the men of Jerusalem to whom they must keep their oaths. In his arrogant fashion, he intended to make it clear that the only oaths that should never be broken were the oaths made to Alexander the Great. When the seven-month siege of Tyre and the two-month siege of Gaza were over, Alexander headed toward Jerusalem. News of Alexander's encroachment upon Jerusalem terrified Jaddua, the high priest. He, therefore, instructed the people to pray, and they should join him in making sacrifices to the Lord. Jaddua sought the Lord to protect the nation and to deliver them from the hand of ruthless Alexander.

The Lord God answered Jaddua in a dream instructing him to take courage. Jaddua was to adorn the city and open the city gates for Alexander. Everyone except the high priest was to meet the king in white garments, and the priest was to adorn himself in his royal garments of purple and red. Once it was known Alexander and his army were just miles from Jerusalem, all the priests and the citizens dressed in the garments as the Lord instructed. They began a processional march to meet the conquering King, Alexander the Great. The troops with Alexander were expecting to plunder the city and terrorize the high priest Jaddua. Instead, they watched in utter amazement as their commander in chief responded differently than the "warrior" they were accustomed him to be. King Alexander approached the procession by himself after seeing people clothed in white garments. The high priest was robed in royal purple and scarlet, and his head crowned in gold with the name of Lord engraved upon it. It is said King Alexander saluted the high priest and adored the name written on the crown. His army, as they witnessed Alexander's behavior, thought their commander had lost his mind.

Parmenio, one of Alexander's generals, inquired of him why he had adored the high priest of the Jews. It was customary for Alexander to require adoration from his subjects. Alexander replied, "I did not adore him, but the God who hath honored him with the high priesthood; for I saw this very person in a dream, in this very habit, when I was at Dios, in Macedonia, who, when I was considering with myself how I might obtain the dominion of Asia, exhorted me to make no delay, but boldly to pass over the sea thither, for that he would conduct my army, and would give me the dominion over the Persians: whence it is, that having seen no other in that habit, and now seeing this person in it, and remembering that vision and exhortation which I had in my dream, I believe that I bring this army under the divine conduct, and shall therewith conquer Darius, and destroy the power of the Persians, and that all things will succeed according to what is in my own mind."[9]

---

[9] *"Josephus The Antiquities of the Jews"* Book 11 Chapter 8, 3-5

The Almighty spared Jerusalem! Jaddua and Alexander were instructed by God in separate dreams, exactly what they were to do. They heard the voice of the Lord, they recognized the voice of the Lord, and they were obedient to the voice of God. God intervened because of their obedience and accomplished His purposes on the earth during this time in history. He spared many lives. On the timeline of history, this happened in 332 BC, during the time called the so-called "silent years." Therefore, this proves that God was not silent, and he did speak during this four-hundred-year period.

We just read the account of Jaddua, the high priest of Jerusalem, receiving instructions from God in a dream. God spoke to the Jewish high priest, Jaddua, and to the Gentile from Macedonia,[10] Alexander the Great. There were many devoted to God that heard His voice during those "silent years." God has never stopped speaking. He is still speaking today. Perhaps the real problem is that people are not listening. I know that this was my problem. I never took the time to listen. God had to get my attention by making a grand entrance with His thundering voice and invading my car. It was not until then that I began to listen. My world turned upside down that day. Little did I know that God would be invading my life, time, and time again.

---

[10] At the time of Alexander, Macedonia was an independent nation located north of Greece. Macedonia is the oldest recorded European nation, although its boundaries have changed significantly through its history.

Chapter 3

JESUS TOOK THE WHEEL

I've decided to call this chapter "Jesus Took the Wheel," because I have had several experiences with the Lord in my car. My life-changing encounter with the living Christ began in my car, although we were not traveling together — He did invade my vehicle. I have had many traveling experiences with Him at the wheel since that day. The first event happened shortly after the Lord said to me, "Choose This Day Who You Will Serve."

I was returning home from an afternoon of shopping at Brookfield Square in Wisconsin, where I resided at the time. The shopping mall was just thirty minutes or so from our home. Usually, when I shopped at the mall, I took the expressway for easy access. I am accustomed to freeway driving, and it was my habit to zip into the mall and zip out again. I can't find a reason for doing this, but this particular day, I found myself taking the back roads home. I drove on a road that I had never traveled before and never visited again. It was late in the day, and I was thinking about what to fix for dinner that night. I was just a little concerned because it was late, and I did not want our dinner hour delayed. My thoughts were about shopping too long, and the need to get right home to prepare dinner at a reasonable hour. For me to be on the back roads when I was in a hurry to get home, made no sense to me. "What are you doing?" I asked myself. So, believe me when I tell you, what was about to happen next was definitely not on my agenda.

Less than halfway home, my car pulled up to a stop sign, and after I came to a full stop, I found myself making a left-hand turn. To continue straight ahead would have been the direction to my home. I drove another quarter of a mile or so and found myself making a right-hand turn into a strip mall that I had never been to before, or ever would again. I can only compare this experience I was having with a movie I saw once called, "The Stepford Wives." I haven't seen the remake. In the original film, the women were walking and talking like robots because they were programmed. They were programmed to do exactly what their husbands wanted them to do. This is precisely how I felt, like a mechanical robot. I felt like someone who was just going through the motions to be obedient to the signals of some specific programming. I parked the car in front of a pharmacy. I opened my car door and marched into the store as if I was on a mission.

Although my mind was not engaged in that mission, apparently, my spirit was. I walked in and continued straight down the center aisle to the back of the pharmacy. Surprisingly, it was as if I had done this many times before. I headed for a revolving book stand. When my arm rose, it rose as if it had a mind of its own. I gave the book stand a spin. Reaching out my hand, I retrieved a book and clutched it in my hand. I then proceeded to the cash register to pay for the book without ever looking at the front cover. Then I returned to my car. My mind was not comprehending any of this strange behavior. For the rest of the ride home, I was asking myself, "What in the world was that all about? Why did you do that? What in the world possessed you to do such a thing?" The answer to those questions did not come to me until later.

The realization that I had been led by the Spirit of God that day would come to me many hours later. It occurred to me after I had several chapters of the book read, and after I began to understand that the personhood of the Holy Spirit is active in the lives of His people. This understanding was something that I was unaware of at the time of this purchase. The only way that I would have believed such a story as this one was because it was happening to me first hand. I experienced a supernatural power leading me around just as if I had a bit in my mouth, and someone else was holding the reins. First, I hear a voice thundering from heaven, and now some power I have never encountered before is leading me around as if I was on a leash. I was soon to learn who the Master was.

After dinner, I sat down to read the book. I vaguely remember the book. It was either a yellow softcover book with four blue letters or a blue softcover book with four yellow letters. The front cover spelled out in large bold letters the word L O V E. I remember thinking to myself, "Well, I guess I could learn more about love," and began to read it. As it turned out, unknown to me, I had purchased a Bible that day. It was the New Testament, written in easy to understand language. It was the Living Bible paraphrased to make it easy for even children to read. It was just the thing that I needed. Had it been in the King James language Bible with all its thee's and thou's, I would have recognized the book to be a Bible. How the Lord managed to drive my car to the pharmacy, march me to the revolving book stand, grab that book and pay for it, I do not know. All I know is it was His intricate design to get this book into my hands. He wanted me to have His Love Letters. His ways are such an awesome mystery and try as I may, I could not reason it out, because His ways are beyond all reason.

As I began to read the book that He had placed in my hand, chills ran up and down my spine. These chills surfacing on my spine were the direct result of the revelation that had come to me. First His voice broke through from eternity present and invaded my car. Then this same being, the God of the Universe had orchestrated the ride home on a strange and unfamiliar road. Then he marched me through the pharmacy, to purchase the book. He had given me His love letters. I was reading the book of all books, the Bible. The revelation of His love began to saturate this wounded soul, and I knew that changes were coming into my life that I did not yet understand. In some respects, I thought I was living in the twilight zone.

His love continues to change me daily. He has imparted many truths to me, and now He wants me to impart them to you and teach His Word. I am writing with an awesome awareness that in the beginning was the Word and the Word was with God, and the Word was God. In the beginning of my glorious walk with Him, He delivered His Word to me personally. Right from the start of our relationship, I stepped into the realm of the supernatural. Because this was my foundation, I fully anticipated to be walking in His miraculous glory and supernatural manifestation from then on, and I have.

I share with you the things that I have learned about His marvelous and mysterious ways, His wondrous miracle-working power, and His intimate encounters with one of His daughters. Walking in His Glory is a normal expectation for any child of God. You can have as much of God as you desire as you prioritize your life for Him. He desires to interact with each of us in an intimate and personal way. May sharing my experiences with our Creator, project you into greater depths and higher heights that will continue to embrace you in His loving arms and glorious presence. If you are reading about my experiences with God, then your heavenly Father has arranged the circumstances that brought you here. He loves you that much. You are not reading this book by accident; the Lord arranged this book to get into your hands, just as He drove my car to the pharmacy and purchased His book. God almighty, the One who created you in your mother's womb has created you for intimacy with Him. You are His heart's desire. You were meant to be the object of His Love.

That mysterious drive that led me to the pharmacy to purchase a Bible that day began a marvelous journey with God through His Word. He began teaching me things about Himself and how to operate in His Kingdom. Those lessons were not just limited to the study of His Word, which became alive to me; much more was learned as Jesus took the wheel of my car, and together, we journeyed through life.

I am convinced our belief system has a lot to do with divine intervention. The Lord in His sovereignty and at His choosing can intervene with anyone at any time. My point, however, is if we know the word and believe what it says and expect divine intervention, we are likely to get the things that we believe. Conversely, I also believe when we have unbelief, it ties the hand of God from moving supernaturally. The reason I say this is because the word of God says that signs and wonders will follow those that believe. (emphasis on the word believe) Each of us has a choice to either believe what the word of God says or believe the negative voices we hear in our minds. Now, I am not saying that I never have moments of doubt or that I never have negative thoughts, because that would not be true. The battle is in the mind, and when these negative impulses arise, I must bring my mind captive under the mind of Christ. I usually have a little talk with myself about what I should and should not believe. At those times, I convince myself to believe the word of the Lord.

When God in His word tells me that He is my protector and that He is my high tower of safety I can run into, I happen to believe Him. When His word indicates to me that my faith is my shield of protection, I happen to believe that too. When His word says He will answer me when I call, I believe that as well. When He says He will never leave me or forsake me, I believe Him. He has proven Himself to be faithful to His word, at so many different times and situations. The following stories were several of those situations when the Lord, my protector, and provider showed up on the road.

The Vision of an Accident

For a while, my children attended a private school until we could no longer afford to support such an education financially. The school was about a twenty-minute drive from our home. I drove them to school and picked them up again at the end of the day. The ride is breathtaking, with its winding roads through the Kettle Moraine Forest in Delafield, Wisconsin.

As I was coming up a small hill and about to make a sharp turn to the right, I had a vision of a car coming around the bend at record speed, and because it was going so fast, it had crossed over into my lane, and a horrible accident took place in the vision. Immediately before I had time to think, I slowed down and pulled my car over onto the shoulder of the road. Just in time, I might add, because just as the vision had shown me, a vehicle traveling ever so fast, came barreling around the curve in the road. Had I not pulled over to the shoulder, there would have been a head-on collision. There is no other explanation, except to say that the Lord in a vision had warned me. Jesus had given me His own personal road sign warning. What a God we serve!

The Hydroplaning of My Car

There was another time my driving companion, Jesus, was with me traveling on a cold winter night during a snowstorm. I was driving on a country road close to my house. There was a slight incline before one would reach the top of the overpass that I was traveling on. On the left side of the viaduct was a railing about 3 feet high. On the right side was solid ground. A car would drop 8 -10 feet to the ground if it broke through the railing. As I traveled, there was a steady stream of traffic ahead of me and behind me. I watched the car ahead of me as it twisted and turned, trying to stay on the slippery road. The minute I reached the top of the incline, I hit a patch of ice, and I had no control over my vehicle. The car turned itself to the left and headed for the railing. I could see in my rear-view mirror the headlights of cars behind me. In those seconds before I would hit the barrier and plummet to the ground, I cried out to Jesus for help. In a flash, He was there, and I felt the car rise as if it were hydroplaning.

My car turned in mid-air and was facing the direction that I needed to go, however instead of going straight ahead; it moved perpendicular to the right side of the road. Then the car was put down on the shoulder of the road just in time to let the other vehicles pass without incident. For any vehicle to move sideways, from left to right, would be an impossible feat, especially since the wheels of my car were not touching the ground; but then nothing is impossible with God. I cannot but wonder what the car behind me must have been thinking as he or she witnessed this phenomenal event. As one would expect, I sat there, praising the Lord before I could gain my senses and drive away safe and sound. Jesus was with me on the road that night!

Like a Green Pea

This next experience with the Lord is not about any accident or near accident, but since it happened in my car, I am telling it here. Through the years, I have been on both sides of the financial spectrum. I know what it is like to have the kind of abundance that allows you to have anything and everything that your heart desires. I also know what it is like to wonder how our bills are going to be paid and still have enough money left over for food. This story is about one of those times when the bank account was empty. My husband's business had failed

BEYOND ALL REASON: Moving Out of Logic Into the Supernatural

due to a domino effect of bankrupt contractors during the building crisis. Therefore, he was without a job. This domino effect closed the doors of my Interior Design Studio as well. Consequently, I had taken employment with a real estate company but had not closed any deals just yet, and since I got paid from the commission of a sale, and there were no sales, we were hurting. I had taken a listing from a couple in our town to sell their house. I needed to drop some paperwork off at their home, and I had just enough gas in the car to drive to their house and back again. I knew I would be able to take care of that transaction, but I didn't know what I was going to do for the rest of the day. I would need my car for the rest of the day to conduct some other business transactions, and there was not enough gas in the car to take me to all the places that I needed to go.

"Lord." I prayed on the way to my client's house. "I do not know how You are going to do this, but I need money for gas, and your word says, You will supply all my needs according to your riches in glory." When I arrived at my destination, I parked the car in front of their house, rolled up the windows, and locked the doors after I got out of the car. After I finished my business, I returned to my car. I unlocked the door and was ready to get in and sit down when I saw something on the driver's seat that looked like a green pea. I thought to myself, "How strange is that, how did a single little pea get into my car?"

I picked it up from the driver's seat and upon further examination, discovered it was not a pea at all. It was as small as a green pea; however, it was not round like a pea but square. It was a green square of paper the size of a pea folded into a perfect tiny little cube. I began to unfold it, and to my great delight and surprise, it was a twenty-dollar bill. I knew instinctively that the Lord or an angel had put it there. It was not there when I got out of the car, and the vehicle was still locked when I returned to it. Besides that, I tried to fold that twenty-dollar bill myself to see if I could fold it into something small as a pea, and found it impossible to do. I couldn't fold it that small, let alone fold it into a perfect cube. Try it yourself sometime!

It was the hand of God that folded a twenty-dollar bill that small. I had said to him, "I don't know how you are going to do this," yet, I did expect him to do something. However, I did not expect to find a pea-sized object turn into a twenty-dollar bill. I sat there in my car and laughed and laughed, and I know that He was laughing too. God was in my driver's seat and having fun with me that day. Amazing! I sat there awhile, grinning, and had a good laugh with the Lord. Then I started my car and headed to the gas station with the twenty-dollar bill in my hand.

The Accident in Corpus Christy, Texas

Another time also involves my daughter and the miracle that God did for her. It was Thanksgiving time, and my husband, Bill, and both of my sons, Billy and Kelly were planning a hunting trip with their grandfather and uncle. They intended to be gone a few days, including Thanksgiving Day. So, Tracey, who worked for an airline at the time, got tickets for her and me. We decided that we would take a trip of our own. For our holiday, we chose to go to Corpus Christi, Texas, and enjoy the beach. Well, we never made it to the beach. On our first day there, we left our hotel room, got in our rented car, and drove through town looking for a grocery store to purchase something to drink. We never made it to the store either. As I approached the intersection, the light was green, and so I proceeded to cross the intersection. A woman in the oncoming traffic turned right in front of me, and I could not stop the car in time, and therefore, I hit her. The collision sent both of our vehicles swirling, and our rental car ended up hitting a light pole head-on. Unfortunately, neither one of us had our seatbelts on, nor did we have the benefit of airbags.

I felt the impact on my legs and particularly in my knees. Although shaken and in pain, I was grateful to be alive. The impact threw Tracey to the windshield, and she hit her head so hard that she became temporarily blind, which scared both of us. When I looked over at my daughter, her pants covered with blood, caused an alarm. Immediately when I saw my daughter Tracey's condition, I began to pray in tongues. I knew there was nothing that I could pray from my conscious mind at that moment that could have the same effect as allowing the Holy Spirit to pray for her. The gift of speaking in tongues and having a prayer language that transcends the natural mind is said to be a mystery because the Holy Spirit makes intercession for us. If ever I needed the Holy Spirit to be praying for us, it was then. This entire subject of praying in tongues can be found in the Bible and will be covered in another chapter.

When the paramedics arrived on the scene, the first thing that Tracey asked was, how were the mother and little child that we hit? We barely got a glimpse of them. Were they all right? They informed us that they were shaken but not hurt badly. We were relieved to hear the news. From the look of their car, we were expecting to hear the worst. The car that we had rented was totaled, and it looked as if theirs was too. The paramedics had difficulty opening up our car doors because of the great amount of damage to the vehicle. Finally, they were able to pull Tracey out, although she was going into shock. They put her on a life support stretcher while transporting her to the hospital. Still praying intensely, I followed her into the ambulance. My legs were in pain, but I was able to walk and did not need the use of a stretcher. At one point, Tracey's blood pressure had dropped significantly. They even thought they had defective equipment. Due to my strong belief that the Lord is in control of all things, and my belief in the power of prayer, I never stopped praying in tongues. I did not care what the paramedics thought, as they were listening. I only cared about whether God was listening. Tracey's blood pressure began to rise. For the entire ride to the hospital, I did what the Bible instructs us to do. I laid my hands on my daughter and prayed in tongues over her.

The paramedics began to cut Tracey's bloody clothes off and clean her up to discover where her injuries were so that they could treat her. One of her pant's leg was a bloody mess. The paramedics washed her leg off and examined her to see where the blood was coming from. In their bewilderment, nothing was found. Her legs were in perfect condition, except for a tiny scar. Tracey says to this day that the scar is a reminder that the Great Physician, Jesus, was with her. He had already taken care of her open wound. There were no open wounds on her body anywhere! The puzzled look on their faces will forever be locked in the memory of my brain as a "Kodak moment." It's evident to me that there was one other person in that ambulance with us. The Great Physician had arrived on the scene. My prayers had summoned Him. Although He was unseen, the healing work of His Holy Spirit was seen by all in total amazement. It was a miracle that took place in that ambulance. Tracey kept the pants that the paramedics cut off of her as a memorial to the Glory of God. We were admitted to the hospital in Corpus Christi, Texas, and both of us were checked over from top to bottom. Not only was it a miracle that we both were alive, but it was a miracle that after Tracey hit head-on into the windshield, she had no concussion or brain injury and that her sight returned. All the tests came back normal. We were dismissed sometime in the wee hours of the morning and sent back to our hotel in a cab. The ride back to our hotel was nothing short of another miracle.

The cab driver was a woman, who after we pulled away from the hospital, turned her head around as she was driving to look at us sitting in the back seat to ask us what had happened and why we were in the hospital. We told her that we had been in an accident and had totaled our rental car. While turning her head around to face us, again not paying attention to the road in front of her, and driving well over the speed limit, she replied, "Oh, I know just what you mean. I totaled my cab just last week." What?? She insisted on having a conversation with us the entire time, mostly with one hand on the steering wheel, and her head turned to look at us while racing to our destination. Tracey and I looked at each other frightened and scared, yet, it was great comic relief, and both of us just busted out laughing. Tracey whispered to me, "Why am I not surprised she was just in a bad accident?" With this statement, we looked at each other, rolled our eyes, and broke into nervous laughter again. It was only the grace of God that got us to our hotel without having another accident on the way. This cab driver's eyes were more focused on us in the back seat than they ever were on the road we traveled. The Lord's protective hand was heavy upon us that day, and it would not surprise me if He had taken control of the steering wheel to make sure we arrived at our hotel safely. I can believe that was the case, from my very first encounter with the Lord taking hold of my steering wheel and driving me to that pharmacy to buy a book, I later learned was the Bible.

We spent the entire vacation in our hotel room recovering from the accident. Each of us in too much pain to even suggest a flight out. We just wanted to be home in our beds, but we were so stiff and sore that we could hardly move. We spent the rest of our vacation in the hotel beds, and had to crawl on the floor to get to the bathroom. That's how bad it was. Finally, after several days in bed, we made ourselves get ready and go to the beach; however, we did not enjoy ourselves very much. We were anxious to get home to be with the rest of our family and celebrate the miracle that we were both still alive.

The Supernatural Drive from Texas to Wisconsin

This episode happened on a trip that I was taking alone in my Oldsmobile. I lived in Dallas at the time, and I was making a trip to Wisconsin, where all three of my children lived. I was making the trip on the weekend, and it was a two-day drive for me. Whenever I traveled alone, I would leave in the wee hours of the morning and pull off the road around 3 or 4 p.m. to avoid the heavy traffic. I would get a nice hotel room, have dinner, retire so that I could get an early start again the following morning. The next morning would have been a Sunday morning. As usual, I was in my car and on the road early. I wasn't on the road long when my car started to over-heat. I exited the interstate and turned off on a country road. Just as soon as I saw a gas station, I pulled over, hoping to get some help. The gentleman holding down the fort was nice and willing to help this lady in distress. I told him that I was coming from Dallas, and I was about halfway to my destination, which was Wisconsin. When I told him that my car had just started to over-heat and I didn't know what to do, he said I needed a mechanic, but that I would be hard-pressed to find anyone to help me on Sunday. Then he said, "OK, this is what we will do. Once your car cools down, I am going to open the hood and tie it down so that there will be an air space of about an inch. This solution will circulate the air over the engine, keeping it cool while you travel. But you will need to get the car to a mechanic as soon as you can. Now, if you notice that the car begins to over-heat again after a while, you will need to pull over and let the car cool down." So, once the car was cooled down, this fine gentleman did just what he said he was going to do, and I drove away with a one-inch air space between my hood and the body of the car.

Once I was back on the interstate headed north, I began to pray. "Father God, I need for you to keep this car running until I get to my daughter's home. Please, Lord, do not let it overheat or stop working." I put my praise tapes in the player and began to sing songs to the Lord for the rest of the trip. Intermittently I prayed for God to keep the car running, sang songs to Him, and prayed in tongues. At the same time, my eyes were glued to the gauge, making sure that the car was not overheating. I know my prayers probably sounded more like begging and desperation, PLEASE GOD, PLEASE, JUST LET ME GET

THERE! The rest of the trip home, I was coupled with faith and fear. I had waves of faith wash over me, and I would think, "God is going to do this, yes, He is." Then out of nowhere would come the thoughts, "But what if He doesn't?" So, to silence the double-minded thoughts, I would sing His praises.

Finally, I saw the sign, "Welcome to Wisconsin," and I began to chant, "Just a little longer, just a little bit longer." When I saw Tracey's apartment complex, I burst into a song of thanksgiving. Then just as I turned on to Tracey's driveway, the car made a loud sputtering noise and gave up the ghost. Now you tell me, was that a coincidence? I think not! The Lord had once again provided me with His traveling mercies.

Remember the Loaves and the Fishes

When the Oldsmobile gave up the ghost, my son Kelly convinced me to get a little Chevy Beretta. Well, this one day after moving to Phoenix, I was on I17 traveling north when the car started to slow down and chug along in spurts. I quickly looked at the gas gauge and found it to be on empty, actually below empty; Since I was near an exit, I tried to move the car to the exit and off the expressway, but to no avail. It sputtered a bit and moved a foot more or so and quit. "Please, God," I prayed, "Help me get off this highway." I turned the key, fully expecting the car to start, but it did not. I bowed my head in prayer again, as the traffic was whizzing by. "Lord," I said, "remember the loaves and the fishes. I need you to put some gas in this car." I turned the key, nothing. I was panic-stricken and near tears. Again, I prayed, "Lord, forgive me for being careless and not checking the gas gauge long before this so that this whole scene could have been avoided. But now I need your help, please Lord, just enough gas to get to the gas station. I turned the ignition key again, and VAARRROOOM, the car started, and I drove another mile or two to the nearest gas station. My near tears had turned to joy as I exited the expressway and drove away. My AAA roadside assistant, Jesus, had helped me once again. That is my Awesome, Ageless, Authority met me with His roadside assistance, but only after I had asked for forgiveness.

There is a really important lesson to be learned here. Often, we find ourselves in jams we have created for ourselves, and when we cry out to God for help, it seems as if our prayers have reached a deaf ear. Next time, you find yourself in a position where help from Heaven does not arrive, take inventory of the circumstance, and examine your contribution to the situation. Then where applicable, ask for forgiveness. You are likely to discover an entirely different outcome.

Got Another Call

The next two encounters with God did not happen to me, but my son Kelly. One day Kelly was on his way to work, he heard the voice of the Holy Spirit whisper to him to go and check his grandfather. He turned his car around and headed for his grandparent's home knowing this action would cause him to be late for work. He was a UPS driver and this action could hurt him, but he did it anyway. Kelly arrived at his grandfather's home just ahead of the paramedics. He was joined by his uncle who had been called by his mother to come quickly. The paramedics transported grandpa to the hospital, where he died shortly after. Kelly's uncle questioned Kelly about how he knew to come to the house at that particular time. "I was the only one mother called," he said. Kelly responded to his uncle by saying, "I got another call!" When relaying this experience with the family, Kelly said you just can't make this stuff up.

Only Mom Will Believe Me

When my son Kelly had his 2nd visitation from the Holy Spirit, he was in his 20s during his partying days. When I answered the phone the day Kelly called and heard the inebriated voice of my son, I was not taken by surprise. As he slurred his words, he said: "Mom, this is Kelly. I have something to tell you. I can't tell no one else cause they won't believe me. You will though cause this stuff happens to you too. Well, first I have to tell you…well you know I drink, right? Well, today, I stopped and had a few drinks with the guys after work. Then I get in my car to go home, and I kid you not, something took hold of the wheel and began to drive my car."

(I began to laugh, remembering the day the Lord drove my car.) He continued, "Mom, I ain't kidding you! Something drove my car!" "Well," I said, "Where did it drive you?" "Well," Kelly responded, "It didn't take me home. No siree, it kept on turning and turning, and then, guess what? It turned right into the church's parking lot, and it drove my car right over the grass. It didn't care if it was driving on the church's grass. It just kept a going until it stopped right at the foot of that big cross." "What did you do then?" I asked. "Gosh, Mom, I didn't know what to do, so I prayed for grandpa because he just died." (I was in stitches on the other end of the line, but I couldn't let him know. I tried to gather my composure, so I could ask my son what he thought all this meant. When I was finally able to ask, I heard him say, "Look Mom I'm not stupid. I know that God is trying to tell me to get my $#!+ together. I gotta quit drinking and go home to my wife. I need to clean up my act."

I hung up the phone rejoicing because the Lord of the Universe had burst into the scene of my son's life, giving him a real live object lesson. The Lord had brought my son along with his sin to the foot of the cross. How incredible is that? How do these things happen? I do not know. All I do know is they do happen, and they are beyond all reason. Long before the Lord drove my son to the foot of the cross, He drove me to a Pharmacy; therefore, it was easy for me to believe my son's story, and as Kelly said, he didn't think anyone else would believe him but me.

As I stated previously, all my children have the characteristics of Christ. Kelly is very generous, thoughtful and kind and puts other's needs before his own. I am very proud of him. My son Kelly now has his personal walk with the Lord, and I have all the faith that I will be hearing more and more miraculous events and testimonies in his life. I just wish I lived closer to him and his family, so I can witness these events.

Each of us needs to leave our sin at the foot of the cross. The price for each and every sin was paid for there. Jesus paid the price with each drop of blood He shed for us at the cross of Calvary. Each drop of blood shed was a gift of love poured out for us so that we can be free from the punishment that sin requires. All that the Lord requires of us is that we respond to this great gift of Love.

Sending Help From Heaven

If my memory serves me correctly, this was the first time my oldest son Billy came face to face with the supernatural realm. My teenage son was driving age and had worked hard to purchase his own car. He was invited to a party a friend from school was having. The drive to his friend's house would cause him to be driving on the same winding roads through the Kettle Moraine Forest, that I drove when a vision spared me from an accident. Driving time to his friend's house was around 30 minutes or so. It was winter in Wisconsin, and when Billy left for the party, the roads were in good condition. When the party was over and it was time to drive home, it began to snow. As he drove, the conditions worsened, and the roads became slippery. So much that Billy lost control of his car. He ended up on the side of the road, backed into a snowbank.

Unable to make his car budge from the snowbank after many tries, he began to get concerned. It was late at night on a deserted road, and he was afraid there would be no one to help him. Being stranded in Wisconsin during the winter could be a dangerous thing, and he was worried. Every time Billy made an effort to get his car out of the snowbank, the only result was spinning wheels. So, he decided he would try to lift the back end of the car, but to no avail, even though he tried, again and again, he just was not strong enough. Therefore, Billy cried out to the Lord for help. He tried again, and sure enough, help was sent! Either an angel or the Lord himself came to the rescue because this time, Billy lifted the car with ease! He got his car back on the road and was relieved that he arrived home safe and sound. My son was so excited to share his experience with me the following morning.

Romans 10:13 *For whoever calls on the name of the LORD shall be saved.* Billy called on the name of the Lord and was saved from what could have been a dangerous outcome.

My Trip to San Francisco

This roadside assistance encounter happened just a little over a decade ago. The Lord had instructed me to go to San Francisco on a prayer vigil. I was to go and pray for the city. I lived, as I do now, in the Metro Phoenix area, so the drive is about seven hundred fifty miles and takes about twelve hours to drive. When the Lord spoke to me three weeks previous to my trip to San Francisco, He did not give me much information except to say, "I want you to pack some things and go to San Francisco." He also said He was going to lead me to green pastures and that there would be a door of opportunity open to me there. The final thing that I heard was that whatever it is to take place would be monumental. Those last words of His I still find hard to comprehend. Nothing that I did from my way of looking at it resulted in anything monumental. However, I know, He is keeping a record, and someday the time will be revealed. I will watch from my first day in San Franciso, October 17, 2006, to the future, and I will see things that are impossible to see now.

During the twelve-hour drive, I prayed for revival to come to every city and town that I passed along the way. I spoke in tongues most of the way. That is when I wasn't singing along to my worship tapes. My car became my private sanctuary. My family had voiced their concerns about me driving alone, each expressing their fears of the things that might go wrong. They were fearful that I might get lost or have a flat tire on the road. To which I gave my standard reply of faith. "God will keep me safe and provide me with the help I will need if I end up needing any help." This type of answer must seem trite to someone who has not walked in the awesome provision of the Lord as I have. In the end, it was with my family's blessing that I hit the road bound for San Francisco. I wasn't on the highway long when I saw a billboard that said, "Are you lost? Read my book. It is your road map." I thought to myself, I should call my daughter Tracey and tell her about this sign. Maybe that will put her fears to rest.

After coming out of the mountains, I looked, and as far as the eye could see, were humongous farms. I saw orange groves planted with such precision, and fields of cotton, and hay. Some fields were green for what seemed like miles. After coming from the desert, it was very refreshing to see so much green stuff. Just as I was commenting to the Lord about how beautiful it was, He said to me, "I told you I was taking you to green pastures." Our Lord has quite a sense of humor! It had not occurred to me that these were the green pastures he had mentioned to me before the trip until He said something right then. This observation made me think about all the things that I may have missed because I was unaware and had not paid attention to detail. It was then that I determined to pay closer attention to the happenings in my life. I do not want to miss the unusual happenings of the Lord. I stopped for a potty break and bought a medium size coke at a Taco Bell. The young man behind the counter asked if there would be anything else, and I responded, "No, that will be all." He handed me my medium drink after I had paid him, and I said to him, "You have a blessed day!" With that statement, he grabbed the container out of my hand and replaced it with the largest one that they sold, saying," Here, this is just between you and me." Our previous pastor, Pastor Michael Maiden, had recently prophesied the Lord was going to be giving His people a double portion. If I had not been determined to keep my eyes open and to be more aware, I might have missed it. The beverage cup in my hand now was at least double the size of the one I had before. I received a double portion of His unmerited favor. The thrill was not that I had more coke to drink; no, I certainly did not need more. It was thrilling to know that I had eyes to see it was from the hand of the Lord, just for speaking a blessing over that young man.

About four o'clock that afternoon, my cell phone rang, and it was my daughter asking how far I had gotten for the day. I told her that I thought that I was about an hour or two from my destination. She inquired was I going to stop for the night and tackle the city in the morning? My reply to her was, "That was my plan until I heard the voice of the Lord say He still wanted me to go into the city today." I could tell in her voice that she was unhappy about this decision. Her concerns were justified; I did not want to go in at night, either. Only a minute or two went by after hanging up the phone when there appeared in the middle of nowhere, on a fence post, an orange and blue sign that read TRUST JESUS. I immediately picked up my cell phone to call her back to share the message of the sign with her.

BEYOND ALL REASON: Moving Out of Logic Into the Supernatural

I arrived in Oakland about sunset and felt that the Lord was directing me to continue into the city. This direction, I did not want to do, because of night falling and me being in a strange city alone. But because I wanted to be obedient to what I perceived to be His voice, I crossed over into San Francisco, taking the Golden Gate Bridge. It was an impressive sight. I kept hearing "9th" over and over in my head, so when I saw 9th Street, I turned and drove down it expecting to receive more directions. Earlier I had heard that voice say He would direct me when I arrived in the city. However, either I was too upset to hear, or there were no more directions.

For the next two hours, I drove around in circles trying to find a place to stay. I had seen a Days Inn and had tried without success to get back to it, but I couldn't find it again. I must have covered every street in my search to get out of the city. As most of you probably know, San Francisco is built on hilly terrain. I was terrified that having to stop on one of those steep hills while waiting for the signal to change that my car would roll back and cause an accident. I just wanted out of the city. I know that God wanted me in the city so that I could overcome my fears and learn to trust Him more for these kinds of situations. If it was a test of faith, I wasn't doing so well. I was about to have an object lesson. I made the mistake of turning down a one-way street where there were cars backed up bumper to bumper. At the bottom of the hill, a truck had gone over the curb and was blocking traffic. The only way out was for everyone to back out and go up the steep hill. This street was pitched several feet below sea level in my estimation. There were two lanes of cars that now had to back up the very steep hill, which was at least two city blocks into the on-coming traffic. The intersection did not have traffic lights that would have at least momentarily stopped the oncoming traffic. My car and the car next to me had to lead the procession of cars backing up into traffic. My heart was in my throat and beating rapidly. The on-coming traffic did not care that forty or so cars were merging backward into traffic; they were instead honking their horns in annoyance and was only concerned for themselves.

Then from out of nowhere, a young man stepped out from the shadows and stood between the approaching traffic and my car. With a wave of his one arm, he held his hand out, and he stopped the on-coming cars, and with the wave of the other arm, he began guiding me as I backed the car into the intersection, turned in the direction that I needed to go, and went on my way. As I pulled away from the stranger who helped me, I looked into my rear-view mirror, and the stranger that was there just a second ago had vanished. Thank you, Jesus was all I could say! It did not occur to me until sometime later that I just may have been helped by an angel.

With this last episode, my frustration with the city had reached its peak. I was thrilled with the possibility that an angel had helped me during such a stressful ordeal, but the stress level of driving at night in this city was overwhelming. I was tired and hungry. I couldn't find a place to spend the night that I thought I would be able to afford. I needed a break. Therefore, I was frantically crying out to God to help me get out of the city. My prayer language was becoming even too loud for my ears. I had decided I would be better off outside of the city in a hotel that would be less costly. I reasoned that I had more time than I had money. Finally, after driving this way and then that way, I saw the signs directing me to the expressway. It was a horrible experience after the long drive, and I was exhausted. Eventually, I found myself out of the city, and still, I was unable to find a hotel. Having them in the view from the expressway, I would exit to find a hotel for the night. However, upon exiting, I would get turned around and could not find it.

Thank goodness for cell phones and computers. I took an exit and pulled off the side of the road and called my daughter. Tracey became my GPS. She got on her laptop and looked up hotels in the area after I gave her my location. Then she directed me, using Yahoo maps, and guided me to the hotel. At long last, I landed in a surprisingly pleasant Budget Hotel a little less than an hour away from the city. It was much further than I had intended to go, but by this late hour, I was happy to have found something as pleasing as it was for the price. The entire adventure left me so exhausted that sleep would not come. I lay in bed, complaining to the Lord about the horrible experience I had just had. At this point, because I had not received further instruction from Him, I was becoming convinced that I had not heard Him at all.

Walking in the Spirit is not always easy, especially when the outcome is different from what you expect. After much pleading with the Lord to make it clear to me what exactly I was doing some seven hundred miles away from home, he spoke to me. "I want you to understand something. Every day I am losing people to homosexuality and drugs in this city." That is all He said, but this is what I perceived He was trying to tell me. "People are lost daily to eternal darkness, and you are complaining to me because you got lost in the city and drove around in circles for two hours, got messed up in a traffic jam, and even though I sent you someone to help, you are complaining. Your little inconvenience isn't even worth mentioning on a scale that measures the difference between life eternal and eternal damnation." Although He didn't say it quite like that, I got the message loud and clear. I was on a mission that had eternal consequences.

The next day I decided to make reservations at the Days Inn that I had seen in the city so that I would have some peace of mind until the Lord made it clear what I was to do next. I called to make a reservation, the person who was on the other end of the line said because I had had an Entertainment Book, I was entitled to a discount. I did have an Entertainment book, but I had not thought about bringing it or using it on this trip. The thing that puzzled me was that my daughter purchased the book under her name, and I could not for the life of me figure out how the hotel knew from my call that I had the book or was entitled to a discount. I had not mentioned my daughter's name, only my own. When I told Tracey what had happened, she was as puzzled by it as I was. Since I had not thought about bringing the Entertainment Book and the card for the discounts with me, Tracey had given me her ID number over the phone when we talked that morning. Right after I hung up the phone from talking with her, I dialed the Inn from my cell phone. I informed the person on the other side of the line that I had an Entertainment Book and was entitled to a discount. I then asked if she wanted my identification number. The receptionist replied it wasn't necessary because she had it. She then proceeded to read it back to me, and she quoted the exact number. I asked her how she knew the number, and she said it was on her computer and tied to the caller ID from my phone. My cell phone is in my name, not my daughter's. I was very puzzled by the entire transaction. Then she proceeded to tell me that everyone calling in for reservations today would also be receiving an additional $20.00 gas voucher. Then she asked if I would be interested in receiving the voucher. With my positive response, she connected me to another operator. By the time I hung up, the gas voucher had increased to $40.00, and the cost of my hotel room reduced to $67.00. By subtracting the $40.00 gas voucher, in essence, my stay for the night in the city of San Francisco cost me $27.00. The entire episode was strange. It is my opinion it was once again the divine intervention of the Lord working in the background, bringing me that double portion of blessing that was prophesied. I was obedient to what the Lord had asked me to do, and just as the Bible says, "blessings follow obedience."

I stopped at a drug store to pick up a map so that I would have a better handle on how to navigate around the city when I arrived. As I approached the destination, the same words from the day before kept swimming in my mind. "9th, 9th, 9th." For several days now, I had also had the Salvation Army on my mind, thinking that I should perhaps contact someone from there while I am in the city. It should not have surprised me when I found the Salvation Army Church on 9th Street, but it did. I immediately pulled the car over to park it in front of their building. I went in and introduced myself and told the woman in charge, why I was in the city. I said, "I was sent by the Lord to pray for revival in the city." She said, "That is interesting because in two weeks there will be people from all over the country coming for a convention that will be meeting in the city. Then from there, they plan to hit the streets with the gospel of salvation. We sure need prayer for that." I asked if there were any prayer houses in the city and indicated I was looking for accommodations and a place to pray, trusting that the Lord would provide. She told me that I could use the chapel for prayer if I like. She said that she would be speaking to her husband and that I should call tomorrow morning about it. I left knowing that my prayers just might be breaking ground for when the army of God would be on the streets in a couple of weeks. I then went on to find the Days Inn that I had booked.

The Days Inn that I saw last night was not the Days Inn, where I booked the hotel. The address given to me turned out to be walking distance to the Civic Center and the government buildings. After checking in, I took a very long walk. I did a prayer walk around all the municipal buildings and theaters, praying in tongues as I went. Since I was hidden in God, no one paid any attention to me. But then it was San Francisco, and I suppose some lone lady praying in tongues as she walked around the city was not weird to those city dwellers. While looking for a grocery store later in the day, I had an opportunity to pray with a woman. She was an attendant from the car lot next to the hotel. I started up a conversation with her, and before I knew it, we were talking about God, and she said she was desperate for prayer because she wanted to be a better person and do more for God. I prayed with her that the Lord would give her the desires of her heart. I left thinking that the doors of opportunity to serve the Lord are everywhere; all one needs to do, is look for them.

The following day I did a prayer walk around Fisherman's Wharf and through several neighborhoods. I prayed in tongues as I walked everywhere I could on those streets in San Francisco. It certainly was more enjoyable than driving them. I was enjoying myself and was hoping that I would be there for a while longer, but then I heard that voice say, "Go home." Wanting to be sure that I had finished my assignment, I drove to San Carlos and spent the night praying there before I headed any further south. In prayer, I got confirmation on the words "Go home," so I began the rather long drive home.

After driving an hour or two, I heard the thud, thud, of an apparent flat tire. Oh, no, I thought, just what my family feared. I pulled over to the shoulder and took the first exit off of the main highway that I could. I pulled my car to a stop right in front of the Soledad Prison. On the property to my left was a row of mobile homes, so I walked over to them to see if I could find someone to help me. As I approached one of the homes, there was a gentleman out in his yard. When I told him, what had happened, he extended his hand of hospitality to me. He asked me to take a seat on one of the lawn chairs, called one of his adult children to get me something to drink, while he made a phone call to a mechanic that he knew in town. He introduced himself and told me that he was an employee of the prison. I joked about having a flat in front of the prison grounds, and he said, "Well, you can be sure you are safe here. Should anyone escape, they would want to get as far away from this place as they could and as fast as possible." We all laughed at that one. While I waited for the mechanic to arrive, another one of his adult children joined us on the lawn. As we sat there, I introduced myself as a minister of the gospel of Jesus Christ and told them about my trip to

San Francisco. He then began to unburden himself and told me that his wife was very ill in a nursing home and that she had been there for over a year now. So, under the shade tree and on the grounds of Soledad Prison, I held a prayer meeting. I prayed for the Lord to do a "healing work" for the wife of this kind gentleman and mother of these kids that I had just met.

I do not believe in coincidences. The fact that I had a flat tire at that moment in time at that particular place was a divine appointment. It can be counted with many situations that I have had at first glance may look as if something bad is happening, when in fact, it is just the opposite. Having a flat tire just then and there; turned out to be a door open for me to minister to someone in need. This experience was not about a tire that needed changing; rather, it was about changing the atmosphere through prayer. Once the tire was changed, and I was back on the highway headed for home, I picked up my cell phone and called my daughter. I put her on speaker, and we prayed for hours on the phone together for revival to break out in California. I purposefully planned the drive to go through Los Angeles and Hollywood because there is a need for repentance and a returning to the Lord. Tracey stayed on the phone and prayed with me as I traveled the California coastline south to Los Angeles, and as I turned east, headed toward Phoenix.

There are assignments that the Lord will give someone; however, they may never know the purpose or the outcome. Except for the things obvious to me, like the people that I prayed with, I was not sure what I had accomplished in my prayer walks around San Francisco. I left that mystery in the hands of the Lord. I was content with the fact that I had obeyed His voice, and He had shown Himself to me while I was there.

Four years later, a good friend of my daughter, Junn Freeman, who also is a spiritual daughter to me, belongs to a prophetic church in Georgia. She called to tell me something exciting. She was aware of my trip to San Francisco to pray for the city, and thought that I would be interested in what she learned in church on Sunday. There was a special guest speaker who had shared with the congregation something that the Lord had shared with him. This speaker was lamenting in prayer over the state of affairs found in the city of San Francisco. He grieved over the gross sin that could be found there and wondered why the Lord had not destroyed the city like He had with Sodom and Gomorrah. When the Lord answered him, He said, "I have sent my prayer warriors into the city to pray for it, for I am not finished with San Francisco." Junn said she sat in church thinking to herself that she knew one of those prayer warriors who were sent, and she couldn't wait to call and tell me what the speaker had to say. I was blessed to hear I would be counted with others who had been called for such a purpose. I consider it an awesome privilege to be in partnership with the God of the Universe, who allows us to rule and reign with Him through prayer and acts of obedience.

Translated

My daughter and I had a driving experience we found difficult to explain. The two of us were involved with GateView Ministries in Mesa, Arizona, headed by Dr. Pamala Smith, that met on Friday evenings. Tracey was part of the worship team, and I taught there occasionally. The drive to Mesa on a Friday night from Phoenix-Glendale, depending on traffic could take an hour and a half to two hours. We always tried to leave the house at least two hours ahead of time due to the rush hour traffic. A couple of times because of extenuating circumstances, we were unable to leave the house in time for Tracey to rehearse before the service. Those times, we prayed together that God would part the traffic and help us get there safe and sound. To our amazement, as we would pull into the parking lot of the ministry and look at the clock, we would discover we had arrived with plenty of time to spare. IMPOSSIBLE!!! Reason would say driving that far in rush hour traffic is impossible to do in that amount of time. However, the Bible says that nothing is impossible with God. The only explanation is we were translated by the supernatural hand of God. Our God is outside of time and apparently for a brief interval, so were we. These encounters are "Beyond Reason."

These "behind the wheel" experiences span decades of awesome encounters with my chauffeur Jesus, who so many years ago, took the wheel and drove me to the pharmacy to purchase a book. That purchase set in motion the course of my life. It began a quest for truth that can only be satisfied by the study of the Word of God.

BEYOND ALL REASON: Moving Out of Logic Into the Supernatural

Chapter 4

WASHING OF THE WORD

As I began to study the Bible, it became clear to me that God is looking to shower His love upon people. He has promised many blessings for His people, and all He asks in return is we love Him back. He wants us to be set apart for His good pleasure. Obedience motivated by love for Him, and His word has many promises of blessings that will follow. The ultimate gift of Salvation is the gift given in His Son Jesus and would have been more than enough. However, our Loving Father in heaven wants to bless us continually. It just doesn't get any better than that!

Conversely, there are consequences for all acts of disobedience. This truth, I'm afraid most of us are not willing to look at or accept. A good share of the problems we have brought upon ourselves, or we are victims of the consequences of someone else's sin. I learned that although the Lord is the essence of love, long-suffering, and full of grace and mercy, He is at the same time full of hatred for all sin. He does move in His anger and judgment when a person or a nation refuses to repent. He, like any good father, will discipline us because He loves us and wants to bring us back to Himself when we have strayed. God will bring judgment to the sons and daughters of disobedience and to those that continue to refuse His gift of mercy given in His Son Jesus. What most people do not understand is that judgment is married to mercy. When judgment does fall, it is His merciful way of causing things to happen that should bring about repentance and forgiveness. It is far better to suffer a little while now than to end up on the wrong side of eternity. Judgment, therefore, is an act of love from the hand of God for the purpose of repentance.

I was entangled for so long by the power of sexual sin, and I wanted to see what the word of God said explicitly about this sin. I discovered that the Bible had a lot to say about sex and what God expected from every believer. What I found was very interesting to me. I started with the New Testament scriptures that I researched concerning the subject, and then many of these scriptures led me to others in the Old Testament. One thing that I learned was that the new gentile converts were given four commandments to observe when they began their walk with the Lord. Only one of these commandments had to do with sexual immorality. We will be examining all four commandments because of their significance and then return to delve more deeply into the commandment to abstain from sexual immorality.

In the early Church, there was no such thing as Christianity. The term Christianity as a religion developed sometime later. The Jewish believers in Jesus or His Hebrew name, Yeshua, did not start a new religion. They still practiced their Judaism in every way and believed

Jesus was their promised Messiah. The gentiles, otherwise known as pagans, also began to believe that Jesus was their promised Messiah. The Jewish believers who saw the Holy Spirit poured out on the pagans, as well as the Jew, were somewhat perplexed in knowing what to do with the gentile believer that joined them on the way. These new gentile believers raised in a pagan culture, would not have been familiar with the many requirements necessary for a life set apart for God. The Jews had spent their lives educating themselves concerning the Torah, the Prophets, and the Writings. The gentiles would not have been familiar with the Hebrew scriptures as instructions that taught them the ways of the Lord and how to walk in them.

It's important to note that the scriptures we are talking about are found in the Old Testament, which I prefer calling The First Covenant. Calling it the Old Testament sends a subliminal message that these scriptures are outdated. They are not out of date. The New Testament writers were continually quoting the First Covenant scriptures, as did Jesus himself.

For familiarity, I will continue to refer to both books of the Bible as the New and Old Testaments. These scriptures found in what is called the Old Testament were the only scriptures that the people had in that day. What we know as the New Testament today is that they were letters circulating and not until late into the 4th century, were they wholly canonized. Therefore, keep in mind as I quote New Testament scripture, they would not have had these references as we do today. Whenever they quoted from the scriptures, they were quoting from the Old Testament. We tend to forget that. When Paul wrote to Timothy saying, *2 Timothy 3:16 16 "All scripture is given by inspiration of God, and is profitable for doctrine, for reproof, for correction, for instruction in righteousness, that the man of God may be complete, thoroughly equipped for every good work,"* Paul was referring to the Old Testament scriptures. These were the only scriptures available at that time. So, to throw out the old is not what is taught in the New Testament.

As I studied the New Testament, I found when the Gentiles came to the Lord, it was problematic for the Jews, because the Gentiles were not familiar with the Old Testament scriptures. The question arose; how on earth would these Gentiles learn what the Jews were taught since childhood? In those days, you were taught a trade, and your formal education was the instruction of the scriptures. The newly converted pagans would have a lot to learn about the ways of the Lord, and it would take time to learn everything that they needed to know. There was a sect of the Pharisees that wanted the new converts to be circumcised. A dispute began, and a council was held in Jerusalem with the apostles and the elders.

The leaders reasoned that the Torah was preached in every city and read in the synagogues every Sabbath. The rest of the commandments would be taught to them as they attended synagogue and imitated the Jewish believers. Altogether the Rabbis tell us there are 613 commandments in the Old Testament to follow, not just the familiar ten that most of us know. It was decided that in order to keep from putting a heavy yoke upon the new believers in the Messiah, only four requirements were made.

They are as follows: 1. To abstain from eating meat that was sacrificed at the altars of demons. 2. Abstain from eating meat that was strangled. 3. Abstain from eating the blood, and lastly, 4. To abstain from sexual immorality. If the new converts could do these few things, they would be doing well, and the rest they would learn along the way.

Let's look at the four commandments that they were given. New believers were to abstain from these four things as they began their walk with the Lord. If only four commands were considered to be so important out of all 613 commandments, it would serve us well to understand why they were prohibited.

First, they were told to abstain from eating any meat that was sacrificed at the altar of demons. The gentile world was an idolatrous society that paid homage to many demon gods. Animals and children were sacrificed at the altars of these demons. Since the creator of the universe is the one and only true God, for one to worship anything or anyone besides Him would be to commit idolatry. If someone innocent ate the meat unknowingly sacrificed at a pagan altar, this would have been a different matter. They would still be innocent compared to someone who ate the meat, knowing it was sacrificed to demons as part of a pagan idol feast.

The act of knowingly partaking of any sacrificed meat would bring defilement to that person and to the entire body of believers. Anyone who did this would have entered into fellowship with the powers of darkness. They were to stop participating in these pagan practices of Satan. His ways are full of darkness, and they were not to have fellowship with demons. They were called out of darkness into the glorious light of God's kingdom. Paul strongly cautioned the Corinthians concerning this matter.

Consider the pagan practice of sacrificing children at the altar Molech. Are we not doing the same thing today as babies are murdered at abortion clinics across this nation? According to the Center for Disease Control, there have been 45,789,558 babies legally aborted from 1970 through 2015 reported in the United States alone. Fortunately, the data compiled since 2015 show a decline in the number of abortions in America. Even though the report now is lower than 45.7 million for today, the figures are still too high, and we must continue to pray and fight against this evil. The demon god of Molech has a stronghold over our nation. When clergy gather to pray at the altar of Planned Parenthood, it becomes clear; demons and witchcraft have influenced the Church.

Then what about the pagan practices of fortune-telling, astrology, seances, acupuncture, magic, hypnosis, yoga, and astral-projection, just to name a few that have crept into the Church with little resistance? Reader, beware! If you are involved in any of these practices, you are practicing witchcraft. There are many demonic influences in the Church today. This subject alone is for another book.

Paul warned the Corinthians that he did not want them to have fellowship with demons. Therefore, the new believers could not drink the "cup of the Lord" and the cup of demons simultaneously. He then went on and told them that they could not partake of the "Lord's table" and the table of demons. To do so, he warned, would provoke the Lord to jealousy. To provoke the Lord to jealousy was referring to the song of Moses that the Lord had given him. He was to teach the song to the people before his death. The song was a witness against the people of Israel who entered the promised land and rebelled against God. They played the harlot with the gods of the foreigners of the land. This prophetic song describes the heart of God. He wanted to set apart the Hebrews he rescued from Egypt for His good pleasure. He wanted to bless them with every good thing in a land flowing with milk and honey. It prophesies of how these same people God called "the apple of His eye" will provoke Him to jealousy and anger. Causing judgment to fall upon them when they would rebel and turn from the one true God, to worship at the altar of demons.

The song ends with a promise of atonement for those who repent. How awesome it is that God created men and women so that He could have a family to love and for them to love Him back. Yet, we see generation after generation turning their back on God and devoting their lives in the pursuit of everything except the One who created them.

Given the background of this first prohibition, it becomes apparent why this commandment was the beginning of the four chosen for the new believer coming out of paganism. They needed to understand just as we do that to provoke the Lord to jealousy had severe consequences. It may seem that the practice of offering and eating the meat that has been sacrificed at the altars of demons is irrelevant since these practices are not as prevalent today. The rise of Satan worship in our society is more and more blatant, and many altars established are to Satan and his demons. Many of us are provoking the Lord to jealousy today because we believe the doctrines of demons, and these doctrines are affecting our daily lives. Many of us in the Church are unknowingly eating at two tables. They are feasting at the table of our Lord and the table of demons, just like some of the new converts could have been doing two thousand years ago. Many churches have departed from the sound doctrine of the scriptures. Some pastors are afraid to preach the truth in fear of losing members, or they don't believe the Word is current. Some have even twisted the interpretation to fit their lifestyle. God has not changed. He remains the same, yesterday, today, and forever. The people of God are to withdraw from all pagan practices, yet some of these practices still continue.

The next two commands I want to examine, are abstaining from eating anything that was strangled or eating from its blood. These prohibitions, I believe, were necessary to make a distinction between the Holy and the unholy. The scriptures tell us that life is in the blood. To take the life of an animal by the strangling of that animal is a very cruel way of killing it for any reason. It cuts off the oxygen and causes a great amount of distress on the animal. The more kosher way of slitting the throat and draining the blood is a much more humane and expedient way of putting an animal to death. Although the Lord has provided certain animals for us to eat, He has instructed us to kill them in the most humane way possible because of His mercy for the animal.

We now have scientific data from Dr. Caroline Leaf's research on how the negative thought processes of the human brain produce toxic chemicals. These toxins poison our system when we are under stressful situations. Fear, she says, of any kind is the leading cause of stress. These toxic chemicals collected within our bodies are said to cause various diseases. She says in her book, "Who Switched Off My Brain," that toxic waste generated by toxic thoughts (like fear) causes the following illnesses: diabetes, cancer, asthma, skin problems, and allergies, to name just a few. If this fear factor is true of humans, I am suspicious it would be true of animals as well. Our little dog shivers when she is fearful. So, was God saying don't eat anything that was strangled due to the animal's fearful stress that could produce extremely toxic chemicals to anyone who ate the meat? I see this as a real possibility. If this is true, then the split-second slaughter by slitting the throat would not give the animal time to produce any toxic chemicals that would harm those that ate the meat. We should question today, what toxic chemicals are in the meat we eat because of the way animals are slaughtered?

God is Holy, and to slaughter an animal in a kosher way is also making a statement, in my opinion, about being compassionate toward the animal. He wants us to be different from the pagans. I believe He did not want the animal to suffer unnecessarily. He gave a law that would and should cause the world to notice. Even in the slaughter of the animals, God was making a distinction between His people and the pagan culture. He was saying, be different, be compassionate, be separated unto me, and be Holy.

The prohibition not to eat the blood, I believe, would have been another counter distinction between the Holy and the common. It was a pagan ritual to eat the blood of the animal and consider it one of the courses of the meal. Those leaving the pagan world and its practices were now instructed to refrain from any of these rituals. Furthermore, I believe when the law was given in Leviticus not to eat the fat or the blood, these things were to be set aside for sacrifices unto God. These blood sacrifices were to be continual reminders that blood was necessary for the atonement of sin. The sacrifices were pointing to the day when Jesus would be the sacrificial lamb, shedding His blood for the atonement of our sin. Since life is in the blood, this prohibition sanctified the blood and set it apart from the more common uses of the pagans. Jesus, during His Passover meal with His disciples, said in Luke 22:19-20,

19 And He took bread, gave thanks and broke it, and gave it to them, saying, "This is My body which is given for you; do this in remembrance of Me." 20 Likewise He also took the cup after supper, saying, "This cup is the new covenant in My blood, which is shed for you.

The significant fact to be aware of here is that all biblical covenants were ratified by shed blood. Those old covenants were promises made by God, and man ratified them by the shedding of blood from the animals that were sacrificed to God. Jeremiah records the promise of a new covenant and says this in Jeremiah 31:33,

33 "But this is the covenant that I will make with the house of Israel after those days, says the LORD: I will put My law in their minds, and write it on their hearts; and I will be their God, and they shall be My people. Jesus, when He took the bread and the wine, was declaring that "those days" are here and that His shed blood will establish the New Covenant. His blood, therefore, is the ransom paid for our redemption. Priceless is the precious blood of our Savior that from the beginning, God intended for the Israelites to make a distinction between the Holy and the unholy use of blood. Therefore, as discussed, it was prohibited to eat the blood. When Jesus took the cup of wine and said, "This is the New Covenant in my blood, which is shed for you," He was announcing His ownership in the new covenant promises. He was saying, I will put my law in your minds, I will write them on your hearts, and I will be your God, and you will be My people. Whenever you drink of this cup, remember me and who "I am" and remember what my shed blood has done for you."

This law that the new converts were given to obey taught them just as it teaches us that the blood of Jesus is Holy and priceless.

This next prohibition I'm saving for last, and it has become a particular interest to me. The converts were instructed to abstain from sexual immorality. As I evaluated the condition of the Church, it has occurred to me that the most difficult challenge we have as a body of believers is to abstain from sexual immorality. Our society today encourages sexual immorality. Couples live together without the benefits of marriage. Sexual deviants flaunt their sin as a lifestyle. Child pregnancies often end in abortion, and pornography websites are readily available for all ages. Sexual immorality is a sin that touches each of our lives in one way or another.

Currently, an international human sex trafficking investigation is uncovering participants that are in high places of government, entertainment, media, the corporate world, as well as the Church. Much of what has been hidden for decades are being uncovered, and the Church is no exception. God is cleaning His house!

Upon searching the different translations for the words sexual immorality, I found some translations use the word "fornication." Fornication is defined as sexual intercourse between two unmarried persons. Another interpretation is the word "whoredom. "The Greek word used here is: porneia, it means fornication and includes adultery as well as incest. The word comes from the root word porneuo, which means: to act the harlot and to indulge in unlawful acts of lust with either sex. It also can be used for practicing idolatry.

Common sense tells us that all activities that indulge in unlawful acts of the lust of the flesh would be idolatry. In other words, anything that entices us away from God is idolatry. Just a little side note here. One day when I was praying, I asked the Lord whether there was anything in my life that He would consider to be idolatry. I wanted to make sure that there was nothing that I was doing that would be displeasing to the Lord. The answer gave me a whole new slant on the subject. He said this: "Anything that occupies your thought life more than I do…is idolatry." Wow! That sure was a large pill to swallow.

The gentile culture of the day was full of all kinds of gods to worship, and their religious practices included much sexual immorality in the worship of these gods. Some women priests were temple prostitutes and held in high esteem in that culture. Sexual orgies were the norm in the worship of their gods. These practices created a culture of sexual immorality of every kind. The various writers of the New Testament were continually warning the new converts to abstain from fornication, adultery, sodomy, homosexuality, and incest. These were standard practices of their culture, just as they are today in our culture. These practices are so commonplace in our society today that our young people are unaware that sexual immorality is a sin and displeasing to a Holy God. Virgins, whether male or female, are mocked and encouraged to sin and join the ranks of their promiscuous friends.

Paul, when writing to the Corinthian believers, warned them not to engage in any sexual immorality as the Israelites did in the ancient of days. Paul was referring to the time when God's judgment came upon the camp, and twenty-three thousand died in one day. This account is recorded in Numbers. However, in Numbers, it is written that twenty-four thousand, not twenty-three thousand, died of a plague. The discrepancy could possibly be explained by the fact that Paul says that twenty-three thousand died in one day. Perhaps the other 1,000 may have died on previous days. His reference to the situation was to warn us that such behavior has consequences.

This timeframe is where the people joined themselves in harlotry with the women of Moab. These women enticed the people to worship Baal of Peor. The ritual or worship involved sensual licentiousness of the most grotesque kind, and these practices angered the Lord to jealousy. Therefore, He instructed Moses to hang the leaders in the sun. Some think that Baal Peor was related to an Egyptian sun god. This may be the reason that God had the leaders hung in the sun.

Moses then instructed the judges of Israel to kill the men that had joined themselves to Baal Peor. The anger of the Lord stopped when Phinehas, in his rage over this spiritual adultery, took his javelin and entered the tent of a defiant man of Israel. This man paraded a woman of whoredom in front of the congregation and at the door of the tabernacle. With a javelin in hand, Phineas thrust it through both adulterer's bodies. The man and the Midianite woman. This stopped the plague that had infected and killed twenty-four thousand people. The Lord was so pleased with Phinehas's righteous act of holy indignation against this horrific wickedness in the camp. God gave him a covenant of peace and an everlasting priesthood to him and the generations to follow that were of his seed. God did this because Phinehas was zealous for his God and made an atonement for the children of Israel, which stopped the Lord from consuming the children of Israel in his jealousy.

This commandment to abstain from sexual immorality was given to teach the new converts that they were no longer citizens of a corrupt society. They were now citizens of a Kingdom of Holiness. As such, they were to take control of their fleshly appetites and to walk in the Spirit. They were, just as Christians are, commanded to be Holy as He is Holy. To be Holy is to be separated or set apart for God. In other words, they were not to participate in any pagan practices. God wanted them pure and undefiled by abstaining from all pagan practices of sexual immorality. In doing so, they would be recognized as belonging to the Lord God of Israel. Sexual sin identifies us as spiritual adulterers.

As I began to study the subject, I discovered that sexual immorality is a grievous snare for the people that God created for himself, from the beginning of time. From cover to cover in my Bible, I found accounts of men and women who succumbed to this weakness in their flesh. I also discovered there were severe consequences for their sexual indulgences. For the new believers to continue in their sexual sin, would bring the judgment of God upon themselves as well as the entire congregation of believers.

It also surprised me when I came across another scripture that said that sexual sin was the only sin that was against my own body. Immediately, I had insight that I would be paying the price of this sin against my body in some way physically. Based on that information, I also believe this commandment was given to protect the new converts from various diseases that would have been the consequences of continued sexual sin.

Our society has grown accustomed to the multiple conditions that are transmitted through sexual contact. We don't even bat an eye when the advertisement for Herpes flashes across our TV screen. It's as if it were advertising for the cure of a common cold. We have accepted STD, HIV, and AIDS as diseases of our culture and time. As a society, we do not look upon these diseases as consequences brought about by sexual sin.

At this point, I want to interject something that I believe to be very important for all of us to understand. It seems it is human nature to rate sin, making one sin worse than another. Let me draw your attention to something in the scriptures that I hope will change the way we think about sin. In the book of Leviticus, we find the penalty for breaking the laws mentioned to be death. The same sentence of death is for these acts, and there is no distinction made as to which sin is worse.

The following acts are:

1. Sacrificing children to Molech, a demon god. We do this with the sin of abortion. 2. Going to a medium or being a medium, which is someone who calls up the dead. Otherwise, known as a séance, and we are not to be listening to familiar spirits either. 3. Cursing your father or mother. 4. Committing adultery. 5. Committing incest with any family member. 6. Committing homosexuality. 7. Committing bestiality. 8. Having sexual intercourse during a woman's menstrual period.

There are many more commandments to observe; however, these are the ones punishable by death if broken. Our society today does not punish the breaking of these laws with the death penalty. However, breaking them does bring spiritual death, and often, premature physical death. Repentance is the answer to a long life where these sins are concerned. We need to make a paradigm shift in our thinking concerning all sin. The sins mentioned previously are all an abomination to a Holy God. We, however, do not look at them as equally condemning.

I believe this is a good place to comment about judging. We are not to judge another person's sin to the point of condemning them for it. Scripture tells us that we are in danger of being judged ourselves when we do this. This type of judgment sets in motion the fall of the person who is making the judgment. I have seen in the ministry people that have judged sexual sin, fall into sexual sin themselves. We are to judge in the sense of recognizing the sin in someone's life. Without condemning them, we are to correct them lovingly when the opportunity presents itself. Hopefully, our love and prayers for that person will turn them around. Let's love them right out of their sin, just like the Lord loved us right out of our sin.

God loves the sinner and hates the sin that they are committing. He loves the homosexual just as much as he loves the person who has just cursed his mother. God hates the act of homosexuality just as much as He hates the sin of cursing one's parents. He hates sin of any kind due to its destructive nature. As imitators of Christ, we are to hate the sin and love the sinner making no distinction between one sin and another. For every one of us has sinned, and fallen short of the Glory of God.

With so much hatred toward the gay community in our world today, I wanted to draw attention to these truths. The gay couple walks in the same blindness to their sin as does a couple having sexual intercourse without the benefits of marriage, (identified in the Bible as fornication). It is a blindness to sin for the man or woman who is committing adultery, unaware of the seriousness of their sin. It's the same as a rebellious teenager who curses his parents, or those kids that hold a seance for the fun of it, or those new age people who confess to having a spirit guide. Blindness to sin is why we need the law in the first place. Love, not condemning judgment, is the answer to all these sins. Leave the judging to the Judge of the Universe. Our love, compassion, and prayers will draw others to God, and the goodness of God leads a man to repentance.

These are the four laws that I learned about concerning the new converts. They were to turn away from their sinful ways and be faithful to the one true God and to obey His commands. Doing this would separate them from the pagan world and its rituals and customs of the day. Keeping these four commands, they would be well on their way to understanding the ways of the one true God, the Lord God of Israel. They had so much to learn, and I realized I did as well the more I studied His Word.

Daily, I was learning more and more about my sinful condition. I was learning that no one sins alone. Every sinful act will touch someone else, and unrepentant sin is passed on from generation to generation. Just look around you. You are your mother's daughter, and you, young man, are your father's son. We are, by nature, sinful people. None of us can break away from wicked things or a sinful lifestyle on our own. Sin is so ingrained within us that we do not even recognize it as sin. We may have our standard for the difference between right and wrong, but that does not mean that our standard measures up with our creator's standard.

That is why we do need a "Savior," Jesus is the only answer to our dilemma. He is the only one that has the power to change our behavior. Anyone that has ever tried to change by using behavior modification techniques knows it does not work for the long haul. Jesus and the Holy Spirit must do the work. It is the Lord's responsibility to sanctify us. He is the only one that can wipe away our sins and cleanse us inside.

My encounters with this Holy Being, Jesus, was changing me daily. He changed the way I thought and felt about things. Just as the Bible teaches, I was becoming a "new creation." The Bible speaks of "the washing of the Word." Every day, as I read the Word of God, there was a supernatural element at work that was washing and cleansing my mind. Many of my old ways were dropping by the wayside, without any effort of my own. I believe this was due to the empowerment of the Lord's phenomenal Grace making internal changes.

When I heard the voice of God for the first time, he was calling me to repent from sexual immorality. He was asking me to separate myself from the ways of the world and to become His child. It was His Love calling me out of the darkness of my soul into His glorious light. It was His love that supernaturally put a book in my hands that contained His love letters to me. These supernatural experiences launched me into a lifelong quest for the truth. The study of His Word became and continues to be a "positive obsession."

BEYOND ALL REASON: Moving Out of Logic Into the Supernatural

Chapter 5

POSITIVE OBSESSION

That Living Bible was the beginning of a search for truth that has become for me what I consider a "positive obsession." I have on my bookshelves, countless translations of the Bible. I love every one of them for the insight that they have given me on my quest for truth. Each translator has contributed their wealth of wisdom and scholarship to my obsession. There has been much controversy surrounding this paraphrased translation, called The Living Bible that I purchased at the Pharmacy. Kenneth Taylor, the founder of Tyndale Publishing, came up with this paraphrased version of the Bible because he wanted to have a Bible with language that even his children could understand. Scholars were upset with the paraphrasing because they did not think that the accuracy was there. After much research, I agree with them about the clarification. However, I found this easy to understand language ministered to my soul. Even though there is an argument concerning the authenticity of an exact translation, I am convinced that it was a tool in the hand of a Holy God. This Bible led this woman on a further quest for the truth. It certainly had the Lord's approval. He went to a lot of trouble to get this particular Bible into my hands. I am so glad that He did, for I found this version so easy to understand, and that is where I needed to start. It was unlike other Bibles that I had attempted to read. The nourishment that I received from reading this version of the New Testament is compared to a newborn babe feeding at its mother's breast. As the child grows, it learns to feed itself, and more foods are introduced to the baby. As I began to grow, I discovered other translations. I was like a child being fed from milk to meat. My learning grew from the Living Bible to the New King James Bible, the Complete Jewish Bible as well as the Messianic Jewish Shared Heritage Bible, the Septuagint and the Pure Word Bible. These are among many other valuable learning tools that line my bookshelves. I have no problem with recommending the Living Bible as anyone's first attempt at reading a Bible.

My quest for truth began long before the purchase of that first Bible that changed my way of thinking. I had been searching for truth in many directions. I was fascinated by astrology and hypnosis. I read many books on the subject, being drawn to the psychics and prophets of our time. I wanted to develop my powers of extrasensory perception. The supernatural was intriguing to me, and I was being drawn deeper and deeper into its perversion of the truth. I wrongly believed the clairvoyant people I read and studied about, were God gifted people with supernatural insight into a realm that I, too, wanted to enter.

The Lord loved me so much that he rescued me out of my darkness. He showed me the difference between the counterfeit supernatural from the devil and the real thing from the Holy Spirit. At the same time, God put the Living Bible and two other books into my hands. These books totally changed my perception of the supernatural. I am an avid reader, and many wonderful books have helped me to grow and to change. However, no other books, outside of the Bible, had as great of an influence as Hal Lindsey's writings did. The two books, "The Late Great Planet Earth," and "Satan is Alive and Well on Planet Earth," created such an impact and dramatic change in my thinking. These books were such eye-openers to me, and they became great motivational tools to study the Word of God for myself. I was so shaken by the things that I was reading that I was determined to find out for myself if these things were true. Because if they were, I was totally deceived, which I found out to be the case. Many of my opinions about life were based on the lies propagated by philosophies and occult practices. I was deceived into thinking that the taste of the supernatural that I had salivated over, was from God. I was shocked to learn that these practices were from Satan, the dark side of the supernatural. Satan is a deceiver and has no problem with letting me or anyone else think his counterfeit gifts are from the God of creation.

The supernatural realm of the Holy Spirit was hidden from me. We are told as Christians to be in the world, but not of it. I was of it! The most horrible thing about deception is a person does not know they are being deceived. Not until they have been set free from the deception. We must be confronted with the truth to receive deliverance from deception. Even then, unless we are open to admitting how wrong we have been, the truth cannot have its intended effect upon our lives. Likewise, the bondage of deception and the prison that keeps us captive does not become a realization until we have been freed from it.

The beautiful wonder of truth is the fact that once it is embraced, it will indeed set us free, just as Jesus promised us. Truth by its very nature can surface above all lies and make inroads into the heart of every sincere seeker. We are, each of us, going to be held accountable for our knowledge of the Word and whether we have believed and obeyed it. If we have not followed our Father's instructions that are spelled out from Genesis to Revelation, we will be without an excuse on that day when we stand before Him.

I thank my God for educated men and women who are His obedient children and write to tell about it. Their books of instruction and clarification of the scriptures have caused me to take responsibility for finding the truth for myself. On that final day, when we all will stand before the Lord and must give an account of our lives, there will be no one else to blame for our disobedient lives but ourselves. To say to HIM on that day that "I did not know any better," or that "no one told me," will be of no avail or excuse.

Romans 1:18-21 18 For the wrath of God is revealed from heaven against all ungodliness and unrighteousness of men, who suppress the truth in unrighteousness, 19 because what may be known of God is manifest in them, for God has shown it to them. 20 For since the creation of the world His invisible attributes are clearly seen, being understood by the things that are made, even His eternal power and Godhead, so that they are without excuse, 21 because, although they knew God, they did not glorify Him as God, nor were thankful, but became futile in their thoughts, and their foolish hearts were darkened.

What a sad day it will be when we realize we have believed the lies of the enemy and have bought into the philosophy of the world. What a sad day it will be when we have to face the fact that we never thought it important enough to take the time to investigate for ourselves whether the things that we believe are true or not and whether these things we believe merit our allegiance.

The lies we believe, keep us in a walled prison maze that we house and protect in our minds. I am sure that you have heard it said: "The road to hell is paved with good intentions." Well, I say, "That the road to hell is paved with lies." The most deadly of all lies is the belief that you are saved when you are not. Many people know very well they are in danger of hell's fire. They are, in my opinion, in better shape than those that think they are saved when they are not. Those people that know their condition can do something about it. They are operating out of the truth that if they do not do something about their situation, then they will be eternally separated from God. These, I believe, have a better chance of finding their way to God. They have a better chance because they are operating out of truth. Those, however, who falsely believe the lie that their salvation is secure for various false reasons, are in grave danger. They are less likely to come out of their deception and ignorant state. The lies that they believe keep them from Heaven's doors. I was in that condition until God came looking for me on that pivotal day of my life.

Many churches on the street corners of the United States and around the world preach a false doctrine. Their doctrines teach every conceivable way to eternal Heaven, except through the blood sacrifice of Jesus Christ. So many religions teach "good works" is your ticket to Heaven. The problem with that doctrine is not ever knowing if you have worked hard enough to make it. Salvation is a free gift, and you cannot do one thing to earn it. This gift can only be obtained by coming through the door named Jesus and applying his blood sacrifice to our lives. THERE IS NO OTHER WAY!

Upon careful study of the scriptures, one discovers the Lord loves to demonstrate the truth in many varied and puzzling ways. Painting pictures, repeating patterns, rehearsing for the main events, hinting at deeper meanings, and solving riddles, are just some of His creative ways of serving the manna of His Word to us. I call these methods, "Sweet Manna, hidden in plain sight." My obsession with discovering the truth contained in His Word eventually birthed the ministry that I founded by the same name, Sweet Manna Ministries. The ministry is dedicated to teaching the Hebraic roots of the Christian faith and uncovering the things in the Word that are hidden in plain sight. Finding these hidden Gems is like a treasure hunt in the Word of God.

I interrupt the telling of my story to bring you one of those hidden gems where the Lord has painted a picture of salvation, framed in Exodus. The Hebrews had been slaves in Egypt for four hundred years before the Lord raised Moses to bring them out. Generation after generation knew nothing but enslavement. Therefore, all self-esteem was lost. What little self-worth remained was based on how much work they were able to do. A slave's value was tied to the number of bricks he could make. The rather grand and miraculous Exodus from Egypt freed the Hebrew slaves from their taskmasters and brought them out of the land. It did not, however, free them from a mentality that related their self-worth with the amount of work that they could produce. The

Lord began introducing the Hebrews to the idea of rest when He instructed them not to gather manna on the seventh day. They were told to gather enough for two days on the sixth day. On the seventh day, they were to do nothing. Shortly after, Moses returns from the mountain with the ten commandments and instructions on how to keep the seventh-day Sabbath. They were not to do any work on the Sabbath. They were to remember how the Lord saved them from their taskmasters. Also, to remember that after the six days of creation, the Lord rested on the seventh day.

The Seventh-day, i.e., the Sabbath, is the Lord's day. Jesus is the Lord of the Sabbath. When we put Jesus in the center of the Sabbath day rest, we see a picture begin to emerge. Just as the shed blood of the sacrificial lambs painted a picture of the Lamb of God shedding blood for us; likewise, the Sabbath day rest paints a picture too. The Hebrews were instructed to honor the Sabbath by doing no work on the Sabbath. It was meant to be a day that they were not to do anything of their own making. The "hidden manna," we see in this picture, are the brush strokes of our Lord proclaiming His people had intrinsic value not based upon work. The picture painted of the Sabbath represents the Day of Salvation; therefore, all work was forbidden. There is no amount of work that we can do to gain our salvation. Salvation has been purchased with the precious blood of Yeshua. Yeshua is Jesus' Hebrew name, and it means "salvation." Jesus is our salvation! The picture of this seventh-day also points to the Sabbath Day rest of the future when the curse pronounced at the fall will be removed. The millennium reign of Christ is thought of as the 7th-day rest. I often proclaim salvation is a free gift that will cost you everything. Jesus told us that we must be "born again," and He is the only doorway that leads us to the Father. Some were not listening then, and some are not listening now.

Before I had my epiphany with God, I attended a Lutheran church and was told things in error that I believed. From the pulpit, the Lutheran denomination told me that I was saved and going to heaven when I died. When I married my husband, we were married in his church by his pastor. I joined the Lutheran church and continued to worship there until the striking realization with God changed the way that I looked at Christianity. This church taught that baptism saved you, and they practiced the sprinkling of water on an infant's head as their method of baptism. So fearful were the people of my denomination that they believed should a baby die before baptism, it would go to hell. Therefore, my children were baptized at three weeks to put their grandparent's fearful minds at ease. This particular belief was not one that I had adopted. They further taught that confirmation reaffirmed your baptism. So then, you were on your way to heaven if you had been baptized and confirmed. According to the teachings of this denomination, these two rituals saved you.

I am not saying that it is impossible to get saved when going through confirmation classes. I am sure it happens to some people. What I am saying is that these rituals do not save anyone. A confirmand is saved when they open the door of their heart. This decision will make room for the Spirit of the Lord to reside there. Then the Holy Spirit will influence one's mind, changing it and conforming one's demeanor into the image of our Lord. The fruit of salvation means a changed life. The other thing that I am saying is baptism and confirmation did nothing for me spiritually. I want to be very clear! In every denomination, some hearts are right with God. Therefore, in every denomination, some saints have become "born again." I know this was true with the Lutheran Church that I attended. Many fine people loved the Lord and whose hearts I believe were right with the Lord. What I am saying is although many seeds were planted in my heart attending service week after week, never-the-less, it was outside of the Lutheran Church God found me and introduced me to the Holy Spirit and filled me with His gifts.

As I entered adulthood, I continued on my merry way, led by sin's deception. I went to church almost every Sunday. I entered the sanctuary each week, sang some songs, listened to the pastor preach a sermon, and left the sanctuary week after week unchanged. That same merry way that trapped me in the grip of deception was the road that was also traveled by my husband and our three children. Each one of us had been baptized and confirmed. The extent of our theology consisted of a little more than "Jesus loves me, this I know. For the Bible tells me so." Each of us continued to embrace our sins, not realizing that the road we were traveling would lead to death. The reason I say the road that we were traveling was leading us to death, is that the Bible says the wages of sin is death. All of us at one time were dead men walking. Unaware that we were dancing to the tune of a dirge. Sin, by its very nature, is cunning and deceptive. It comes to us wrapped up in many pleasurable packages. Like honey, it tastes so sweet and delicious with its first tantalizing mouthful that we want more and more until that final disgusting taste, like too much honey, it causes us to vomit. This deceptive sickness of the soul leads to death unless the Divine Physician intervenes and brings healing and restoration to our sin-sick souls.

One of the first things I learned when I studied the Word of God, was that I was lied to even about the circumstances surrounding Jesus' birth and the visitation of the wise men. The second chapter of the New Testament states the Magi followed the star they saw in the East to a HOUSE. Our tradition had us believing that they followed the star to the manger where he was born. When in fact, they had followed the star to a house where Jesus lived with his mother and Joseph. Some scholars suggest Jesus may have been as old as two years when the Magi arrived. It could take a couple of years to follow that bright star of Bethlehem from the East traveling on foot. That star was proclaiming that a King had been born, and this is where He resides.

Now I had to ask myself if I had been deceived about this little-known fact, how many other things were presented to me as truth when it was nothing more than tradition? I discovered celebrating the birth of Christ on December 25th is nothing more than a tradition. The evidence in the Word of God supports Jesus' birth to be in September. See the book that I authored, "Jesus and Hanukkah," for more information on that subject. Much of what we do in our daily lives is nothing more than tradition, and there is nothing wrong with tradition as long as we know why we do the things that we do. We need to make sure that our traditions have a purpose and are not unbiblical.

I once heard a story that brings this point home. A young woman was in the kitchen, helping her mother with Sunday dinner. She watched her mother take the ham from the refrigerator and place it on the cutting board, which was on the kitchen countertop. She then took a butcher knife from its holder and began to slice three to four inches off of the end of the ham shank. Her mother then placed the ham shank in the roasting pan and put it in the oven to bake for dinner. As she was returning the sliced end piece to the refrigerator, her daughter asked her the question, "Why did you slice the end of that ham? Her mother replied, "I don't know. My mother always did it that way." Puzzled, the young girl went to the phone to call her grandmother. "Nana, she said, why did you always cut the end off of the ham when you prepared it?" Her grandmother, chuckling, said, "Why, honey, I always cut the end of the ham off because my roasting pan was not large enough for the whole ham." Do you see the point? Often, we continue to do things out of tradition, without investigating how that tradition started in the first place. Jesus was continually confronting the people of his day about their traditions. Many of their traditions were leading them astray. We do not want our traditions to lead us astray. Let's take a look at what is written concerning one such instance when Jesus confronted the traditions of the Scribes and the Pharisees.

Mark 7:1-23 1 Then the Pharisees and some of the scribes came together to Him, having come from Jerusalem. 2 Now when they saw some of His disciples eat bread with defiled, that is, with unwashed hands, they found fault. 3 For the Pharisees and all the Jews do not eat unless they wash their hands in a special way, holding the tradition of the elders. 4 When they come from the marketplace, they do not eat unless they wash. And there are many other things which they have received and hold, like the washing of cups, pitchers, copper vessels, and couches. 5 Then the Pharisees and scribes asked Him, "Why do Your disciples not walk according to the tradition of the elders, but eat bread with unwashed hands?" 6 He answered and said to them, "Well did Isaiah prophesy of you hypocrites, as it is written:'This people honors Me with their lips, But their heart is far from Me. 7 And in vain they worship Me, Teaching as doctrines the commandments of men.' 8 For laying aside the commandment of God, you hold the tradition of men—the washing of pitchers and cups, and many other such things you do." 9 He said to them, "All too well you reject the commandment of God, that you may keep your tradition. 10 For Moses said, 'Honor your father and your mother'; and, 'He who curses father or mother, let him be put to death.' 11 But you say, 'If a man says to his father or mother, "Whatever profit you might have received from me is Corban"—' (that is, a gift to God), 12 then you no longer let him do anything for his father or his mother, 13 making the word of God of no effect through your tradition which you have handed down. And many such things you do." 14 When He had called all the multitude to Himself, He said to them, "Hear Me, everyone, and understand: 15 There is nothing that enters a man from outside which can defile him; but the things which come out of him, those are the things that defile a man. 16 If anyone has ears to hear, let him hear!" 17 When He had entered a house away from the crowd, His disciples asked Him concerning the parable. 18 So He said to them, "Are you thus without understanding also? Do you not perceive that whatever enters a man from outside cannot defile him, 19 because it does not enter his heart but his stomach, and is eliminated, thus purifying all foods?" 20 And He said, "What comes out of a man, that defiles a man. 21 For from within, out of the heart of men, proceed evil thoughts, adulteries, fornications, murders, 22 thefts, covetousness, wickedness, deceit, lewdness, an evil eye, blasphemy, pride, foolishness. 23 All these evil things come from within and defile a man."

The traditions of man and the doctrines of man can keep us from the essential truth of our existence, and that is the Word of the Lord that says we must be "born again." Nicodemus was a Pharisee, steeped in tradition. His tradition made it difficult to grab hold of the spiritual concept of being "born again."

Jesus made it clear to Nicodemus, an influential member of the Sanhedrin, that to see the Kingdom of God, one must be born again. One must be born of the Spirit. Nicodemus, although he was a Torah scholar, could not understand how we could be born all over again. This most quintessential truth could not penetrate his unregenerate mind. His question to Jesus revealed he was in the dark as to how it would be possible to be born again. He asked, "How can we be put back into the womb of our mother to be born once again? His question had the assumption that this would be impossible. He, like each of us, was blind to the new birth in the Spirit. We remain blind until the Spirit of God resurrects us into a new life by infusing His Spirit within us. Until that happens, we are blind and deaf; and each of us, dead men walking. Without the Holy Spirit residing within us, our knowledge of God's Word is nothing more than history lessons. At another time, Thomas, one of the disciples, spoke to Jesus, saying, "Lord, we do not know where you are going. And how can we know the way?" Jesus responded to Thomas by saying, "I am the way, the truth, and the life. No one comes to the Father except through me." Jesus was confronting another tradition, the belief that because the Jews were the sons of Abraham, they had an automatic passage to heaven. There is no reconciliation with God the Father, except through His Son, Jesus Christ. He is the promise of salvation and the promised Messiah.

Satan has done an excellent job of perverting this truth. He has created all sorts of different kinds of religions that teach there is another way to this place we call heaven. There are many religions and, therefore, many doors available to us in this world that we live in. They all hold a measure of the truth, and that is why they are so appealing to us. Satan uses a standard of truth as a bait to trap us. However, there is only one door that opens to the whole truth; that door is the door that opens up to a relationship with Jesus, the Son of God. He and He alone is the door to the Father. According to the scriptures, Jesus said he is standing at the door of your heart, knocking. He will not force Himself upon you. Jesus stands waiting for you to open your heart's door. Once you open that door and invite Him in, he has promised to fellowship with you. Also, He has promised never to leave you or forsake you. The choice is yours to make.

I do not know the exact time I went through the door that leads to the Father. I do not know the day or the hour that I was born again. There is not one moment in time that I can point my finger to and exclaim it to be the pivotal moment of my rebirth. Unlike many others that I know, my born again experience had a very long pregnancy and a rather unnoticeable easy birth. Some people explain their born again experience as a life-changing moment; when the finger of God was upon them. They were never to be the same again. This type of instantaneous change did not happen to me. I grew and was nurtured in the spiritual womb of my Father until I was full term. The exact hour of my rebirth is only known to God. I never confessed in a prayer that I was a sinner needing to be saved. I never pleaded with God to forgive me for all the sinful things that I had done in my life. The day the Lord's thundering voice invaded my car was a pivotal moment because, from that point on, my heart's cry was to know HIM. I pleaded to know His heart. I begged to see His face. I wanted intimacy with the one who had created me. I wanted intimacy with the one who knew me better than I knew myself. It wasn't until this relationship with the Living Christ that

I began to develop and became aware of my sinful condition and my need to be forgiven.

The secular society that we live in has taken on the Christian term "born again" to express several new and different experiences that are far from the born again experience that Jesus was referring to. When someone has a new lease on life, they are said to be born again. Another may be free from a life-long addiction, and they express it as having been reborn. I've heard it said that one is born again when they fall in love. Many wonderful and exciting life-changing experiences are expressed today, "as having been born again." It's an expression used so often that it has diluted the significance of the Spiritual born again experience Jesus was talking about. The born again experience that Jesus was speaking of is a spiritual experience, unlike the born again experience the world speaks of. Jesus tells us that without it, we are unable to see the kingdom of God. We must be born of the Spirit of God.

Nicodemus was a learned man, very knowledgeable of the Torah. He recognized Jesus as an authoritative and wise teacher; therefore, he came at night alone, to be taught by Jesus. Yet, he did not seem to grasp the concept of being born of the Spirit. In other words, Nicodemus had the knowledge but did not understand. He had eyes but could not see. So, did I. I had eyes but could not see. I had the knowledge but did not understand. I was spiritually blind and unable to discern spiritual things. I couldn't discern spiritual things without the help of the Holy Spirit. The Bible makes it clear that you must have spiritual discernment to see spiritual things. Indeed, these things are "beyond all reason."

Paul states in 1 Corinthians 2:14, *14 But the natural man does not receive the things of the Spirit of God, for they are foolishness to him; nor can he know them, because they are spiritually discerned.*

Up until the time of my rebirth, I had been searching for truth in all the wrong places. Once the Word of God became alive to me, it became the standard for truth in my life. I began to search for answers to my many questions in the Bible. According to Hal Lindsey and the influence of the book he wrote, "Satan is Alive on Planet Earth," much of my life was spent in Satan's kingdom, and I did not know it. My house was full of books inspired by the Prince of Darkness. One does not have to be a Satan worshiper to be influenced by his deceptive practices. Until we accept Jesus as our Lord and Savior, and until we are reconciled to God as our Father, we have, even if we have not been unaware of it, been serving our Father Satan. Satan is, after all, the "head of this world system." It is his system and philosophy that we have bought. It is a system that continues to shout at us that all roads lead to heaven and that there are no consequences for sin; therefore, anything goes, if it feels good, do it, and love of self, rules supreme.

Those who are ruled by the King of Kings have entered a kingdom that is not of this world. We are admonished in the commandments "to love our neighbor as ourselves." We are instructed to lay our lives down for another. We are taught to put other people's needs before our own. Contrary to this selfish world that we live in, Christians are to live selfless lives. We are to be motivated by LOVE. Our neighbor does not only mean people living next store to us but anyone that we come in contact with. We are to love all the people that we come in contact with, and it becomes a genuine challenge in this day and age.

Perhaps the little corner of the planet that you live on, love for one another abounds. On the far side of the desert where I live, someone is getting murdered daily. Our house is locked like Fort Knox at night because of the lawlessness prevailing in our neighborhood and city. Today as I write this chapter, I have just returned from Walmart, where I went to pick up a few items for our home to discover upon my return that a shooter has just shot and killed 20 people and injured 26 at a Walmart in El Paso, Texas. And it is also being reported that a Satanist shooter just killed nine people in Dayton, Ohio.

Furthermore, Chicago reports nine killed and thirty-nine injured over the weekend, which is around what is said for Chicago every weekend. Violence is spiking all over the world. I believe the kindest and most loving act we can do for our neighbor today is to pray for them. This Nation needs an awakening! We need an outpouring of the Holy Spirit from one coast to the other because it is our only hope. The hearts of men and women need to be changed, and the Lord is the only one that can do this. Fear for our safety is a far cry from the days, as a little girl, when we never locked our doors, and I slept outside on a blanket in the back yard. In those days, we fell asleep, gazing at the stars, safe and sound, and free from the fear of being harmed. Not so today. Never-the-less to obey the scriptures, we are to look for opportunities to love our neighbor with acts of thoughtful behavior and kind deeds. Doing so allows us to be the hands of Jesus, expressing His love. Then as I said before, an even greater gift of love to a wounded hurting world is to pray for an outpouring of the Holy Spirit. Our biggest problem here and abroad is that a significant part of humanity is without God. The commandment to love our neighbor as one's self was reiterated in the gospels by Jesus. Once a Pharisee asked Jesus, "Of all the commandments which is the most important?" Jesus answered, making the entire Torah so simple. Matthew 22:37-40

37 Jesus said to him, "You shall love the LORD your God with all your heart, with all your soul, and with all your mind.' 38 This is the first and great commandment. 39 And the second is like it: 'You shall love your neighbor as yourself.' 40 On these two commandments hang all the Law and the Prophets."

The Word of God has become for me a "positive obsession" since the first day the Living Bible was put in my hand by the Almighty. I love digging for the truth embedded within the chapters of this incredible book. Yet, Jesus summed everything up with Love. Love the Lord God with everything within you, and love your neighbor in the same way that you love yourself. This truth has guided me for years now. It is simple and profound. Truth can be easy and at the same time, very difficult. I have had great success, and I have failed miserably. Although I have failed the Lord time and time again, he has never failed me. Jesus also made another wonderful promise for us. He promised to send us the Holy Spirit, whose job it is to lead us into all truth. A study of the Word of God is not enough, and we need the help of the Holy Spirit as we study the Word and apply what we have learned to our lives.

Chapter 6

HE IS ALIVE

One moment in time can change your life forever. This chapter is an account of that momentous period that changed this author for eternity. I had many moments in time that changed the course of my life. None, however, as monumental as this one. I have had many experiences with the Lord that have built my faith, none yet, this profound. Many of those experiences happened before this particular moment. Not one of them has left such an indelible mark upon my soul. This one moment has turned out to be the defining factor of who I am, why I was born, and what I am called to do. Here is the account of "that moment."

For many years I suffered from gallbladder attacks. They seemed to come on after overtaxing my system with fatty foods. The worst attack came after overeating home-made toffee, loaded with butter, and one of my favorite indulgences. Because of the excruciating pain, I was taken this time to the E.R. Eventually, the stone passed, and I was dismissed from the hospital with instructions to see my doctor. I left thinking that I never wanted to go through that again. Previous to this attack, I had prayed for the Lord to heal me and was confident that He would. I had been a witness to many supernatural interventions from the Lord on my behalf and was satisfied He would take care of this gallbladder problem as well. But, because this attack was so awful, I decided that it was time to go the medical route. I picked up the phone and made a call to my doctor to set up an appointment to see him.

After the exam in the doctor's office, my doctor began to schedule the surgery that, according to him, was long overdue. In addition to the gallbladder surgery needed, I also needed rectal surgery that my doctor had wanted to do for some time. I asked him whether he could do both operations at the same time. "Because," I said, "You'll never get me to go under the knife again." He said that doing both surgeries would be too hard on me. I insisted that I did not care. If I was going to be miserable, I would rather be miserable this one time instead of being miserable again with another surgery. He said, "OK, I will consider it, but only if you are doing well after the gallbladder surgery." I then asked him if he was a praying man, and he said that he was. I proceeded to ask him if he would pray for me and for the surgery to go well. He laughed and said, "I pray, but never for gallbladder surgery."

I left his office thinking that his job had become somewhat routine for him, so much so that the gallbladder surgery at least in his mind, was a "walk in the park." For me, however, this was a serious business that needed to be covered in prayer. This experience I am sharing with you was back in the day when gallbladder surgery left you with a 6-inch scar from the incision, and the recovering time for the operation was six weeks or more. The day before the scheduled surgery, I packed my suitcase with the things that I would need for my stay in the hospital. I expected to be there a week or so. I was ever so careful not to forget the typed note I had prepared as a surprise for my doctor. The following day, the day of the scheduled operation, I was cautious to keep the note that I had typed hidden in my hand as they rolled me down the hall of the hospital getting prepped for the surgery. They opened my gown and did the prepping necessary to assure that my midriff was sterilized and ready for the procedure.

Once I was left alone, I opened my gown and secured the note I had typed to my midriff with scotch tape prepared ahead of time. I closed my gown, smiling as I remembered the words that I had typed for the doctor to see when they rolled me into his theater unconscious.

"Please handle this body with care and prayer;

For it is the temple of the Holy Spirit"

After the surgery, and after I had gained consciousness, my doctor came into my hospital room.

"Young Lady," he said, "You have no idea how much commotion you caused in the operating room. We opened your gown and found the note you had left us. That note caused quite a disturbance. First, we had to prep you all over again so you would not get infected. Then, I had everyone join hands in a circle around your unconscious body. We prayed just as your note had instructed. Because the gallbladder surgery went so very well, and because your vital signs were strong, I decided that I would do the rectal surgery just as you had requested. So, I rolled you over and slapped the note you wrote on your bare butt, and proceeded to take care of your rectal problem. Now, if you will turn around."

I turned around to find that they had scotch-taped the note on the wall above my bed. It remained there for the duration of my stay. I was pretty miserable from the pain of both incisions, but the steady stream of visitors helped me to keep my mind off of the pain. For the next two days, I had one visitor after another come into my room to introduce themselves to me. They were doctors and nurses who were either involved in my doctor's theater or had come to investigate and meet the woman that so boldly proclaimed her body was the temple of the Holy Spirit. The story had spread through the hospital like wildfire. But that is not the end of the story or the end of the visitors.

On the third day, another visitor stood at the open door of my room, and I could not believe my eyes. THIS VISITOR WAS JESUS! It was the risen Lord standing in the doorway of my hospital room. I was so awestruck by His Holy presence that I hid under my covers, unable to move or to speak. As the Lord walked closer to my bed, the power of His anointing enveloped me. I lay there in petrified awe. I kid you not. Being surrounded by His Glory caused my body to feel like it was petrified wood. I could not move or even blink an eye. My mind was running wild with all the things that I would like to say to Him, and with all the questions I would like to ask Him, but I was paralyzed and could not open my mouth even to utter a sound. I was barely able to breathe, and time seemed to stand still. Could this be happening?

God was no longer at the door. He was now standing at the side of my bed! How could this be? Trembling, I could feel the touch of His hand upon the raw incision on my bare midriff. It felt as if an electrical charge with megavolts of frequency were vibrating as it ran across the incision, first from right to left and then back again from left to right. Zizzz, Zizzz. Likewise, that same electrical charge was then moving along my private parts where the other incision was. Zizzz, Zizzz. Jesus was touching me, and I could not move my body or protest. His very presence had anesthetized me.

"I have become undone. I am going to die. I made it through two surgeries, but now I am going to die," were the thoughts racing across my mind as I lay in total submission to the Lord's eternal touch. Once He had finished with his miraculous touch, He disappeared — gone in a flash, and I was free from pain. Someone else disappeared at that same moment in time. This "Awesome Eternal Touch" had changed the woman who lay there paralyzed under the Master's touch. I was correct to be thinking about the thoughts that I had because I did die that day. Somehow, and I do not understand how, but something supernatural and beyond all reason happened to me spiritually. I know that I was crucified with Christ, buried, and resurrected into a new life. I began a new life thoroughly devoted to HIM. I WAS RUINED. Totally and completely ruined for the things of this world, never to be the same. Since I was no longer paralyzed, I sat up and got out of bed, ran down the hall to tell the nurses at the nurse's station that I was pain-free and that the Lord had healed me. I did not tell them Jesus was actually in my room in all HIS GLORY AND MAJESTY. HIS visitation was too sacred to share with them or anyone for that matter.

The Lord did indeed heal me because immediately upon dismissal from the hospital, I returned to work without any repercussions. Eventually, I began to share HIS visitation with the Body of Christ and found the telling to be a powerful faith builder.

One might ask why didn't the Lord heal me previously to the surgeries? I think this is a rather tricky question to answer. God's ways are often mysterious and beyond reason. I like to think that my bold note pleased the Lord, and He showed up to bless me because of it. One thing that I do know for sure is not nearly as many people would have been affected had He healed me before the surgeries. The Lord of Glory did indeed glorify Himself in that hospital that week. A prayer meeting was held in my doctor's theater, which was probably a first. The Lord's visitation to heal me also touched many, and they were encouraged in their faith. Unbelievers became believers, and a glorious story continues to be told years later.

This was not the first time Jesus appeared to me. He appeared to me in the clouds when I was just a child. It was during the time of my parent's divorce. I had been uprooted from my home and sent to live with my grandparents. His appearance frightened me so much that I talked myself out of it. I told myself that Jesus would not just show up in the clouds for me to see, and yet no one else could see him. I decided it was my imagination or that the clouds moved in such a way that they made a figure to look just like him. I convinced myself it never happened. It was not until I began to hear the voice of the Lord that I realized my vision was for real. For, the Lord Himself reminded me that He was with me during my painful years of separation from my mother. He also brought the memory back to me of His appearance in the clouds, and told me that I had not imagined what I had seen, it was HIM, out-stretched arms and in a white robe. I had dismissed His first appearance as not being real, denying His second appearance is an impossibility. So sacred was this visitation in the hospital that even writing about it causes me to pause and reflect upon how truly Gloriously Majestic is our Savior and King. Words are inadequate to describe His Holiness! Being bathed in His Presence birthed a desire for nothing less than He and He alone — everything this world has to offer pales compared to His Glorious Essence.

We live in a time when Christianity is mocked, and Bible Stories are thought to be fiction. The foundation of Christianity is the death, burial, and resurrection of Jesus the Messiah. We have absolutely nothing to base our faith on if Jesus did not rise from the grave. WELL I AM HERE TO TELL YOU, HE IS ALIVE, I SAW HIM, AND HE TOUCHED AND MADE ME WHOLE! There is nothing or no one that will ever convince me that my faith is based on fairy tales and that God is not who He has said He is in the Bible. He is Creator, Provider, Protector, Healer, Friend, Savior, and soon coming King. He is all these things and so much more. Our God is Alive! I SAW HIM; I RECOGNIZED IT WAS JESUS STANDING AT THE DOOR OF MY HOSPITAL ROOM! I have been called to tell you that Jesus is alive. I am a witness to this fact. I am writing this book to share the life experiences I have had with the RISEN LORD. This encounter with Jesus was by far the most awesome of visitations that I have had the privilege of having, been the recipient!

He is alive and longing to have a personal relationship with each one that desires to know Him better. You may be searching for the truth without even realizing that truth is found in the person of Jesus Christ. If your heart is seeking after Jesus, who is the Truth, regardless of what it might cost you, I can guarantee that truth will find you. You may be searching for Jesus, who is love and determined to find it. If your heart is sincere, I can guarantee that the essence of love will find you. Jesus is a gentleman, standing at the door of your heart, knocking, waiting for an invitation to come in. Invite Him in!

Chapter 7

DIVINE APPOINTMENT

You have read about the various times when the Gifts of the Holy Spirit have been flowing through me freely. But it has not always been this way. Let's go back to where it all started during my interior decorating days. While consulting with a customer, I shared with her about the awesome things happening in my life. I had gone over to measure for the interior designing changes that would spruce up her home. In those days, I still owned and operated a small interior design firm in my hometown, which I mentioned previously. For some reason, after I finished measuring for the new carpet that was going to be installed, I began to share with her about the most recent miracle that had just happened because of answered prayer. I had no idea where she was spiritually, but because I was so excited about what God had just done, I decided to tell her all about it.

My teenage daughter, Tracey, had been invited to spend the weekend with a girlfriend whose parents owned a home on a near-by lake west of us. She was very excited about spending time with her friend because they had a boat, and the two of them loved to water ski. I dropped Tracey, off at her friend's house on a Friday night, and Saturday around noon, dark clouds began to roll in from the west. Concerned, because I heard the sound of the howling wind as it began to rattle our windows, I went to the window to watch the storm that was brewing. As I stood there watching the trees swaying from the force of the wind, it occurred to me that my daughter and her friend would likely be out on the lake as this storm was gathering strength. So, I began to pray for the safety of my daughter and her friend. Knowing then that I had put my daughter in good hands, I went about my business with little concern.

The following day I received a phone call from my daughter. She was all excited to tell me what had happened to her. "Mom, she said, you will never believe what happened to us." She proceeded to tell me that she and her friend were standing on the shore next to the pier, trying to blow up the inflatable two-passenger paddle boat they were going to be taking out into the lake to sunbathe in. She said, every time they tried to blow the boat up with their air pump, nothing would happen. It just would not take the air. They tried several times without success. Finally, with the last try, they saw that the storm was coming and decided to give it up. They went into the house to wait for the storm to pass. Hours later, after the wind and rain had passed, they came outside to survey the damage the storm had left behind. The thunderstorm was pretty severe, with high winds that had demolished property and uprooted a strong tree. The storm had left a lot of damage from tree branches that had crashed to the ground or damaged the hood of cars where they landed. The girls found a large branch that was torn off a large tree. The branch had fallen next to the pier covering the paddle boat where they had left it; after trying to inflate it. I said to her after hearing her story, "Well, praise God, the Lord was looking out for you and sent you guys into the house before that branch fell on you." She continued, "But mother, that is not all…you will never believe this. When we went to blow up the raft to see if we could find the holes so that we could patch them, there was nothing wrong with it, and we had absolutely no trouble blowing it up this time," she shouted, all excited. "The boat held the air, and we were paddling around on it today without any problems. Mom, we could have been killed or hurt really bad. What if we would have still been trying to inflate that boat when the branch fell? God saved us, and He wouldn't let us blow up that boat. Isn't that awesome?"

After hearing this story and a few others about answered prayer, my customer began to share her faith in the Lord Jesus with me. "As a matter of fact," she said, "I meet with a group of Christian women once a month, and I would like to invite you to our next meeting. We meet once a month for lunch and enjoy a speaker after lunch. We will be meeting this Wednesday at the Ramada Inn in Milwaukee, Wisconsin. This month's speaker is Helena Curtis, the cosmetic queen. Would you be interested in going with me?" she asked. I told her, "Yes, I would like that." She then went to the phone to see if there were any tickets left for Wednesday. Since this was such short notice, she was afraid that they might be all sold out because of having such a well-known speaker. I watched a big smile come across her face as I heard her say, "You have got to be kidding me," and then… "I'll take it." Hanging the phone up, she turned to me and said. "There is just one ticket left!"

It wasn't until after Wednesday's meeting that I realized this had been another one of God's ways of orchestrating my life. I had begun to get suspicious since there was just one ticket left. Upon entering the banquet room where the meeting was held, I was very surprised by the attendance. I was expecting a small group of women, maybe 40 or 50. However, there must have been at least three hundred or more women gathering around the tables for lunch that day. The banner on the wall above the head table said, "Women's Aglow."

After lunch, someone got up and began to lead the women in song. I thought that I had died and gone to heaven. These women worshiped our Savior like nothing that I had ever heard before. Their angelic voices took me into a realm that my spirit had never traveled before. It wasn't long before I could hear them singing in what sounded to me like many languages. I looked around, trying to take all this in; everyone had their hands raised to heaven worshiping the King of Kings. I felt a little uncomfortable because all this was not something that I was accustomed to. I was a Lutheran, and we did not worship like this in my church. I'm sure that no one noticed I was the only one that did not have their hands raised. They would not have seen because they were lost in the worship of their Savior. There were no eyes on me; they were all on Him. I felt teary-eyed and did not understand why. Standing there, listening to these women sing one beautiful song after another to Jesus stirred up all sorts of emotions within me. I kept asking myself, where have I been? I have never heard of or experienced anything like this before. I wished it would never end. I kept wondering how something like this could be going on in this world, and I knew nothing about it. It felt as if my life was on another planet or something.

Why have I been left in the dark when something this Holy and beautiful was being experienced? These women seemed to be so alive and so free. I learned of a cliché years later that speaks to the experience I was having then. "When the student is ready, the teacher will appear." The Lord had been getting this student of His ready. Little did I know, this was only the beginning.

When Maxine, which was her real name, began to speak, she shared her testimony of how God rescued her after her husband Louis Stein, the love of her life, had died. Louis and his partner founded the Helena Curtis cosmetic empire. He had named the company after his wife Maxine and his son. Maxine introduced herself to us as Helena Curtis, The Cosmetic Queen. She lived a life as an atheist after marrying Louis, who had influenced her to believe that there was no God. Maxine had come from a Christian home and had denied the existence of Christ when she married Louis. She told us how she was in a suicidal state and was determined to take her own life because life was not worth living without Louis. She planned on taking a cruise and jumping ship somewhere in the middle of the ocean. Those were her plans, but the Lord had other plans. Although she had turned her back on Him, He had not let go of her. In her darkest hour, the Lord rescued her. He appeared to her as a brilliant light in her cabin, changing her mind about jumping overboard.

As Maxine shared her testimony, I began to realize that Maxine's life was being directed by the voice of the Lord. She shared how God showed up and gave her a purpose for living. She was obviously in love with her Savior and very determined to do His bidding. Her life was now full and exciting as she traveled, declaring the reality that Jesus is alive and well, speaking to those who would give her their ear. It occurred to me while she was speaking that I was not alone. Her story aroused something within me not to settle for the limited knowledge that I had about God, because of hearing her, I knew that there was so much more.

After she spoke, she invited people to come forward for prayer. I stood and watched for a while, and then little by little, I inched my way toward her. I was not even sure just what it was that I was after or what it was that I needed prayer for. All I knew was that I was drawn to her and wanted to know the Lord with the same intimacy that she had. Maybe if she prayed for me, I could have it too. I waited and listened to her praying with the other women. I realized she was praying in another language as well as in English. I became aware that there were many voices throughout the room. Several women were also praying in English and other languages as well. Like a flash of lightning, the revelation came to me that they were speaking in tongues. In an instant, I realized that the beautiful sounds that I had been listening to when these women were singing were the sounds of singing in an unknown tongue, just like the Bible described. I knew from what I had read in the Bible; this was one of many gifts of the Holy Spirit. I had heard a little about these gifts being poured out in our day from watching the 700 Club on TV. However, I had never met anyone that had this experience themselves. That is until this particular day when I stood listening to some three hundred or so women who were speaking in tongues and who obviously knew a whole lot more about my Jesus than I did. Eventually, she turned and saw me standing there and asked,

"What is it dear?" I said, "I don't know, I guess I just want whatever it is that all of you have and I don't." She took my hands and began to pray for me. She prayed in tongues for a couple of minutes, and then she looked up and said, "What is it child that you have been into?" At first, I did not understand what she was getting at. But then this realization came over me. One by one, I recalled all the things that I experimented with in my quest for finding the truth and the meaning of life. All of these practices flashed within my mind, much like I would suppose someone's life flashes before them at the moment of a near-death experience. I had been searching for truth in all the wrong places, and she knew it somehow. I later learned she was operating in one of the gifts of the Holy Spirit, called the gift of knowledge.

In answer to her question, I began to confess to her all the things that I had been into. It was as if she were a priest behind the curtain of a confessional booth. I was unaware until that moment that any of these things needed my confession. My confession spilled out of my mouth like rushing water from a dam that had just burst. Maxine's eyes looked into my eyes as if she were staring straight into the depths of my soul. She continued to hold my hands in hers while her eyes pierced mine. I felt as if she had just undressed me. She then said with great tenderness that I was going to have to renounce Satan and all his works of darkness before I would be able to receive the Holy Spirit in power. Then she led me in a prayer to renounce Satan and his deceptive practices of astrology, numerology, clairvoyance, transcendental meditation, yoga, and hypnosis. All these things, I had dabbled in looking for what I perceived as the truth. Unaware, I had entered into the wrong side of the supernatural, the dark side.

After a little bit, she said," There is still something more," as if she had inside information about me. "What is it?" I could not imagine what it could be. Then a memory flashed before my eyes of a weekend seminar that I had attended. It was an enlightenment seminar hosted by Warner Ehrhard, the Scientology guru. I asked her if attending this seminar could be it. She smiled, she shook her head, and said sweetly, "Jesus is the truth and the Light, and that I must ask God to forgive me for getting myself mixed up in the occult even if it was done out of ignorance." Together we prayed a prayer asking for forgiveness, and before I could get the last words out of my mouth ---It happened! The power of the Holy Spirit came upon me, and I found myself floating to the floor as if a strong but gentle wind had blown me down. I was unable to stand up against this awesome and Holy power, nor did I want to. I did not know what had just happened to me. All I did know was that an incredible sense of peace had overtaken me, and I had floated to the ground like a fall leaf freed from its branch. This experience I learned later was called being "slain in the Spirit." Tears from my leaking eyes began to flow down the sides of my face all on their own. Several women were on their knees surrounding me on the floor, all of them praying for me to be baptized in the Holy Spirit. Someone said, "Just speak it out; you've got it."

Just speak what out? I thought to myself. I don't have anything! I wanted to have something, but I could not figure out what on earth these ladies were talking about. As I was lying on the floor, overwhelmed by the power of the Holy Spirit, I wondered what to expect next. A word kept repeating over and over in my mind. Instinctively I knew that it was not a word I had thought on my own. I did not know what the word meant. So, I said to the women surrounding me, "Abba, Abba, is Abba anything?" One precious woman bent down and, in a voice, next to a whisper, and said, "You are saying daddy, daddy. It most certainly is something! You are crying out to your daddy in heaven!"

It wasn't until later that day when I was alone in my car that I did release the rest of my prayer language that the Holy Spirit had given me while lying there on the floor. I was so thrilled that I had been baptized in the Holy Spirit, which was evidenced to me by my speaking in tongues, even if it was just this one word, "Abba!" I kept repeating over and over again the one word I had, Abba, Abba, Abba. Soon other strange-sounding words began to flow without any effort on my part. Before I knew it, I was singing to the Lord in my new-found gift, the gift of speaking in tongues that the Bible speaks of. From my innermost being, arose the most beautiful melody and words that were heaven sent and heaven-bound. I thought to myself, I was now a "woman aglow." Little did I know at that moment in time that the Lord had plans for my future concerning this organization, called "Women's Aglow." For somewhere on His calendar of time, were plans for me to be the President of Women's Aglow in my local chapter. That day, far off into my future dawned for me several years later, when I resided as President of Women's Aglow for my local branch.

After dinner that night, I sat down and opened my Bible to the passage that the women had given to me earlier that day. Oh, my goodness, I just experienced this today in real-time, I thought to myself as I read it over and over again.

Romans 8:14-17, 14 For as many as are led by the Spirit of God, these are sons of God. 15 For you did not receive the spirit of bondage again to fear, but you received the Spirit of adoption by whom we cry out, "Abba, Father." 16 The Spirit Himself bears witness with our spirit that we are children of God, 17 and if children, then heirs—heirs of God and joint heirs with Christ, if indeed we suffer with Him, that we may also be glorified together.

God in His mercy met me where I was, ignorant that the supernatural realm was not exclusive to God alone. I had opened the door to Satan and his deceptive practices without ever knowing that I was committing spiritual adultery. We cannot have one foot in the Kingdom of Light and one foot in the kingdom of darkness at the same time. I did not know that the following scriptures were even in the Bible when I was dabbling with the very things that are forbidden. We cannot drink from the cup of the Lord and from the cup of demons at the same time. Dare I say this, but because of gross ignorance of the Word of God, vast numbers of professing Christians have one foot in the Kingdom of Light and the other foot in Satan's kingdom of darkness!

Deuteronomy 18:9-14 9"When you come into the land which the LORD your God is giving you, you shall not learn to follow the abominations of those nations. 10 There shall not be found among you anyone who makes his son or his daughter pass through the fire, or one who practices witchcraft, or a soothsayer, (astrologer) or one who interprets omens, or a sorcerer, 11 or one who conjures spells, or a medium, or a spiritist, or one who calls up the dead. 12 For all who do these things are an abomination to the LORD, and because of these abominations the LORD your God drives them out from before you. 13 You shall be blameless before the LORD your God. 14 For these nations which you will dispossess listened to soothsayers and diviners; but as for you, the LORD your God has not appointed such for you.

God will meet us in our ignorance when our hearts are set to know the truth, never-the-less we have no excuse for our ignorance. The Lord has given us His Word, and it is all right there in our Bibles for us to accept and obey. Disobedience because of ignorance is still disobedience. Blessings follow obedience. My incapacity to recognize the occult practices that I was into almost kept me from the most precious blessings of my life, the Gifts of the Holy Spirit. I was at that time, believing that many of the practices of this world system were harmless. I was wrong. They are deceptive practices that keep us in bondage, and they bring curses with them. These curses though, can be broken through repentance, obedience, and the protective shed blood of Christ. Jesus became accursed for us so that we could be free from all curses. God has made it very clear in His Word that if we obey Him, He will bless us. Conversely, He has also made it very clear that if we disobey, we will bring a curse upon ourselves. It's our choice.

However, Jesus accomplished an exchange on the cross for us. He redeemed us from the curse by becoming a curse for us so that we might walk in faith and receive the blessings of God. All we need to do is to apply that shed blood to our lives. It is His shed blood that makes atonement for all the sins committed that brought on the curses. If you have been involved in forbidden things mentioned, all you need to do is ask for forgiveness. Then walk away from those practices. These things are nothing but counterfeits of the real thing. God and His gifts are the real thing! Seek Him instead.

Throughout my life, there have been pivotal moments in time that have changed the course of my life. This divine appointment with the Holy Spirit and His servant Helena Curtis was one of those days that set the stage for a radical revolution to take place in the History of my life. My experience with the Holy Spirit that day caused me to study the work of the Holy Spirit and to investigate the gifts of the Spirit. What I discovered was most of my life, I had believed a lie that had actually come from the pulpit. That lie of Satan was that these gifts of the Holy Spirit had ceased with the apostles and that they were not for today. If it were not for the new programs that I had been listening to on the 700 Club and my own experience, I might have continued believing the lie.

My experience and the experience of all those women at the Aglow meeting told me differently. It most definitely was for today, and I was living proof. However, I wanted to know what the Bible had to say about the Holy Spirit and His gifts. The first thing that I learned was that before Jesus accomplished His mission, He prepared his disciples as to what was going to happen when he ascended to the Father. He told them that he would send a Helper, a Comforter that would lead them into all truth, and He the Spirit of Truth would tell them things to come. I would later learn that "telling them things to come" was the gift of prophecy.

Upon further investigation, I discovered there are nine gifts of the Holy Spirit, and speaking in tongues is only one of them. Paul makes it clear that these gifts are the manifestation of the Holy Spirit and that operating in them transcends any natural ability. When the body of Christ is working together in unity for ministry and for the benefit of someone, the Holy Spirit will manifest these gifts in a particular way. To one He will give the gift of the word of wisdom, to another a word of knowledge, to another the gift of faith, to another the gifts of healing, to another the working of miracles, to another prophecy, to another discerning of spirits, to another different kinds of tongues, and to another the interpretation of tongues. Paul goes on to say that the Lord distributes these gifts at will.

I can attest to this fact in my own life of ministry. The Spirit has distributed each one of these gifts to me at one time or another. When I was baptized in the Holy Spirit, He took residence in my heart in His fullness. He deposited all the gifts of the Spirit. What an awesome miracle. The first gift of the Spirit that manifested through me was **the gift of tongues.**

1 Corinthians 14:39, Therefore, brethren, desire earnestly to prophesy, and do not forbid to speak with tongues

I noticed when speaking in tongues, from time to time, it was clear the language changes. Although I do not know what language I am speaking, there are times when I hear myself speaking sounds that sound familiar to me. I may not know what the words are, but I can guess it is Chinese or some other oriental language, and at other times, it sounds a little like Hebrew or Spanish and even African. I rarely have been given **the gift of interpretation of tongues** for myself or someone else's tongue, but it has happened on occasion.

I believe the gift of tongues, although Paul speaks of it as the least of the gifts, is the door that opens for all the other gifts to be in operation. I believe this because it is how it happened to me. First, I received the gift of speaking in tongues, and the more that I spoke in tongues, the more the other gifts began to be made manifest to me until every one of them has been operating in my life as the Spirit of God has seen fit. When Paul speaks of one having this gift and another having a different gift, I believe He is speaking about how we are to move together in ministry with our gifts.

When I am ministering with others, I may move out with a word of knowledge, and someone else will have a word from the gift of wisdom on how to apply that word of knowledge. Another may have a prophecy for an individual or the entire group, while yet another person may feel led to lay hands on someone for healing. At another time, I may feel the leading of the Holy Spirit to pray for a miracle instead of healing. **The gift of discerning of spirits** is a wonderful gift because it discerns between the things that are of the Holy Spirit and those that are not. For instance, someone in the church or a meeting may bring forth a prophetic word, and the pastor who has the gift of discerning of spirits recognizes the word is not from God. This pastor should handle this situation in a gentle manner, take the individual aside, and not let them continue. This gift is an essential gift, especially in the "last days" because Satan is a deceiver and loves to disguise himself as God.

And so it goes, each of us supplying a particular gift as the Lord distributes them. I wanted to make it clear that if you have a gift from the Holy Spirit, by no means does it limit you to just that one gift. I believe every one of the gifts is available to you. The Lord is no respecter of persons, and if I have experienced every gift at one time or another, so can you. When Paul was speaking about one person having this gift and another person having another gift, he was talking about how the gifts operate in a meeting. He was not saying that just one gift is for this person, and just one gift is for that person. The Holy Spirit is generous in distributing His gifts. Just press into more of Jesus and use the gifts that you have been given. If you have not received any of the gifts of the Spirit, just ask for them. They are for all who are called. They are yours for the asking.

Each gift manifested has a purpose in the plan of God to allow us to work in partnership with Him; as He touches His own and reveals Himself to us in supernatural ways. **The gift of wisdom** reveals the mind of God for any given situation. **The gift of knowledge** reveals information supernaturally that one does not have previous knowledge about often for an immediate need. It has been my experience that most often, these two gifts work together. A word of knowledge may be deposited into your mind, followed by the gift of wisdom that teaches how to apply that knowledge. The gift of knowledge is not always received well and with appreciation from those in the family of God. I have had some hurtful experiences when sharing with someone what the Lord has shown me through a word of knowledge.

Some people do not like it that the Lord has revealed certain aspects of their lives to another. They consider this an invasion of their privacy. What they fail to comprehend is God is a loving Father. Any information that He passes on to another is either to reveal Himself or to reveal a truth. It is for our benefit. The revelation will either be a blessing or an answer to the situation. For instance, during the years that I was raising my children and even into their adulthood, the Holy Spirit would tell me what sin they were currently committing so that I could confront them with it. This knowledge was not well-received! However, they began to realize that God was real, because how else could I know the things revealed to me.

The gift of Faith is different from having faith to believe for salvation. It is a supernatural gift imparted to an individual for a specific situation. It goes beyond the natural ability to believe for something. It is a knowing that transcends reasoning. When God deposits this gift for the scenario at hand, there is absolutely no doubt that God will do what He has given you the faith to believe for, regardless of how hopeless it may look.

An example of the "gift of faith" happened when the doctor gave my son Bill, a death sentence and did not think that he would find my son alive in December when he returned from his vacation. My daughter Tracey had the gift of faith that God was going to raise her brother out of his death bed, even in November, when he was first admitted, and all the negative reports about how poorly he was doing would not shake her belief. She was also operating in the word of knowledge. I was so worried about my son, and my daughter kept telling me, "Don't worry, mom, he will be home for Christmas Eve," and Praise the Lord, he was!

The gift of healing is a gift from God that the Holy Spirit distributes for the supernatural intervention by the Holy Spirit for the healing of many illnesses and various diseases. When this gift is in operation, it releases the power of the Holy Spirit to heal and make whole the victims of a multitude of various maladies. It is a gift that overrules any medical diagnosis or treatment. In my opinion, this gift is one of the most difficult gifts to understand. I think everyone who operates in this gift has the same question. "Why are some healed, and others are not?" In this Spiritual walk of mine, I have laid my hands on several people, and they were healed. Conversely, and to my great disappointment, many that I have prayed with have had to endure their suffering. Through the years, the Lord has instructed me to understand that there are many hindrances to divine healing. Unconfessed sin and unforgiveness, as well as doubt, are the ring leaders that block the supernatural healing. Another key that will unlock the reason that healing does not manifest is the individual receiving the healing prayer may believe a lie of Satan. The key is to discover the lie and replace it with the truth. Some healings are hindered because there is a legal accusation against us in the Courts of Heaven that need to be resolved. Satan is a legalist, and if any legal claim is legitimate, it can hold us in bondage. For instance, there was a lie on my birth certificate that held me in bondage for years. My mother had lied about her age on my birth certificate, to cover up the fact that she had gotten pregnant at such a young age. Secrets like this give Satan an open door to mess with your life.

I want to interject something right here of great importance, spiritually. Never, ever keep secrets from your children or spouse. If you are keeping a secret because you think you are protecting them, YOU ARE NOT! This belief is a lie from Satan. That secret, whatever it might be, is an open door for the devil to wreak havoc with you and your family. Let me give you just one example to drive this truth home. I was once praying for a young child who had been given a death sentence by his doctors. It did not look good, but several of us were banging on the doors of heaven for his healing. Long story shortened, the Lord revealed to the child's mother that her husband had been with a prostitute, and if her husband confessed his sin to her and his children, the Lord would heal their little boy. Fortunately, this story has a happy ending. Her husband did confess his sin, and miraculously the child was healed. Hiding your sin from your family, thinking you are protecting them, is the worst thing that you can do. Tell the truth, for it is the truth that sets us free. The Bible is very clear about this being the action necessary to receive healing.

James 5:16, 16 Confess your trespasses to one another, and pray for one another, that you may be healed. The effective, fervent prayer of a righteous man avails much.

Even though the Lord has revealed many hindrances to healing, I have seen God override all these hindrances in order to reveal His mercy and love. So, the same question that haunted Kathryn Kuhlman haunts me, "Why are some healed and others are not?"

The gift of miracles is different from the gift of healing. This gift of working miracles is a creative gift. It is a gift when in operation lengthens legs, creates limbs where there were no limbs, drops off weight supernaturally, creates eyeballs where there were none, caps teeth with gold where needed, raises people from the dead, creates organs where there were none, and countless other supernatural creative miracles that can only be credited to the glorious workings of the Holy Spirit as He transcends the natural in order to reveal Himself.

My son Bill was a recipient of one of these creative miracles, during a church service he was attending, there was an anointing for the working of miracles, and he received a gold tooth. He was so excited when he called me to tell me all about it. All of these types of manifestations are way beyond all reason.

The gift of prophecy is a gift from the Holy Spirit for the purpose of edifying the Church. This gift operates by bringing a word of comfort through the revelation of the written word or speaking the oracles of God prompted through the Holy Spirit. With this gift, there is an intimate connection with the God of the Universe and his creation. Prophecy is a gift that allows us to know what is on God's mind at that very moment in time. Sometimes, His word to us is for that moment, and sometimes it is in preparation for the future. At times, it is a gift that will bring a personal word to an individual, and at other times He will bring a word to the entire congregation. The Bible says the testimony of Jesus is the Spirit of prophecy.

The entire Bible is a prophetic word given by God and recorded for us, and it testifies of Jesus from cover to cover. Today when a word is given in a prophecy, it too is a testimony of Jesus. It testifies He is the Spirit of Truth; therefore, all that comes from the mouth of God will be confirmed as truth. It testifies that all that Jesus has promised about the gifts of the Spirit are true. It testifies Jesus is alive and communicating with His people through the gift of prophecy. Having the gift of prophecy enables an individual to speak the oracles of God today in both realms, first from the written word in clarity and secondly a fresh Rhema word from the Holy Spirit.

As stated earlier, I believe the gift of speaking in tongues is the door that opens all other doors to the nine gifts of the Holy Spirit. All these awesome gifts from God are operative through the Holy Spirit. We are nothing more than the vessels that are willing to allow the Holy Spirit to work His will through us. We must never lose sight of the fact that we do nothing more than to submit our tongue to Him for prayer and worship. It is the voice of the Holy Spirit that interprets our tongue. We are to submit our hands to Him for healing and submit our spiritual ears to hear what He has to say. He is the one that builds our faith to believe for miracles, and He is the one that gives us wisdom and knowledge about things that we do not know about. We must never take credit for any of the works done by the Holy Spirit. His work transcends the working of our natural minds. All that the Holy Spirit accomplishes is done in the realm of the supernatural, and for Jesus to be glorified on the earth.

Even scientists came to the conclusion what Christians have been saying all along. Their research proves the Holy Spirit prays through us when we pray in tongues. It is now supported by scientific evidence. In November 2006, the New York Times reported about the research being done at the University of Pennsylvania on the brain activity of Christians as they spoke in tongues. The study supports that speaking in tongues is not an intentional function of the brain, but rather, the language is coming from the spirit of the man as if someone else is doing it. It is my opinion that the study supports the fact that indeed, the Holy Spirit is "DOING IT." HE is praying through the believer and that the gift of speaking in tongues transcends the mind. The following is a quote from Principal Investigator of the study, Andrew Newberg, MD, Associate Professor of Radiology, Psychiatry, and Religious Studies, and Director for the Center for Spirituality and the Mind, at Penn. "Our finding of decreased activity in the frontal lobes during the practice of speaking in tongues is fascinating because these subjects truly believe that the spirit of God is moving through them and controlling them to speak. Our brain imaging research shows us that these subjects are not in control of the usual language centers during this activity, which is consistent with their description of a lack of intentional control while speaking in tongues."

I hope you find some of these little rabbit trails I take are interesting to you. Although I will always consider myself to be a student of the word, I love to share the things that I learn. When you are a teacher, you are not satisfied with just reading the word of God. I have to dig and take every word apart, find the meaning of Hebrew or the Greek. Ask the questions of who, what, where, and when. I sometimes drive my friends crazy when answering a biblical question for them. They often say, "Please, get to the point." I, on the other hand, just love to be around other teachers of the word. They will share some of the most unknown and interesting facts that they have diligently dug for. You see, I find the pursuit of God and the hidden treasures in His word is the most fulfilling of all pursuits that I have engaged in.

I will always treasure the day that this door to the gifts of the Spirit was opened to me. It was the beginning of the most exciting journey of intimacy with the Lord. I did not need to have scientific proof this was the Holy Spirit. I knew by faith that God had opened the door to the supernatural to me. It always thrills me, though, when science confirms what faith has already established. Not only did the Lord open the door to the nine gifts of the Spirit, but He also opened the door to visions and prophetic dreams. Every day became a new adventure for me. Plus, finding the golden nuggets sometimes hidden in the Word is amazing!

When I was baptized in the Holy Spirit and began to walk in the Supernatural realm, my children were teenagers. Bill was nineteen, soon to be twenty. Kelly was sixteen turning seventeen with a birthday coming up at the end of the month. Tracey was fourteen and wouldn't have her fifteenth birthday for several months. Our children were in church with us every Sunday, and they attended Sunday School before the service. They had never experienced anything supernatural. They believed in God and in Jesus as their Savior of the world. They loved Jesus and knew Jesus loved them. When we said our bedtime prayers, they blessed everybody they could think of. I wanted my teenage children to experience God in the same way that I had.

I knew I only had a few years left to influence them before they would be out on their own. I could see that their peers had way more influence over them than I did. This was especially true with my two sons. Billy had a full-time job and was gone from our home a good share of the time. Likewise, with Kelly, he was still in school and holding down a part-time job. My time with my sons was limited. This was not true with Tracey, she was around more for me to influence.

Proverbs 22:6, Train up a child in the way he should go, And when he is old he will not depart from it.

One of my favorite memories of my son Kelly, who was just a little tyke at the time, assured me that some good seed had been planted in his heart. My two boys shared a room, and every night was a battle to get these "energized bunnies" to settle down and go to sleep. After our bedtime prayers, I would leave their room, only to return another time to scold them for their bad behavior. One evening after many scoldings, I returned to their room angry and said some harsh things to them. I closed the door and stood there to listen. I heard my oldest son Billy say to his brother, "Oh Kelly, I think we did it this time. I don't think mommy loves us anymore." Kelly's response to his older brother melted my heart. I heard him say, "Billy don't you know? Moms are just like God; they love you no matter what you do."

My kids would even play church after service when we would arrive home and it caused me to think that surely those seeds would mature into good fruit one day. They would set up chairs and a little table for the pulpit. They would take turns being the preacher, retelling the Bible stories they had learned in Sunday School and church. Billy would bring his guitar and lead worship. The memory of their precious sermons told me that more seeds were planted than I had anticipated.

Another favorite memory that shaped their character, and trained them in the way they should go happened at Christmas time one year when they were all in grade school. After opening all their presents, I noticed something in my children I did not like. They seemed to be ungrateful and wanting more. Then I noticed they decided to count how many gifts they had received. They wanted to make sure that one of their siblings did not receive more than they had. I was unhappy with their ungrateful attitudes. I sat them down and had a little talk with them. I told them that as far as I was concerned, they were not acting as if they were very thankful for the things they had received. I went on to say that I knew some children who would be very grateful for just a gift or two at Christmas. These children were orphans in an orphanage. "So," I said, "This is what I want each of you to do. I want you to pick out three gifts a piece from your pile of presents. Tomorrow we are going to drive to Milwaukee to the Orphanage, and deliver the toys that you have selected to the orphan children who will appreciate whatever they are given."

The following day, we loaded up the back of my station wagon with toys to be delivered to the Lutheran Home where the orphan children lived. In the back seat of my wagon, sat my three children. As I drove away and glanced into my rear-view mirror, I saw three very sad faces. When we arrived, they hand-delivered their gifts to the director of the Lutheran Home. This life lesson changed all three of my kids. In the following years, they wanted to go Christmas shopping for the orphans and drop the gifts off so the children could open them on Christmas day. This experience has had a lasting effect on my offspring. As adults, each one of them has the most generous heart, reflecting the character of their Heavenly Father.

James 5:16, The effective, fervent prayer of a righteous man avails much.

That scripture verse kept me going during those teenage years and beyond. I spent hours and hours praying for my family because I believed this scripture, and in time it became a reality. The Lord began to reveal Himself to my teenagers and continued to do so into their adulthood. First, it was in small ways, and then it increased just like the verse promised. The prayers for my kids was indeed availing much. Those encounters have been woven into the fabric of this book.

Let me encourage you to expect your prayer to be answered. If you have rebellious children regardless of their age, or children that are just walking a far distance from their creator, never ever give up on them. Prayer is a powerful thing, especially the prayers of parents. The only one that loves your children more than you do is the Lord. He has plans and a destiny for the children of righteous parents. I believe the Lord wants to partnership with you concerning your children. Your job is to pray for them, and His job is to woo them into His Kingdom!

BEYOND ALL REASON: Moving Out of Logic Into the Supernatural

Chapter 8

GO TELL JESSE

As of this writing, I have had five separate audiences with Jesus. I have already shared some of those events.

Now I want to share when Jesus appeared to me in a dream. The dream was so vivid and so real that I sat right up in bed and shook my husband to wake him up. Trembling, I said," Jesus was talking to me in my dream," He asked, "Well, what did He say?" I told him, "He was standing before me in a white gown with outstretched arms, and he said to me, "Margie, go tell Jesse." My husband responded by saying, "It sounds like you have work to do."

Jesse was my grandfather and lived alone after my grandmother's death. My grandparents raised me after my parents divorced. They divorced when I was quite young, and I was seven years old when I went to live with my grandma and my grandpa. These were my paternal grandparents, mom, and dad to my daddy. My grandparents had hired an attorney, and they persevered in a court custody battle over me because they did not believe that either one of my parents was fit to raise me. The judge ruled in their favor, and I grew up under their guardianship. As one might expect, this action put a breach in the relationship between my father and his parents. This distance seemed to heal after time. I would not learn of the circumstances of my parent's divorce or the custody battle until many years later.

I did not know the significance of the memories surrounding the divorce that I did have until I was old enough to understand and make sense of them. Before I went to live with my grandma and grandpa, I lived in Milwaukee, Wisconsin, with my mother and little baby brother, Kenny. There were five years between my brother and myself. The three of us lived on the second floor of an apartment building on the north side of the city. My brother was still on a bottle when he was left alone on a blanket in the middle of the living room floor until I came home from school. My mother would leave for work, and my brother would be unattended until I returned home. How long he was left alone is not part of my memory. There would always be a bottle out, and I would feed it to him upon my return from school. I was my baby brother's little mother in my mother's absence. I fed him, I rocked him, and I mothered him. I was just a little over the age of six.

I had been told not to go to the door and not to let anyone in. I was an obedient six-year-old and did exactly what my mother had asked me to do. That is until one day when the door-bell rang, and I did open the door. I opened it after recognizing my father's voice calling to me. He began calling after there had not been a response from the bell. Hearing his voice, I went to the door. After discovering that we were alone, my father began to question me about where I thought my mother was and about how often my brother and I were left alone? The next thing I knew, my brother and I were living at my grandma and grandpa's house.

One day when I came home from school, my brother was gone. My grandmother told me when I was older; my brother cried so much that they decided this little baby boy needed his mother. The loss of my mother and my brother broke my heart; my brother was not the only one who wept. My silent screams in the night for my mother and my brother could only be heard through the ears of heaven. My father lived with us, although it was not for very long. He soon remarried and moved into an apartment walking distance from his parent's home. The separation from my father did not have the same effect upon me, as did the separation from my mother and brother. I had not bonded with him as strongly as I had to my mother and baby brother. The courts gave my mother visitation rights some years later. She was remarried and had given birth to my half-sister when I saw her and my brother again.

My mother lived in Milwaukee, Wisconsin, about twenty-five minutes from my grandparents. The arrangement made for visitation was I could spend every third Saturday with her. Since my grandmother did not drive, she accompanied me on a bus to Milwaukee every third Saturday. After escorting me to my mother's home, she returned on another bus back to Waukesha, where we lived. There were also times when my aunt Doreen would drive my grandmother and me to Milwaukee, drop me off at my mother's home, and they would return to Waukesha. At the end of the day, my mother and her husband would then drive me home to Waukesha. It was always an emotional parting of the ways. These visits did not continue for long because my mother found them to be too difficult for her to handle emotionally.

Although the visits ended, she was faithful to write me letters and send me cards, always remembering my birthday. It was not in God's plan that I should see her again for many more years. The sorrow and grief lodged in my heart over feelings of rejection and abandonment followed me long into my adulthood. I doubt whether anyone was aware of the pain that I carried because I was a very good actress.

I believe I was providentially placed in the home of my grandparents. I may never know all the reasons that this was the Lord's plan for me, but this I do know, his hand was upon me from the time of my birth. I was nurtured and loved and had many advantages that my grandparents were able to give me that they had not been able to provide for their own children.

My father was the second son of seven children. At the time I moved to my grandparent's home, my father, and their three youngest children were also still at home. I shared a bedroom with my aunt, their youngest daughter, until she got married. Their two youngest sons shared a bedroom together with my dad upstairs until he remarried. The modest Cape Cod home where my grandparents raised seven of their children and me was a four-bedroom home with one bath. There were two bedrooms downstairs and two bedrooms up. The one rather large bedroom upstairs housed the boys in dormitory-style. There was another smaller bedroom at the top of the stairs that one would need to walk through to get to the main bedroom. This bedroom was the one I slept in after my aunt got married. She and her new husband were now occupying the downstairs bedroom that she and I had shared previously.

My two uncles out of respect for me and my privacy would open the door at the bottom of the stairs and call to me, asking if I was dressed before they would climb those stairs two at a time. Isn't it funny how the littlest things creep through and surface as memories, when you least expect them to? This gesture these young men made to protect the privacy of a little girl in a new environment means much more to me today than it did at the time.

My grandfather was a factory worker and not a man of means. In retrospect, I find it to be an amazing story of how he and his wife supported their rather large family. Their lives were devoted to their children. My grandfather had a beautiful garden he tended to during the gardening season to help with the grocery bills. For the winter, my grandmother canned vegetables from the garden. She was an excellent self-taught seamstress and made her children's clothes to stretch the budget. She also made clothes for me, including my prom dress. There was always good quality food on the table, and every chair occupied around it. Guests were always welcome at dinner time. "Just throw another potato in the pot," is what they would say if someone showed up unexpectedly at dinner time.

My grandparents were not in a position to help any of their children monetarily. So, in order to help them financially, they insisted their married children live with them until they saved enough money for a home of their own. The home my grandparents provided for me was filled with activity and support. The Lord had arranged a support system for me of loving and caring aunts and uncles as well as grandparents that all adored me. The house was full of life.

The only time I ever saw my grandparents together in the church was for funerals and weddings. My grandmother did occasionally go by herself. However, I noticed through the years; this happened less and less. Even at the very young age that I arrived at their doorstep, they saw to it that I attended Sunday school each Sunday. So, you see, the Lord had His Hand upon me from the start.

So much time had passed since the hand of the Lord placed me in the home of my grandfather. Now, so many years later, the Lord was sending me on a mission. "Go tell Jesse," is all He had said. As I drove to my destination, I rehearsed what I would "tell" my grandfather a hundred different ways. When I pulled into the driveway of the house I was raised in, pink petunias that my grandfather had planted in the flower boxes were all in full bloom. So were those pink petunias that lined the white picket fence he had built surrounding the house. I found my grandfather sitting in a lawn chair under a canopy of grapevines. The grapevines filled the trellises that he had built over his two-car garage. They provided shade for the chair that he sat in when I arrived. For as long as I can remember, one side of the garage housed a fishing boat he was either repairing or building for himself or one of his sons, and the other side housed his car. It was the side of the garage that housed the boat where a couple of lawn chairs were placed during the summer months. This area is where he visited with his neighbors, his friends, and his family. Under the shade of the grapevines. This place was the location of my grandfather's "city gates."

As I approached to sit beside him in the empty chair, I was nervous and self-conscious. This would be my first experience in sharing the gospel of Jesus Christ. I was instructed to share the gospel to a man that I never saw go to church except for someone's wedding or funeral. I was instructed in my dream by Jesus Himself to share the gospel of Jesus Christ with a man that never spoke the name of Jesus except to use it to curse. I was fearful that I might be the one that would soon be cursed if I opened my mouth to speak about Jesus with Jesse. I was also afraid of the consequences that may happen if I did not share what I had learned to be true. There is no salvation or way into heaven except through the Son of God. If Jesus sent me to tell Jesse, if His love for my grandfather compelled Him to come to me in a dream so Jesse would know the truth, I was even more afraid not to do what I had been instructed to do. I just had no idea how I was going to do it. Satan's favorite weapon is fear, and he was successful using this weapon on me, for I was indeed fearful.

I sat there with my grandfather under the shade of the grapevines. I was silently praying to the Lord for help. I prayed for an open door to discuss what I had come for. We talked about the kids, my husband's construction business, and who had been by to visit. We talked, I silently prayed. We talked some more, and I prayed some more. We sat there together for a very long time talking. He surely must have been wondering what had gotten into me this day. We had never spent this much time in conversation before, not just the two of us. I was determined to sit there visiting with him until a door was open for me to go through so that I could talk about Jesus. He chatted, I prayed. Then it happened, he was in the middle of a sentence about his garden and how bountiful this year's crop of potatoes was, when the bells of the church on the corner behind his house began to chime. He turned to me and said, "Those church bells chime every day about this time, and I think it is the best thing that has happened to this neighborhood." The hair on my arms stood straight up; they were standing to the attention of the Holy Spirit.

It was the opening that I had been waiting for. I asked my grandfather if he had ever visited the little church that was ringing those bells? I learned something about him that day. I learned that at some point in his life, probably when he was a young man, he had been introduced to the gospel of Jesus Christ and had been a churchgoer. He shared with me that he stopped going because he felt Christians were nothing but a bunch of hypocrites and that they just wanted your money. I responded to him by saying, "Grandpa, you are not the only one that thinks like that, you are in good company. The Bible tells us Jesus himself chastised the religious leaders of his day for being hypocrites. They professed their righteousness; however, it was their unjust conduct he was upset about. He called them hypocrites to their faces."

This conversation led to talk about the Bible, and he shared with me how difficult he found it to read. I introduced him to the Bible that I had fallen in love with, The Living Bible, and told him that I would purchase one for him in large easy to read print. This I did and returned with the purchased Bible marked with a yellow marker where Jesus addressed the religious hypocrites in Matthew, Chapter 23. He had been open to having me purchase a Bible just for him when we talked that day; however, when I returned with it, his heart had turned cold. My grandfather told me that he didn't want it and that I should take it home with me. This I did not do; instead, I said to him that I was going to leave it there with him just in case he ever changed his mind. Satan had entered his mind stealing the seed I had planted. His heart had waxed cold. I left feeling defeated. It had been such a glorious victory just a few days earlier, and I had left his home on a mountain top high, but this day, I was leaving from a valley so low. This began the engagement of war over the soul of my grandfather.

I began to pray and intercede for my grandfather, asking God to soften his hardened heart. I prayed that the Lord would instill a curiosity within him to find out what that Bible had to say. I prayed that he would accept Jesus as his Lord and Savior. Months went by, and nothing was ever said by him when we visited that would give me any indication that my prayers were being answered. My aunt, Grandpa's oldest daughter, lived on a cul-de-sac directly behind his property. She was in the habit of checking on him daily since the death of her mother. She often brought him his dinner or groceries that she knew that he needed. One day after making her daily rounds and dropping off a few groceries, she gave me a call. What a sweet gift that phone call was. "Margie," she said, "Today, when I stopped by the house to check on my dad, I found him reading the Bible that you bought him. He did not hear me come in right away, and when he finally heard me, he quickly put it down. He acted a little embarrassed, so I just pretended like I didn't see a thing. I thought you would like to know."

Sometimes when you pray for other people, you are not privileged to know the outcome. Sometimes the answer to your prayers does not come for many years. I was new at this. I had gone over and over in my mind what I might have said or done differently to get a different result then what had happened that day that I brought the Bible to him. My faith had been shattered momentarily, when I heard, "You just need to take that Bible home with you." There is nothing that can restore faith that has been weakened, like an answered prayer. The Lord was letting me know through this phone call that He was at work, answering my prayer. I was so grateful to have learned the Holy Spirit was at work within my grandpa and that for at least this one time, he had opened the book of life. How often and for how long the book was opened is written in the scrolls of heaven. I did not need to know.

Sometime later, my grandpa became ill with Prostate Cancer and was in and out of the hospital many times. During one of my hospital visits with him, we were alone, and I asked him if it would be all right with him if I would pray for him. He consented, and I prayed a very short prayer out loud for his healing and his release from the hospital. I left the hospital thinking to myself how vulnerable he had become and how frail he looked. He was dismissed a few days later. My aunt insisted that he return to her home where she could care for him during this time. I visited with him at her home after he was released to her care. I have a Kodak snapshot in my mind. I can still see him sitting beside her kitchen table, and I saw a man whose countenance had softened considerably during his illness. He was a gentler, kinder man. When I said to him, "I bet you are glad to be home from that hospital." He said, "Thanks to the good Lord."

Eventually, my grandfather ended up in the hospital for the last time. It was my final visit with him. He was in and out of consciousness the day that I stood alone with him by his bedside. I took his hand and began to pray. I was scared. It had now been several years since I had obeyed the instructions that had come to me through a dream. I was frightened, and doubts began to flood my mind. I was so afraid that maybe he wasn't saved. Perhaps he was at the end of his life, and he wouldn't end up in heaven. After all, I reasoned, I never did pray the prayer of salvation with him. I never told him to ask God to forgive him for his sins. I never gave him the "born again" message. I never told him that Jesus stands at the door of our hearts, knocking gently, waiting to be asked in. "Oh, dear God, if he's not saved, it would be all my fault. I did not do what you asked me to do." My mind was spinning. "I should have done this. I should have done that!" "Please God," I begged, you must show me, somehow someway, does he belong to you?"

My grandpa's breathing was labored while I stood there, holding his hand. Yet, I thought I heard him say something ever so softly. So, I bent my ear to his mouth and listened. No, I cannot be hearing what I think I am hearing, I thought to myself. I bent my ear to his mouth again. He said it again. He never came out of his state of unconsciousness, and yet he kept repeating it over and over again. Abba, Abba, Abba. Had I not been familiar with the scriptures and because of my own personal experience some years earlier with the word Abba, I would have missed the sign God had given me. Yet, I continued to bend my ear to hear those ever so soft utterances. This is just unbelievable. I said to myself, he is crying out from his spirit: "Daddy, daddy," to his heavenly Father. I left the hospital with tears streaming down my face.

You would think that after an experience like this one, there could not possibly be any room for doubt. However, by the time I arrived home, I began to doubt what I had heard. Maybe that was just my imagination because I wanted it so much. It was so faint how could I be sure. Maybe his labored breathing just happened to sound a little like aaaaabbbbbbbaaaaa. Satan was playing with my mind planting seeds of doubt, and I was letting him. Gripped with fear and doubt, I went into my prayer closet. I mean that literally. We had a walk-in closet off of the master bedroom where I would go to pray. It was an excellent hideaway place! I got down on the floor with my face to the floor and prayed my heart out. However, my prayer was totally motivated by fear. A fear I had not heard what I thought I had heard. Fear that my grandfather was not saved after all. With deep groans of intercession and with many tears, I cried out to God for some answers.

After some time in prayer, I heard the voice of the Holy Spirit say to me. "Read Psalm 91", I jumped up from my prone position on the floor and ran for my Bible. I began paging through the Psalms until my eyes rested upon 91. I began to read,

Psalm 91, 1 He who dwells in the secret place of the Most High shall abide under the shadow of the Almighty. 2 I will say of the LORD,

"He is my refuge and my fortress; My God, in Him I will trust." 3 Surely He shall deliver you from the snare of the fowler and from the perilous pestilence. 4 He shall cover you with His feathers, and under His wings you shall take refuge; His truth shall be your shield and buckler. 5 You shall not be afraid of the terror by night, Nor of the arrow that flies by day, 6 Nor of the pestilence that walks in darkness, nor of the destruction that lays waste at noonday. 7 A thousand may fall at your side, And ten thousand at your right hand; But it shall not come near you. 8 Only with your eyes shall you look, And see the reward of the wicked. 9 Because you have made the LORD, who is my refuge, Even the Most High, your dwelling place, 10 No evil shall befall you, Nor shall any plague come near your dwelling; 11 For He shall give His angels charge over you, To keep you in all your ways. 12 In their hands they shall bear you up, Lest you dash your foot against a stone. 13 You shall tread upon the lion and the cobra, The young lion and the serpent you shall trample underfoot.

Nothing in this Psalm was making any sense to me in regard to my grandfather's salvation. I began to question as I was reading why God wanted me to read this particular Psalm. Then, it became very clear to me as I read the end of the Psalm continuing on with verse 14.

14 "Because he has set his love upon Me, therefore I will deliver him; I will set him on high, because he has known My name. 15 He shall call upon Me, and I will answer him; I will be with him in trouble; I will deliver him and honor him. 16 With long life I will satisfy him, And show him My salvation."

At last, I was at peace. The Lord took me to this Psalm to clearly tell me that God would show my grandpa His salvation. I was thrilled with this knowledge.

The road to Jesse's salvation took me from the grapevines to the gravesite. It was a long journey, and it took several years to get there. I was not the same woman standing at his grave that had started down this road under the shade of the grapevines. I had changed, just like he had changed. Both of us were being transformed day by day. Nor do I now recognize the woman that stood at the gravesite; she is not the same woman that is the author of this book. I had been so fearful that I had not done everything correctly, concerning the assignment that I was given in the dream. I had taken on the responsibility of his salvation as if it all depended on me. His salvation did not depend on the power and might of the things that I could say and do. *It is not by power, it is not by might, but by my Spirit says the Lord,* was not a scripture that I was leaning on at the time. It was my responsibility to be obedient to the call of the Lord, to go and tell the good news, and to put the good book in the hands of my grandfather, but salvation belongs to the Lord. It was my responsibility to pray for the Lord's will to be accomplished, but how and when is the work of the Lord. He and only He can do the work of the Holy Spirit. It was His work of gently and lovingly wooing the soul of my grandfather into the Kingdom of Light because God is the lover of his soul. Upon reflection, I believe the Lord was calling my grandfather back to Him. He was calling him back home.

I was unaware at the time, but now upon remembrance, I realize that my Christian witness to my grandfather was not empowered because I knew just the right scriptures to quote to him. He was not desirous for God because I could expound on just the right spiritual principle for every situation. Instead, so much more was being said by the way that I was expressing my love for him. Sometimes it seemed that love was demonstrated in the smallest of ways. My changed life empowered my witness to him. My life was an open Bible to him. He may or may not have been reading the Bible that I gave him, but this I know, he was reading me.

There are wounded unbelieving people in all our lives that will never pick up the word of God to read it for themselves. If they are reading about you and I, and our lives are an open Bible for them, will they read about love? The littlest jester of love will be remembered long after the scripture we quoted has been forgotten.

John 3:16-17, 16 For God so loved the world that He gave His only begotten Son, that whoever believes in Him should not perish but have everlasting life. 17 For God did not send His Son into the world to condemn the world, but that the world through Him might be saved.

Jesus is the Savior of the world. He came looking for my grandfather, just like He came looking for me. Even though my life was in bondage to sin, I never felt condemned, and I know my grandfather never did either. God's love empowers us to walk away from the sin that may be entangling us. I guarantee the Lord wants to love on you as well. He wants to show Himself to you and take you higher in Him than you have ever been. Just let Him know that you are willing. Then expect supernatural happenings that are beyond all reason.

My purpose in this book is to encourage you to take a step closer to God. He wants to have a close relationship with you. My prayer is for Him to reveal Himself to you, perhaps in a dream or a vision, in an answered prayer, or even in a book you read. Pick up a Bible and begin to read the love letters that are written there for you. Ask God to help you to understand what you have read. He wants to bring you revelation.

It is written in the text in Proverbs 25:2, *2 It is the glory of God to conceal a matter, But the glory of kings is to search out a matter.*

There are things hidden in the Word of God that only are understandable when the light of the Holy Spirit is shed upon it. There are things hidden from you that only God can show you. Only God can open your eyes to see spiritually. Only God can open your spiritual ears to hear His voice. May each new day of your journey with the Lord be more exciting than the day before.

Chapter 9

EVERYTHING HIDDEN WILL BE UNCOVERED

One day when I was around nine years old, a letter came to me from my mother. She wrote to tell me that due to her health that she would no longer be able to spend any time with me on Saturdays. She said that she had a nervous breakdown and that spending time with me and then having to let me go at the end of our visit was just too hard on her. This thinking is not something that a nine-year-old girl who wants to be with her mother could possibly understand. As the years went by, I began to understand how this would be a difficult situation for any mother. Many years later, I discovered the things that my mother had told me in the letter were not even truthful.

Over time, my mother and I kept in contact through letters. The next time I saw her, I was fourteen. I had convinced a girlfriend of mine to go with me and go to Milwaukee and find my mother. I remembered how to navigate to her home by bus from my town to the city of Milwaukee. We needed to transfer from one bus to another to arrive at our destination. How I remembered to do this is a mystery to me now that I am looking back. I was only eight or nine years old when I traveled those bus lines with my grandmother.

We arrived at the home that I remembered her living in when I would visit, only to discover that she had moved. This house was now being occupied by an aunt who then drove my girlfriend and me to my mother. The visit turned out to be nothing but tears and sobbing on my part. Because upon questioning her why she did not want to see me anymore, her answers could not satisfy the need that I had to be with my mother. It was determined my mother and her husband would drive us back home at the end of the day. That was the last time I saw my mother until I was married and had children of my own. However, the letters from her kept coming, not regularly, but they kept coming periodically. I knew that she had another child just a little older than my eldest. She had sent me a baby picture of my half-sister in one of her letters. In each letter, my siblings were referred to as HER children. She spoke of them as if I had no relationship to them whatsoever.

I had tried many times to restore our relationship, thinking that I was an adult now, and I saw no reason why we couldn't meet for lunch or just sit and have a cup of coffee together and chat. There was always some excuse for why she would not be able to do that. She had made it very clear she just wanted to leave things the way that they were. She often blamed her husband and said he wanted her just to devote her time to their little family. I often questioned her about my brother. I was most anxious to find him and to connect with him again. She did keep me up to date about his marriage and children, but she never released to me any contact information. She was always telling me it would not be a good idea for me to contact him now after all these years.

During one Christmas season, my husband and I were with our children walking through the Southridge Shopping Mall in Milwaukee. Wisconsin. The mall was not very busy for being the most active shopping season of the year. While we were in the mall, I saw this woman and a man together on the farthest part of the mall walking towards us. I said to my husband, "See that woman way down there with a scarf on her head? That woman is my mother." My husband had never met my mother, but he turned to me and said, "How on earth can you tell whether that is your mother or not? She is so far away," "Oh, that is my mother, alright, I said. You will see." I kept my eye on her as they began to approach us, getting closer and closer. Finally, when she was about 12 feet away, I walked up to her and looked her straight in the eye and said, "Hello Mother, its Marjorie, your daughter!" With that "Hello," I could tell that I startled her, and she didn't know what to say or what to do. I introduced her to my family, and for a few minutes, we stood there staring at each other, trying to make small talk. We exchanged a few pleasantries, and then we parted ways. A few days later, I received a phone call from her with an invitation to come with the family for dinner at her home. This invite surprised me. She always had some excuse for why that could not happen.

I accepted her invitation and thought to myself that at long last, I was going to begin to have a real relationship with my mother. When we arrived, she had a Christmas gift for each of my three children. We actually had a very nice time and enjoyed dinner and our time together. The only thing that seemed a little awkward was during this time, Roxanne, my half-sister, who was now a teenager, came home in the middle of our visit. My mother introduced her as Roxanne, and I was introduced to Roxanne as Marjorie. That's all that was said. Roxanne then went to her room, and I was unable to have any conversation with her. After what I thought was a nice time together, my mother began again to make excuses for why we could not get together. Sometimes in her letters, she would say things like I was all about money now and that she just did not fit into my lifestyle. Or she would say that John, her husband, just did not want to mix up the two families. When her daughters were grown, she would tell me that her daughters were the jealous type and that they could not handle her paying attention to me. Mostly though, she blamed her husband and said he did not think it was a good idea for her to become involved with me. However, the letters kept coming.

One day, a letter came. In the letter, she talked about grieving over the death of a man that she was engaged to. According to the letter, her husband John had been dead for five years, and she was first getting around to telling me that. Then I was informed she was engaged to another man and it angered me. I was irritated when I wrote back and called her on it, saying something like, "John has been dead for five years, your kids are all grown, and out of the house. What is your excuse now for not wanting me in your life?" My mother wrote back and said she feared I had turned into a very bitter and angry person.

It may have taken years for me to see the truth, but I finally saw the truth about why my mother did not want a relationship with me. She was the one that did not want it. If she had wanted to see me and build a relationship, she very well could have. Her husband, whom she blamed, had been dead for five years. Five years, and she was just telling me now! Was I a bitter and angry person? You bet I was. Especially with her! She had been lying to me all these years. So, for many years, I just stopped corresponding with her altogether. What was the use? I had made all sorts of excuses for her lack of involvement with me. I wasn't going to do that anymore.

After some thirty years of marriage, my husband and I moved from Wisconsin to Illinois, and it was in Illinois that our marriage began to fall apart. When we separated, I moved back to Wisconsin, and my daughter and I got an apartment together. I was at a place in my spiritual journey with the Lord that I did not want this division between my mother and me to continue. She was, after all, getting up in years, and I believed the Lord would want me to try to reconcile with her. I had worked through forgiving her because I needed to do that for myself. I knew, however, that reconciliation would complete the process of that forgiveness, not just for me, but for her as well. Once we were settled in, I sat down and wrote her a little note. I told her that my husband and I were separated and that I had moved back to Wisconsin. I gave her my telephone number and where I could be reached should she want to contact me. I left the ball in her court.

I was actually very surprised when the call came. My mother wanted to meet me for lunch. We met at a Chinese restaurant, and we had a long talk about life, and we talked at length about the Lord. She assured me that she read her Bible every day and prayed to the Lord. She said that with all the things that she had to go through in her life that she would not have made it if it were not for Jesus. I left feeling really good about everything because my main concern was about her salvation. From the things we shared that day, I was sure that her life was in the Lord's hands and that I need not worry about whether she was saved or not. I felt certain that she was.

I received a call from my mother, shortly after we met for lunch that day. She wanted to meet me for lunch again, and she said she had someone that she wanted me to meet. We made arrangements as to where we would have lunch along with the date and the time. When I arrived, she was standing in the doorway of the restaurant with two other women. Those two women turned out to be my two half-sisters, Karen and Roxanne. She introduced us to each other. This time she made it quite clear that I was her first-born daughter. We had a very nice lunch, but I am afraid that the three of us sisters did monopolize the conversation. We had so much to catch up on.

It was later on that I learned from my sisters that our mother had kept me a secret from them. It was not until she announced to them that she had someone that she wanted them to meet that they learned about me. They said they were shocked to learn that they would be meeting their sister. They did not know that I even existed until then. She had never mentioned me to them before. Roxanne said that when we were introduced at that one Christmas when I was visiting with my children, she had no idea that I was her half-sister. She thought that I was some friend of her mother's. My mother had been denying my existence to her other children all those years. I had just turned the corner of my 50th birthday when she was finally able to tell the truth about a daughter that she had with her first husband.

My brother, Kenny, was raised as the son of my mother's second husband and positioned as the eldest child in the family. Both of the girls had no idea that their brother was the son of my father and not their dad. My sisters had no idea that their mother had two children before she met their dad. My brother did not find out that he had a different last name than the rest of the family until a letter came in the mail from the United States Armed Forces, drafting him into service by another last name. This news came as quite a shock to my brother.

I so wanted to connect with my brother, but my mother protected all contact information about my brother from me. Then to my surprise, my brother came to visit me one time during the summer after I met my mother at the mall. I was so thrilled because I thought that he and I had made a wonderful connection during his visit. However, nothing more developed, and my mother told me that he had indicated to her that we had nothing in common and that he was not interested in seeing me again. I tried unsuccessfully to get any contact information from her so that I could try to pursue him in spite of what she said. I regretted not getting any of that information from him on our visit. I knew the community that he lived in, but I was not successful in finding him on my own. A couple of times, I had driven my car to his town and just drove around, hoping to find him walking around or standing in his front yard. I kept trying to find him because something did not feel right. I could not reconcile how warm and friendly he was with me the day of our visit with the information that my mother had given me. It just did not make sense to me, so I tried to find my brother on my own.

The truth has a way of surfacing at some time or another. Scriptures tell us that those things that are hidden shall be revealed or uncovered. Most times, the things that are hidden do more harm to those that they are hidden from than it does when speaking the truth. Believing the lie that the truth will be harmful in some way and that one is better off not knowing the truth is a lie that keeps us in bondage. Satan convinces us to keep things a secret because he knows the secret when it is known will set us free. For indeed, the truth will set us free. My mother carried her secret and lies for over 50 years and what a great burden lifted when she was finally able to tell the truth about me.

What seemed to me to be a strange turn of events after this wonderful meeting with my sisters; it was not clear until after the death of my mother. You see, after we had such a fabulous time together, I was told by my mother that my sisters were not at all interested in having a relationship with me. I was certainly surprised because they were not at all standoffish the day that we shared lunch. They seemed genuinely warm and friendly, just as my brother had been. Believing my mother, I did not make any further effort to contact my sisters or my brother, thinking that if they wanted to develop a relationship with me, they knew how to find me. I never heard from any of my siblings; although I was disappointed, I figured it was just too hard to pick up and develop a lasting relationship after all these years.

BEYOND ALL REASON: Moving Out of Logic Into the Supernatural

One Christmas, not all that long ago, when I was addressing a Christmas card to my mother, the thought crossed my mind that I would not be sending any more Christmas cards to her because her time on this earth was soon to expire. A few months after Christmas, I received a phone call from my sisters, Karen and Roxanne, telling me that my mother had passed away. They were able to locate me because of the Christmas card I had sent mother. Several years had passed since our luncheon date, and I had moved to Arizona, so without the card, they would not have known where I was. We spent the entire afternoon on the phone together and again the next day. The horrors of what was hidden in the closet were uncovered with my mother's death.

I discovered that my brother and sisters were lied to, just as I had been. They were told I wanted nothing to do with them. My sisters explained to me that our mother had always put a wedge between the three of them, dividing and isolating each one, not allowing them to build relationships with one another. I was told that I was spared from insidious abuse. The abuse that my siblings suffered is unconscionable and diabolic, and the only reason they survived is that the same divine arm of intervention, was in their lives just as it was in mine. I was relieved to learn that my brother Kenny had a divine visitation from the Lord before his death. I know now that we will meet again.

My mother was diagnosed as having a narcissistic schizophrenic personality disorder, making her incapable of loving anyone. She was jealous of everyone and everything. This reason is why she kept her children apart. She was jealous of any relationship that they had outside of her. Her every action was motivated by what was best for her. She also imagined things to be true that were not, and vice versa, she thought things that were not true to be true. In my research on Narcissistic behavior, I found that most Psychologists believe that pathological narcissism results from a child deprived of a loving personal relationship with their parents. Parents that are unable to form a healthy, emotional attachment to their children; can result in the child's perception of himself or herself as unimportant and unconnected to other people, usually family, community, and society. Typically, the child comes to believe that they have a personality defect that makes him or her an unvalued and unwanted person.[11]

My heart aches for my mother because I believe she was miserable and unhappy for her entire life. She grew up not knowing who her mother or father was. The story goes that there were two sisters, and the family is not sure which one of the sisters actually gave birth to my mother. It seems the older sister may have taken the role of mother to protect the younger sister and the family name because the younger of the two was much too young to have been in a family way. Neither one of the sisters raised my mother; she was instead handed over to another aunt and uncle who raised her, never to know who her parents really were. She was never nurtured and loved in a way that would cause her to develop normally. She then found herself repeating the same sin as her mother before her. My mother gave birth to me at the age of fifteen, another thing that I learned after her death. My birth certificate states she was older. Lies and deceit followed her all her life.

---

[11] *"Wikipedia,"* Narcissistic Personality Disorder" (Environment

Because of the conversation that she and I had about Jesus, I hope that somewhere in that mixed up psyche of hers; she understood the message of salvation.

As adults, narcissistic people become very controlling, shifting blame to others, intolerant of others, and oblivious to the needs of others or how their own behavior affects anyone around them. They are self-absorbed, and masters of manipulation to satisfy their individual needs. The children of narcissistic parents are placed in an intolerable position. They are expected to meet the emotional needs of the parent, which is an impossible thing to accomplish, and when they fail, they are punished severely. The punishment is manifested in a variety of abuses; including outbursts of rage, blame, instilling guilt, emotional withdrawal, criticism, and physical abuse.[12]

My sisters were brought up in this type of environment. One of my sisters told me that my brother suffered most of all. This realization is hard to comprehend since the pain and suffering that my sisters had to endure was horrific. For reasons only known by God, I grew up not having the care of my mother. I chose to tell this part of my life story because there is a powerful and profound lesson to be learned from it. We live in a wounded and hurting world. For many, life is not easy, and even when we walk with God, we never-the-less find ourselves in situations where we question God. We wonder where is God; in our current circumstances. We may ask, why did I have to go through that? Or what is this suffering all about? We may even question God's love

---

[12] ibid

for us, not understanding why we continue to suffer. I carried the pain of being rejected time and time again by my mother well into my adulthood. I never realized then, why there was a separation from her since the age of seven. After her death, God revealed the answers. It became so clear to me that the pain that I had suffered being apart from my mother was insignificant compared to the pain I would have endured being raised by her.

The love of the Lord is so profound that each one of us must trust His love even in the middle of the most excruciating set of circumstances. Why? Because He knows the beginning from the end, and His hand may very well be protecting each of us who suffer from something or someone that would be even more intolerable. His love is sparing you and me from unknown things. At just the right time, the Lord revealed the answers to my many questions about my mother. I am just so overwhelmed when I consider the mercy of the Lord and the remarkable way that He snatched me from an environment that could have destroyed me.

For years, I pined for my mother to be a mother to me and was rejected by the very one who brought me into this world. Thankfully, El Shaddai, "the double-breasted one," filled that void. All the rejection and abandonment was replaced with acceptance. I spent many hours with my head upon the breast of God. He accepts me. He and He alone brought healing to this wounded soul. The many tears shed upon my bed as He held my head are now kept safely in a bottle marked surrendered. He holds my tears in a bottle as a priceless treasure of total and complete surrender to Him. He is the only answer to a wounded and sin-sick soul. Trust that no matter what your past has been or what your future holds, God loves you, and even when life is difficult, He is working things out for your good. As for me, God has indeed turned my mourning into dancing, and He can do the same for you.

Father, I pray for everyone who has been rejected or abandoned by one or both of their parents. May you, the Father of all creation, be revealed to all who do not know you as their loving Father. May they rest their heads upon your breast until the beat of their heartbeat beats in perfect harmony with yours. I pray that each one of my readers comes to know the comfort that can only be found in your loving arms. My prayer is everyone reading this will discover the father's heart of their God. I pray that they will come to understand that you will never reject them or abandon them and that your promise to your children is you will never ever leave us or forsake us. Amen

BEYOND ALL REASON: Moving Out of Logic Into the Supernatural

Chapter 10

THE SUDDENLIES OF GOD

The intricate timing that the hand of God has orchestrated time and time again in my life blows my mind. I do not believe in coincidences. It was no coincidence that on the exact same day and in the exact same hour, a mother and daughter who had not seen one another in decades and lived miles away from one another would suddenly meet in a deserted mall at Christmas time. This moment was a divine appointment. Only God could pull something like this off. As I think about HIS providential hand upon my life, I am in awe of the ONE who has guided me and provided for me since childhood. This meeting in the mall took place long before I became "born again," telling me that He was always there, even when I did not have eyes to see or ears to hear.

There have been so many timely instances that flood my mind as I write. These memories are encounters that only God could have orchestrated. I like to call these happenstances "The Suddenlies of God," even though it is a made-up word. It is when He does something unexpectedly to reveal Himself in some Glorious way. Praise and worship often precede His suddenlies. Such was the case with Paul and Silas when they were in jail. They were in prison, praising the Lord regardless of their circumstances, and the Lord caused an earthquake to open the prison doors.[13] It certainly was a "suddenly" when Jesus showed up at my hospital bedside in all HIS Glory. The following are "suddenlies" that have happened after I received the Holy Spirit, and I had eyes to see and ears to hear. This chapter is a collection of those glorious visitations.

In the Name of Jesus

When my daughter, Tracey, was a teenager, there had been reports of several rape victims in our community. Therefore, she was fearful. So, I began to teach her about using the authority that she had in the name of Jesus. I told her all the same authority Jesus had was passed on to those who believe and follow Him. Jesus told us that even greater things would we do than He did. I also explained our battle is not against flesh and blood, but against evil powers and principalities; the demons of Satan's kingdom. I explained to her it was not enough that she had this authority because she was a believer, but that she had to exercise her authority by speaking things into existence or commanding the spirits to leave in Jesus's name. I told her that if someone actually tried to take advantage of her, the most powerful weapon that she had against that person would be the words that came out of her mouth. Just say this, "In the name of Jesus, I command you

---

[13] Acts 16: 25-26

to stop, and I bind you Satan and all of your powers against me. I command you to flee, in the name of Jesus."

To bring this truth home to Tracey, I told her about a story I just heard the day before on the 700 Club about what had happened to two young teenage girls. After shopping at a mall, they returned to their parked car in the parking lot. Unknown to them was the fact that a group of young men were waiting for them in a somewhat isolated area of the lot. These men were laughing and jeering and harassing the girls. The girls were unaware that these young men had removed the carburetor from the hood of the car. Somehow the girls managed to get into the car and lock the doors, while the young men stood outside of the car laughing because they knew that their car was going nowhere. Their ultimate plans for the girls was only known to the men and God.

The young driver put her keys into the ignition to start the car, and it would not turn over. So, the girls bowed their heads in prayer, and then they commanded the car to start in Jesus' Name. She then turned the key a second time and, no doubt, to the young men's bewilderment, the car started, and she drove away. Once these young girls got home and told their father what had happened, he, of course, was relieved they had the presence of mind to pray for help and use their authority. What he did not know was that the carburetor was missing from his car. This observation, he discovered later when he was unable to start the car.

My daughter sat there in amazement and thrilled to hear about how the Lord had supernaturally rescued these girls. I told the story intending to build her faith and remove her fear, and it did just that.

Tracey, I said, "These are the kinds of things that happen when we exercise our authority Christ gave us and believe our words have power." People with authority speak words that are obeyed by others because they recognize the authority of the one that is speaking. This is how it is when we recognize our authority in the Kingdom of God. We can put the devil to flight and create miracles by the words of our mouth, in the authority of the name that is above every other name, Jesus.

    That afternoon Tracey and I decided to go horseback riding at a riding stable not too far from our home. Neither one of us were expert horsemen, but we thought that we had ridden enough that we could be left alone on the trails without a guide. They would not let us go alone, although the guide said that once we were out in the open, she would allow us to open up if we chose to. So, the three of us started on the trails. First was the guide, then my daughter and myself, with my horse in the rear. For whatever reason, my horse decided he wanted to lead this parade, and he began to race with my daughter's horse. Both horses, in their quest for the lead, passed the guide. Tracey's horse was not about to be outdone and took off in a full gallop, with my horse close behind. It was frightening, and although I had been pulling on the reins to stop him, my horse just kept on going. Then, my saddle, which was not fastened tight enough, slipped off of the horse's back and turned me upside down, and I fell under the horse and was watching his back hooves as they were about to trample me. This incident happened in a flash, and all I could think to do was call out the name JESUS!

Suddenly, I felt the powerful arms of a supernatural being take hold of me and roll me and stand me up on my feet. My horse kept going trying to outrun my daughter's horse. The guide, who was now behind us, witnessed the fall and the miraculous recovery. She was quickly by my side to see if I was OK. She then said to me, "Well, you said you guys had experience riding, but that fall and recovery was done like a pro." Little did she know that I had nothing to do with it, and indeed it had been done by a pro, albeit, a divine pro!

I stood there trying to take it all in because it would have been just seconds, and those hooves and all the strength of this magnificent animal would have come crashing down on me. Yet, there I stood upright without a scratch. I stood there speechless, when Tracey my teenage daughter, came cantering back to where I was standing, with her horse totally under control. "Mom," she says, "Why didn't you do what I did? I commanded my horse to stop in the name of Jesus, and he did! Just like you said!"

Jesus, the Tailor

When I was a young woman, I did quite a bit of sewing. I had shopped and bought the most beautiful soft linen in a gray-blue color I knew would be just stunning in the pattern design I had chosen. I spent several days cutting out the pieces and sewing everything together. It was a two-piece suit, skirt, and jacket with quarter length sleeves. I had decided I would trim the sleeves edge and the jacket opening with a dark beige thread to give the jacket more detail and pizzazz. The detailing I did by hand, and I was so happy with the results. When I finished sewing, I ironed the garments and then tried them on. The skirt fit me just fine, but to my great disappointment, the jacket was not tailored to fit me right. It looked like I just got off the boat! I sat down and cried. After all that work, I didn't want to look like Eleanor Roosevelt! After a while, I began to pray. "Lord," I said, "I am going to spray this jacket with water, then I am going to iron it again, and what I need for you to do, is to shrink it to fit my body perfectly." With the faith that Jesus would do what I asked, I stopped crying, took the spray bottle in my hand, sprayed the jacket, picked up the iron, and pressed the jacket once again. Suddenly, and without me noticing a thing, the jacket was shrunk to fit me. Jesus, the tailor, had come to my rescue. I wore it until the design was no longer fashionable. Then it went to the Goodwill. One great regret is I did not keep the suit as a memorial to the goodness of God.

Jesus, the Winemaker

We had sold our home and moved into a duplex during the construction crisis. My husband was between jobs, and there was little income during this time in our lives. Even though this was the case, I became aware that something supernatural was taking place. The first thing that I noticed was there seemed to be a multiplication of the food that I prepared. I would cook what I thought would be enough for our family for one meal, and there would be plenty left over. I would make a pot of soup for us that would usually be gone in a day or two, and it would last for several days instead. I began to notice something strange at the grocery store too. After years of shopping for groceries, most women can come pretty close to what the total cost will be just by eyeballing the shopping cart full, half full, and so on. I was usually within a few dollars one way or the other. But during this time, the clerk would ring me up, and it was always way less than what I had anticipated. Yet, we were eating good, and I had not changed the quality of the food that I purchased. This provision happened so often that I decided I was going to check the cost of every item and add things up to compare the total price with my receipt.

As I was ready to do just that, I heard the Holy Spirit say, "Don't Do It." I was thinking of the possibility that the Lord was doing something supernaturally, and that is why I intended to prove it by adding everything up. Now that He said, "Don't Do It," I knew for sure that my suspicion that something supernatural was taking place, was right. Believe me, I was praising God for His provision every day. Next, I noticed that the gas in the car was lasting longer between refills. Not having learned my lesson, I decided I was going to start keeping track of my mileage. Again, I heard the voice of the Holy Spirit say, "Don't You Dare." Well, I didn't because, "Don't You Dare," spoke volumes to me. Those few words told me that He was indeed multiplying my gas, but He did not want me to keep any records to prove it. My job was to trust Him to provide.

It was during this time that one of my favorite and fun, "Suddenlies of God" took place. I was making dinner for the family and went to the cupboard for a bottle of cooking wine that I thought was there, but it wasn't. So, I grabbed my car keys and headed for the grocery store a short distance from our duplex. At the grocery store, there was a section where the cooking wines were displayed. As I remember it, there were four different cooking wines. Each for a different purpose and each had a different colored label. The wine that I needed was the one with the blue label. There was a row of green labeled wine, and a row of yellow labeled wine. There was also a row of red labeled wine, but no sign of the blue labeled wine. It had been sold out. So, I decided to look at each row more carefully, just in case the blue labeled wine I was looking for was misplaced in the wrong row. I took hold of one of the green-labeled bottles of wine and held it in my hand. Removing it gave me a clearer view of the row it was in to see if, by chance, a blue label was there. It was not. I did the same with the yellow labeled wine. Not having any luck finding a blue labeled wine bottle, I removed the first red labeled wine bottle to look closer at that row.

No, nothing there. Disappointed, I went to return the red labeled wine bottle in my hand, but when I looked at it in my hand, it was a "blue labeled bottle of wine." Don't ask me how this could have happened, because my answer will always be the same; I don't know. But what I do know is that it was a creative miracle of God! "IT WAS A SUDDENLY OF GOD THAT IS BEYOND ALL REASON!" His ways are mysterious, and they are often hidden, somehow supernaturally. It is not for us to try to figure it out. We are merely to trust and believe.

Jesus and the Alarm Clock

My husband and I were going to be gone for the weekend. As I remember it, Kelly and Tracey were going to be spending the weekend with friends and Billy; my eldest was old enough to stay home alone. I had just finished reading the Cross and the Switchblade written by

BEYOND ALL REASON: Moving Out of Logic Into the Supernatural

David Wilkerson, and I gave the book to Billy to read, hoping that it just might ignite a desire in him to reach out to the Lord. You never know what method will intrigue a child and bring their curiosity to a peak. I thought this book might do it. When we returned home from our trip, our son had a story to tell. Billy told us that after reading the book, he was encouraged to ask God for a sign. He went on to say, "On Saturday night, when I went to bed, I prayed. I asked the Lord to give me a sign if He wanted me to get up on Sunday morning and go to church." Curious, we asked whether or not Billy received his sign. He said, "Well, early Sunday morning, there was such a loud crash of thunder that it woke me up! "Did you go to church?" I asked. "No, I was too tired," replied my son. At this point, his father said, "Let me tell you something, if that had happened to me, I would have hightailed it to church as fast as I could!"

Here Comes the Judge

One of the most amazing "suddenlies of God" happened in a courtroom. My son Billy was picked up for shoplifting when he was in his 20's. He had been out having fun with his friends and had one too many beers when he went to the grocery store in the wee hours of the morning. He put a small jar of celery salt in his sock and proceeded to leave without paying for it. WHAT IN THE WORLD WAS HE THINKING? He had invited his friends over to his apartment for breakfast, and he didn't have any celery salt. He got caught, arrested, and a court date was set. I praise God that he did not get away with it because this began a series of events that brought him to his knees in repentance before he had to stand before the judge. Shortly after he was arrested, he lost his job and moved home to live with us. During this time, he went to church with me at the Charismatic fellowship that I was attending. My pastor took Billy under his wing and discipled him.

While he was looking for another job, he began mowing lawns in the neighborhood for pocket change. One day while he was mowing, he came home all excited. While mowing the lawn the Holy Spirit came upon him and baptized him in power and he began speaking in tongues.

Our fellowship was just a small group of people, and we did not have a worship leader, so we worshiped along with worship tapes, that is until Billy joined us. My son brought his guitar with him to our services and led the worship. Much had changed in his life in such a short period of time. He was listening to Christian music in the house all the time that he was there. He tried without success to convince his sister that she would love listening to his Amy Grant tapes. Tracey, however, was not interested in Christian music at this point in her life.

A baptism service was planned for a Sunday morning service at a lake not far from where we lived. Although both Billy and I were baptized as infants, we decided that we wanted to be immersed in the waters of baptism just as Jesus was. Billy's court date was set for the Friday before the baptism was to take place. Our entire church was praying for the Lord to have mercy and that the favor of the Lord would rest upon Billy when he went to court. Friday came, and my pastor and his wife accompanied Billy and me to the Court. We sat in the back praying while the proceedings went on. Billy's name was near the end of the doc, therefore, we watched one individual after another stand before the judge and get sentenced to various times in jail. Watching, this, I must admit, it shot arrows of doubt into my faith. Finally, my son's name was called, and he approached the bench.

When the judge saw my son, he said, "Young man, this is not the first time that you have stood here before me. I think that it is about time that we teach you a lesson." My mouth hung open, what in the world was this child of mine up to that I had not been informed about? Then the judge asked if there was anyone in the courtroom that had anything to say before he would sentence Billy. I stood up and said that I had something to say. "Your honor," I said, "I understand your reason for believing that my son needs to be taught a lesson, however, much has changed since he was arrested. He has become "born again" and has turned his life around. In fact, he has plans to be baptized this Sunday. The judge said something like, "Well that is all well and good, but your son needs to learn that there are consequences to his actions. I will, however, delay the sentencing until Monday morning so that he can be baptized on Sunday." A time was set for us to return on Monday, and the four of us exited the courtroom very discouraged.

Over the weekend we went before the Judge of heaven and asked for favor concerning the sentencing. My son and I were baptized together, but the fear of what the sentencing might be was hanging over our heads like a dark cloud. Monday came and a very nervous young man stood before this judge for his decision. On the judge's desk were all sorts of cases and papers in little piles. Then, SUDDENLY something awesomely supernatural happened, the JUDGE of Heaven arrived, and the judge residing in this earthly courtroom became very confused. In his confusion, and with both hands, he began to mess up all the papers on his desk, so much so that some papers fell to the floor. Then without another word, he picked up his gavel and said, "CASE DISMISSED!"

It is said, "The greatest lessons in life are learned by our mistakes." My son Billy grew closer to the Lord through this experience. He now serves his Savior and prays and ministers to others in his workplace. I get great pleasure from the stories he tells me about how the Lord intervenes in his life.

Without a Trace of Tracks

A precious sister in the Lord and Prophetess, Ruth Carneal, brought a word of the Lord to my daughter Tracey some time ago that she was to be watching for the suddenlies of God. She has experienced several, but I would like to share a suddenly of God that happened with my daughter's little Lhasa Poo, dog Sadie. Sadie was a miracle dog. I say that because many things happened to her, which are not explainable in the natural. The Lord's hand has been upon this dog from the beginning. He gave Tracey this dog, and He told her what to name her. Sadly, Sadie is no longer with us. As she was getting older, she became diabetic and blind. Tracey was trusting the Lord to heal her dog, but she was never-the-less at this point, blind. She may have seen shadows, but for all intents and purposes, she was blind. Sadie had memorized the house and navigated pretty well inside the house. Sometimes she got confused and would walk right into a wall. Other times she began scratching on a closet door as if to say, "let me in."

Sadie had a little doggie door, so she could get to the backyard by herself to do her duty. Because Tracey was fearful that Sadie, being blind, might fall into the pool. She had put a little lattice fence across the patio, preventing Sadie from getting anywhere near the pool. Twice now, while Tracey and I were interceding for some friends of ours, we had witnessed what we believe to be "Suddenlies of God."

Tracey and I had spent some time singing and worshiping when the phone rang. It was a friend with a need, we were in Tracey's bedroom, and we were doing some spiritual warfare for this dear friend who has been oppressed by the spirit of shame for many years. We began to do some serious damage to Satan's kingdom by blowing the shofar and praying in the Spirit over the situation for our friend's deliverance. We were in another zone when a "Suddenly of God" occurred. It was as if Sadie was suddenly just dropped off in the room. One second ago, she was not there, and the next second, I heard Sadie making a rumpus, and she was running around the bedroom like she was crazy. I looked, and she was soaking wet. I said to Tracey, "Look, Sadie must have fallen into the pool; she looks like a drowned rat." With that, Tracey got a towel to dry her off, and I went to examine the patio and the pool to see if I could figure out what might have happened.

Sure enough, the barrier was moved, and Sadie must have pranced around near the edge of the pool until she fell in. Nothing so unusual about a dog taking a dip in the pool, except that Sadie hates the water, and Tracey was unable to teach her to swim, although she tried many times before she lost her sight. Whenever she tried, the dog, unlike other dogs, would panic, paddle a little, turn on her side and go under the water. This outcome is why Tracey was so fearful of having Sadie exposed to the pool. Before Sadie went blind and the fence was put up, we experienced what we believed to be our first "Suddenly of God." One day Sadie come flying into the house, dripping wet and running wild. There was no doubt; she had fallen into the pool. Upon investigation, it was obvious as to what had happened, because starting from the pool and across the patio, she left a water trail of paw prints. She also left a water trail through the doggie door and into the house wherever her little paws took her. Sadie had definitely fallen into the pool. The question, though, remains, "How did this little dog get herself out of the pool and back into the house? We had to dry her off and clean up the water that she had dripped from one end of the house to the other. We were suspicious that Sadie was rescued and guided to the house by either an angel or the Lord Himself.

This time, however, we were not suspicious, we were confident that we had a "Suddenly of God" because there was no water trail, therefore no water to mop up. Not one wet paw print across the patio, not even one drop of water anywhere to be seen except at the edge of the pool where she had fallen in. Sadie was soaked, and there was no water trail on the concrete patio from the pool to the house. There was no trace of water anywhere, not outside, not inside, not at the doggie door, which by the way, is the only way that Sadie can come into the house by herself. Sadie just appeared in the bedroom, literally dripping water from her body and shaking like a leaf. There are two possible explanations as to how she was retrieved from the pool and carried to Tracey's bedroom. But either way, it had to have been "a suddenly of

God!" An angel or Jesus rescued Sadie and brought her to our worship. Or she was translated by the supernatural power of the Holy Spirit. One day we will find out what really happened from the Throne Room of Heaven.

Another Close Call

I am reminded of the scripture in Proverbs 18:10 that says, *10 The name of the LORD is a strong tower; The righteous run to it and are safe.* Just think about how safe we are when we are trusting the Lord with our whole hearts. If He is concerned about the safety of a little dog, how much more is He concerned about the safety of those that He loves and knows that are trusting in Him for their protection.

I have saved the most awesome "Suddenly of God" for last. This one is about a time when the Lord was concerned for the safety of His two daughters. There are benefits that can only be obtained by having a personal relationship with Jesus. Having head knowledge does not allow one to walk in His glorious provision, and safety is one of those provisions. One must tune in to the divine voice of the Almighty, and that ability only comes by spending time with Him. Not just the time you might spend at a worship service at church, but the time spent every day in prayer, reading and studying the Bible, having Q & A with the Lord, so you learn to hear His voice. It was our custom to spend quality time with the Lord, and fortunately, it has paid off for us in so many incredible ways.

This particular "Suddenly" happened in Arizona after I moved to join my daughter, who had moved there from Chicago, Illinois. We lived in a small apartment complex at the time. The living room, kitchen, and eating area were all open as one large room with no walls dividing the space. The living room had large sliding glass patio doors overlooking the parking lot and driveway. Tracey and I were having a conversation, she was standing with her back to the patio windows, and I was standing behind the kitchen island facing her as we talked. Then suddenly, Tracey screams at me to "DUCK!" As she screamed, she flung herself to the floor, as I did. Just in time, because what followed was the deafening sound of a bullet from a gun that shattered the glass of our patio doors.

The Lord warned Tracey with a word of knowledge of the impending danger, and she relayed it to me. We both obeyed the command, and God saved us from a situation that could have had a severe outcome. We were praising the Lord for His divine intervention after that close call. It wasn't long before we heard the sound of the sirens of the police cars approaching. Within minutes several police officers were standing in our living room to investigate the shooting. The area was blocked off with the infamous yellow crime tape, and a crowd had gathered. Fortunately, for us, among the group was one of our neighbors, who was a carpenter and good friend of Tracey's. He took over and had the patio doors boarded up in no time. The experience shook us, but never-the-less, with grateful hearts, we continued to praise the Lord for His Goodness!

I often wonder how many blessings we miss because we are not listening or how many mishaps we could have avoided. Pondering this, as I write, reminds me of a "Suddenly" that happened somewhat recently that drives this point home. My daughter and I were ready to leave the house to go shopping and out for lunch and enjoy the day together. I had my car keys in my hand and was prepared to leave when suddenly that voice spoke to me. "Do not leave the house today." We obeyed and stayed home, both of us wondering what kind of danger the Lord was saving us from? We will never know what harm was avoided by staying home, but this we do know, blessings follow obedience, and we obeyed the word of the Lord that day.

His voice said, "DUCK," and we obeyed. His voice said, "Do not leave the house today," and we obeyed. In both cases, the Lord was protecting us. Had we taken the time to reason we would never have ducked. Reasoning could have cost one of us our life. Reasoning could have convinced us to leave the house, and only God knows what would have happened had we reasoned ourselves out the door. His ways are "Beyond all Reason."

BEYOND ALL REASON: Moving Out of Logic Into the Supernatural

Chapter 11

DISCERNING THE VOICE OF GOD

Although I attended church regularly and even taught Sunday school, I seemed to be powerless over the many sins in my life. However, significant changes began to happen in my life after the day I was baptized in the Holy Spirit. It all started at that first meeting that I had attended with the "Women's Aglow" conference at the Ramada Inn in Milwaukee, Wisconsin. After that meeting, I went home all excited to tell my husband what had happened to me, just sure that he would be as enthusiastic about it as I was. I was wrong!

The following days and weeks, I could not wait for convenient times to be alone with the Lord and speak to him in my new language. Raising three children, tending to the needs of my husband, and operating an interior design business did not give me many opportunities to be alone with the Lord. So occasionally I would get in my car and drive somewhere, park my car, and pray for a while. For some time after I was baptized in the Holy Spirit, whenever I would close my eyes for prayer, my eyelids would be full of golden shafts of light. These shafts of golden lights danced and sparkled, putting on quite a light show for several weeks. I was experiencing my first exposure to the Glory of God. Having this glorious manifestation of the Lord's presence take place when I closed my eyes, thrilled, and delighted me. I was so disappointed when the curtains for the light show closed. At other times when it wasn't possible to slip away or be alone in my prayer closet, I would have my nose in the Bible or some book authored by a spirit-filled Christian. I wanted to learn as much as I could about God. I felt cheated. Here I was thirty-eight years old, and until now, no one in my church or any of my family or friends had ever told me that these experiences with God were even possible. I felt like I had missed a lot and that I needed to catch up somehow. I prayed and studied every spare moment that I had.

The idea that the third part of the trinity, the Holy Spirit, actually had invaded my life and chose to live in my heart was more awesome to me than any words could ever express. The more that I spoke in tongues, the more things began to happen in the supernatural realm. It wasn't long until I began to hear God speak to me. Here's the thing though, He didn't talk to me in an audible voice. It was not a voice thundering from heaven, like the Voice that spoke to me in my car. No, it was a very still, small voice from within me. It was more like the sound of my voice when I am thinking about something. The only reason I knew it wasn't me thinking was that He said things to me that I would never say to myself. He also told me things that I did not know of. The second time the Lord spoke to me, it was in His still small voice, He said: "I Love You, Margie." Now those words are not words I would ever say to myself! Upon hearing "I Love You Margie." the tears began to stream down my cheeks. You know God loves you, but it is a whole different thing when you hear Him say it. It is kind of like the times you hear those words from someone that you are romantically involved with. You know that he loves you because of his behavior towards you. However, when he says those three little words, "I love you," it melts your heart, and it means so much more to you just to hear it said out loud. Hearing my heavenly Father say these words, "I Love You, Margie," gave me a very real sense of self-worth. This feeling was something that I had been trying to achieve by all my "good works" my entire life.

When I was removed from my mother's apartment and taken to live with my grandparents, I was too young to understand what was happening to me. All I knew was that my mommy didn't come to get me and take me home with her, and my daddy moved out, got married, and only visited occasionally. Surely, there must be something wrong with me that mommy or daddy didn't want me anymore.

This confusion is where the work of Satan began. A door opened for the spirit of worthlessness as well as a spirit of abandonment. These spirits tormented me for a good share of my life. Until the day that I heard those words, "I love you," for the first time. I had worked very hard at being the best I could be about everything that I endeavored to do. I needed the praise of people around me to feel good about myself. I went to great lengths to get the "approval of men." I was an excellent role model for a people pleaser. It wasn't until I heard God, the Father of all fathers, tell me that He loved me that the strongholds of Satan began to lose their grip. Also, having the knowledge that Father God had adopted me from the kingdom of darkness into His Household, His Kingdom of Light, gave me a sense of real value and a sense of belonging. Remember, the first scripture that I looked up after my experience at the Woman's Aglow meeting? I needed to find the location of the word "Abba." That section of scripture became such a great comfort to me because it spoke to what was very much a part of my own experience.

Romans 8:14-17 14 For as many as are led by the Spirit of God, these are sons of God. 15 For you did not receive the spirit of bondage again to fear, but you received the Spirit of adoption by whom we cry out, "Abba, Father." 16 The Spirit Himself bears witness with our spirit that we are children of God, 17 and if children, then heirs—heirs of God and joint heirs with Christ, if indeed we suffer with Him, that we may also be glorified together.

The Holy Spirit of God chose to live within my heart and was indeed the Spirit of adoption that the Bible speaks of, and the first word I uttered when I received my prayer language, was "Abba."

The Lord began to instruct me about many things. One day I heard Him say that he loved people who tithed. I had not been tithing my income at that time. I, however, wanted to do everything that I knew to do that would please the Lord. So, I began writing checks to the church for 10% of my income. This coupled with the fact that my husband did not believe I was hearing the voice of God, caused a rather troublesome atmosphere in our home. He was not only upset with the amount of money that I was giving to our church. He was upset with the fact that he had lost his partner in crime. I wish I had a dollar for every time I heard him say to me, "You are just not any fun anymore;

why don't you go and join a convent and become a Nun!" You see, I had stopped drinking with him, and he had to drink alone, and my abstinence really bothered him. I was not even aware of how much I was changing. I was not making any conscious effort to be different. The changes happening were very subtle. I just didn't want to do some of the things that I did before. I stopped lying, and a quest for truth became a motivating factor in this new life that the Lord was creating within me. Therefore, I was reading the Bible and any books by Christian authors that I could get my hands on.

One morning before my husband left for work, he took me in his arms and in a very gentle and tender voice (which by the way was not his style) said; "Now, honey, I don't want you to read anything today OK? I just want you to rest and take it easy. Can you do that for me?" Oh, my God, he thinks I'm crazy, I thought to myself. "You think I'm "losing it, don't you?" I said to him. Well, of course he does, in his mind, people who hear voices are crazy people. I can't blame him, and if I were him, I'd think I was crazy too. Once he was out the door, I dropped to my knees. "Lord I need some help here; my husband thinks I'm ready for the funny farm," Bill had grown up in the Lutheran Church. However, the things happening to me were outside the sphere of his spiritual knowledge, and they were definitely not something coming from the pulpit on Sunday mornings in the church that we attended. I knew from my husband's tone that he was really worried about me.

Lord, I repeated. "I need some help here." Then I heard the voice that I had become accustomed to hearing, say "Go get the Yellow

Pages phone book," I got up went to the closet and reached for the phone book on the top shelf and returned to my place on the floor where I had been kneeling. "Turn to page 278." He said. I did, and to my surprise, it was in the section where churches were listed. Then He said, "Go over three columns and count down 12." I did, and I stopped counting at a Lutheran Church in Brookfield, Wisconsin, which was number 12 of the churches listed. The address told me that the church was maybe 30 minutes away from our home. "Go visit that church," the voice said.

Sunday morning came, and I informed my husband that I was going to visit another Lutheran Church that morning. I didn't dare tell him that I was instructed to go there by "that voice" because he would have called the men in white jackets. I had checked the time for the service in the phone book, where it was listed, and I gave myself plenty of driving time to get there. When I arrived, the parking lot was full. I found a place to park some distance from the door. As I walked approaching the entrance to the church, I kept wondering why the Lord wanted me here this morning. I entered the main vestibule, and no one was mingling, so I peeked into the sanctuary. It was a full house. From the sound of it, I could tell the pastor was wrapping up his message, so I didn't go in. I should have called for the service time instead of trusting the phone book; I thought to myself as I began to observe the main entry of the church.

On one of the main walls in the vestibule was an enormous bulletin board. I meandered over to read what was on the board. Alongside of the bulletin board was a book table that caught my eye before I looked at the message board. To my delight, I found many books that I had read about the Spirit-filled life, writings about speaking in tongues, and the gifts of the Spirit. Then glancing at the bulletin board, I saw an announcement of some coming event sponsored by the 700 Club. "This is a Charismatic Lutheran Church," I said under my breath to myself. "Oh my, God, you are too much!" "I asked for help, and you sent me here." This time was another one of those supernatural divine interventions.

Since I had missed the service, I decided to wait for the pastor and see if he had time to speak with me. After the last congregant shook hands with the pastor and disappeared behind the solid oak doors that opened to the parking lot, I introduced myself to the pastor. "Well, welcome," he responded, "What brings you here this morning?" he asked. "You'll never believe why I am here this morning," I said. "Well, try me! Let's go into my office where we can sit down and have a little chat." He motioned in the direction of the office, and I followed his lead. After I told him the story of how the Lord had directed me to his church, a big smile stretched across his face, and he began to praise the Lord for His mysterious ways. I told him that I attended a Lutheran church, but as far as I knew, I was the only one in our congregation that was baptized in the Holy Spirit with the evidence of speaking in tongues. I shared with him several of the awesome miracles taking place in my life and how they were affecting my marriage. I told him that my husband thought I was crazy. With this statement, he began to laugh. "Join the club; it has happened to all of us at first. The natural mind does not understand these Spiritual things. Therefore, the mind rejects them and labels them crazy," was his response.

Then he began to share his own experiences with the Holy Spirit. "When I received the Spirit and began speaking in tongues, I considered leaving the Lutheran Church because my denomination did not believe that these things were for today. They believed that speaking in tongues and the other gifts of the Spirit, such as prophecy, ended at the time of the apostles and it is not for today. I was faced with a dilemma. What to do? After much prayer and consideration, I decided to stay and let my experience speak for itself. After a time, the denomination accepted this was indeed a move of God. I received their blessing to teach on the gifts of the Spirit that are definitely for today." He told me about many miracles that he experienced, as well as his wife and members of his congregation. We talked and shared our experiences with God with excitement and with awe for over an hour or more. It felt so good to speak with someone in the clergy that understood where I was coming from. I told the pastor as we were starting to say our goodbyes, "I cannot wait to go home and tell my husband that you do not think that I am crazy." With that, he chuckled and invited me to bring my husband back with me some Sunday morning, which never did happen.

When I arrived home in the middle of the afternoon, I was greeted with, "Where have you been? Church surely didn't last this long." "Wait until I tell you!" I said. I could tell by the look on Bill's face, after I shared with him my conversation with the pastor, that he was relieved I was not the only crazy person in the Lutheran church. I knew that there would be no more talk about having me committed. God had solved that problem. I suggested to him that we visit this Charismatic Lutheran church together on some Sunday. "We'll see," he said. Experience had shown me that what he really was saying was, "No, I don't think so." I had yet to see one of his "we'll see" turn out to be a "yes."

In the days that followed, my excitement about the Lord seemed to be contagious when it came to my friends. However, not with my own family. I think they thought that I was going through another phase of some kind. After all, my epiphany had come on the heels of the recent seminar with Werner Erhard. I had been equally excited about his enlightenment seminars. I had learned later that what he was promoting was nothing more than Hinduism, disguised under a new name and part of the new-age movement. It has developed into the occult religion known today as Scientology. False religions always give us some truth mixed in with the deceptive doctrines of demons presented as the whole truth. I searched for the truth in many directions. Unfortunately, all those roads led to occult practices that would enslave me. My family was not so willing to swallow everything that I was feeding them right away. They were waiting and watching. Besides, none of them had the same need as I did. They were content with the way things were. I was not. I knew that there had to be more. Thank God that I had finally found what I had been looking for. Once that empty vacuum in my heart had been filled with God Himself, I found such an incredible peace enter my soul. I knew that I had finally found the "truth." In the beginning, I went overboard with the preaching and the teaching. My family would find scripture verses scotch-taped to the mirrors, to the refrigerator, to this and to that. I wanted so much for them to have the same wonderful experience with God that I had, I became obnoxious. Eventually, I learned that I could not be the Holy

Spirit to them. In fact, I learned from God that I was actually getting in His way. I became less vocal about my relationship with the Lord and began to pray for my family more. I knew that my family would have to find their own way in their own time.

In the meantime, Claudia, the woman that had invited me to my first Women's Aglow meeting, invited me to attend a Bible study a friend of hers, Jan, was having in her home. She suggested that if I wanted to bring anyone with me, they would be welcome. I called my friend Rita, my sister-in-law Jeanne and my secretary Julie, and we made a date to meet on Thursday evening for Bible study. Since these three women were the closest to me, they were the ones sharing in my enthusiasm. There were six of us in all, and we sat comfortably around Jan's kitchen table. It was an exciting time of learning the word of God and sharing the things that the Lord was teaching us. I remember this one time before the meeting, I was in prayer, and I heard a voice say several things to me instructing me about this and about that. I wrote the words down that I was hearing, tucked the piece of paper in my Bible to share later at the Bible study. When the opportune time came, I pulled the sheet of paper out and read it to the group. Everyone seemed receptive; then, after reading it, we went on to discuss some other things. After Jan served a snack, we reluctantly began to gather up our things to go home when we saw that the clock on the wall was ticking its way toward ten o'clock.

When I answered the phone the following day and heard Claudia's voice on the other end of the line, I had no idea it would be the beginning of a series of lessons and tests that would serve me well for the rest of my life. "Marjorie," she said, "I don't know how to tell you this, but I have been in prayer all morning, and I believe very strongly that the Lord wants me to tell you something. I am not sure how you will take this, but it must be said." "Claudia," I responded, "It's OK. Just go ahead and say whatever you have to say." So, she began, "I need to tell you that every voice that you hear is not the Lord's. I believe you are listening to a familiar spirit. I asked the Lord how it is that you, such a babe in the Lord, are getting all these words of instructions? I then heard Him say, "You wouldn't give an infant the keys to a car, would you? I'm so sorry to be the one that must tell you this." I heard what she said, but my mind could not take it in. It was spinning around like in a whirlwind. "No, Claudia," I was finally able to utter, "Really, it's all right. I am glad you told me. I don't want to be listening to any wrong voices." It was a bittersweet call. I was upset because I wasn't sure what all this meant. Had I not heard God at all? No, that can't be true. I know what I have heard. Yet, I did not want to be in deception. Now I was baffled; what was from God, and what was not? All these thoughts were swimming in my head while Claudia was still on the line. Whatever she said after that, I really can't remember.

After I hung up the phone, I could not concentrate on anything. All I could think of was that she did not think the things that I shared the previous evening were from God. I felt like a fool, embarrassed, and humiliated. If not from God, then from whom? Could Satan have been playing with my mind? I just could not wrap my mind around that thought. The call was bitter because of all the negative feelings that I was having, and it was sweet because it was correcting me and leading me away from any deception. I decided that from now on, I would keep the things that I hear to myself and test them as to whether or not they came from God.

Well, it wasn't long after that I got tested. Unfortunately, I was not true to myself. I did not ponder the next thing I heard and, instead, acted on it. My teenage daughter, Tracey, was in braces, and the orthodontist thought she would need to wear them for around two years. She was scheduled for a check-up at the dentist right around the one-year mark. Since I believed in the supernatural intervention of God, I began to pray that He would speed up the process and remove the braces early, because she was so tired of having to wear these braces. Just a few days before the scheduled appointment, I heard these words ever so distinctly, "I have healed Tracey. When you go to the dentist, tell him to remove the braces. She is healed." Well, the woman of faith that I am, I marched into his office and declared, "She is healed!!! Off with the braces!!!" OK, I wasn't that brazen. But I did explain to the orthodontist that I believed I had heard the Lord's voice speak to me and tell me that Tracey was healed and that the braces could come off. The doctor was kind, and although I am sure that he wanted to roll his eyes, he didn't. He just wisely said he would examine Tracey's teeth and see if I was correct.

When I saw the look on my daughter's face after the examination, my stomach sunk, and I began to feel sick. I knew before the doctor opened his mouth, what he was going to say. "I regret having to inform you that your daughter's teeth will still need to remain with braces because there is no evidence that her teeth have shifted to the degree that would warrant taking off the braces." Oh, my God, Claudia was right, I have been listening to a wrong voice, I thought to myself. Jesus would never tell me something that would embarrass and humiliate my daughter like this. Anything that the Holy Spirit would speak would be correct. Although I was also embarrassed and humiliated at my mistake, my heart was much more concerned about how I had put my daughter in such a vulnerable position. She, after all, had to return for several more visits to the orthodontist before the braces could be removed. Every time she would have to face him, she would have a reminder that her mother is known in this office as some whacked-out religious nut case. Tracey's eyes were telling me that if she could kill me, she would. She could not get out of that office fast enough.

Some lessons are learned the hard way, and this was one of them. I had not yet learned about what the scriptures say. It says in I John 4:1

1 Beloved, do not believe every spirit, but test the spirits to see whether they are from God, for many false prophets have gone out into the world.

One way I could have tested the spirit was a wait and see what the orthodontist had to say. If she really was healed, the doctor would have told me, instead of me telling him. Oh, what a fool I had been. Satan, the father of lies, had just lied to me, but worse than that was the fact that I had listened to the wrong voice and believed his lies. This example is just one of the many strategies that Satan uses to try and deceive the people of God. He comes as an angel of light, looking for those that he can deceive. When I was baptized in the Holy Spirit, it opened the door to the supernatural. What I did not know until later was that I had not just entered the spiritual realm of the Holy Spirit, but that I had also entered the spiritual realm of the unholy spirits, the demons.

One of the gifts of the spirit that I also received when I received the gift of speaking in tongues was the gift of discernment. This gift is given as one of the power gifts to help the believer to differentiate between the Holy Spirit and the many fallen angels or evil spirits of their offspring who serve Satan; that we call demons. I was not using this gift of discernment, or I would have been able to distinguish the difference between the voice of God and His arch enemy. This lesson that not every voice is the voice of God was a hard lesson to learn, but I am grateful that I discovered it early in my walk. The humiliating experience at the orthodontist has kept me on guard for my entire spiritual walk with the Holy Spirit. Little did I know then that the Lord was just beginning His boot camp training. I had been drafted to be trained as a warrior in an unseen spiritual battle.

It was my habit to start and end the day with scripture reading and with prayer. It wasn't long after our visit to the orthodontist that I found myself snuggled up in my favorite chair to do just that. It was a Queen Anne Wingback chair we had inherited from a relative. It wasn't old enough to become an antique, but it was old. I had it reupholstered in a beautiful green damask fabric. I loved the chair because it was very comfortable and yet stylish. I was sitting there all comfy reading my Bible and enjoying my cup of coffee when I heard this audible voice say to me, "Put that book down, I can teach you everything that you need to know." I could not believe my ears. "How dare you Satan," I replied. "I will not put down this Bible, it is the word of God, and God will teach me everything that I need to know. I bind you now in Jesus name you are not to speak to me or counsel me in any way, be gone." The word of God says that if we resist the devil, he must flee. Now I was angry, and I was not going to be deceived by the devil this time.

It didn't take a lot of discernment to figure out that God would never tell me to put down the Bible. It is His Word to us. He has gone through great pains through the ages to place His inspired Word into our hands. I had to laugh to myself because I thought that it was really a very stupid thing for the devil to say these things to me. He might have just as well identified himself and said, "Hey, look, Marjorie, it's me, Satan, and I want to teach you everything that you need to know." It's a fearful thing to consider what might have happened to me had I believed this voice to be God. I might have been the one penning the book Conversations with God instead of Neale Walsch. This poor misguided man believed the voice that he has been listening to was the voice of God when, in actuality, it is the voice of a familiar spirit guiding him with the doctrines of demons. It is the voice of the god of this world's system.

I heard about this book on some TV show, and since I was interested in finding out what type of conversations someone else was having with God, I bought the book. As it is with all that Satan does, that is, baiting you with some truth, in the book "Conversations with God," he does the same thing. He intertwines the book with some truth so that you will buy the entire concept, hook line, and sinker. I found the book to be contrary to the Word of God on almost every page. At one point, the author even says there is no such thing as sin. Be careful whose voice you believe. Satan's plan is to lead us away from God, and he will even pretend to be God to do so. Neale Walsch is not the only one that believes he is hearing from God because he hears a supernatural voice outside of his voice. Many people today think they are being guided by God when, in fact, it is not God, but familiar spirits that have come to deceive and lead people away from the ways of God.

A few years ago, I was in the park walking my dog, and I overheard a conversation of two women who were discussing their spirit guides. One woman was saying to the other that she had several spirit guides. She said that every morning, one of them came to her and told her what she should do for the day. She went on to say that she would not be able to go on without them. There is only one Holy Spirit; all other spirits are unholy and cannot be trusted to tell the truth. They will lead us astray if we give them any audience. This deceived woman was saying that she would not be able to go on without them. I fear for her because the truth is "with them," she will not go on into eternity. Jesus is the only answer for her. I fear that I failed to be a witness for the Lord that day. Perhaps I should have stopped and joined in on the conversation, just maybe I could have planted a seed of truth. At the time, however, I just wanted to get as far away from that conversation as I could.

These early experiences of listening and believing a wrong voice taught me so much. I thank God for them, even though they were hard and sometimes embarrassing lessons to learn. I learned that when the Holy Spirit speaks to us, He will always confirm what He has said again and again. He would never say anything contrary to the written word. His job is to lead us into all truth. Furthermore, the Holy Spirit will always point us to Jesus as the only way to be reconciled with God the Father, and the Holy Spirit will convict us of our sinful nature. Only the devil would try to convince us that there is no such thing as sin. If the concept of sin is missing the mark, then doesn't just plain old fashion common sense tell us that we miss the mark all the time? None of us are perfect, except, of course, the man Jesus, who is God.

We can all have conversations with God. He is speaking to us all the time, and it's up to us to listen. First and foremost, He speaks to us from His written word, which is logos. The Bible is a remarkable book, indeed. It is a book that has recorded God's thoughts, words, and instructions, and His purpose through history, to a people that He calls His own. It shares His redemption plan through the ages, and it reveals Jesus from cover to cover. It is His love letters to us, and yet so many of us put those love letters up on a shelf and never read them. He also speaks to us in His Rhema word, which is that still small voice in our hearts. The most significant defense any Christian can have against the deceptive strategies of the enemy is to be familiar with the Word of God. That way, when the devil whispers his lies into your ear, you will recognize the lie because it will be contrary to the scriptures. There are many voices in our society that are shouting for your attention. Much of what the screaming is all about are lies that are parading around as truth. The enemy of your soul knows if you hear a lie over and over again, eventually you will believe it to be true. Guard yourself with the only standard that there is to measure truth, the Word of God.

Much of my life, I was walking in the truth as I knew it. However, circumstances proved to me that what I thought was the truth, was not. Or that I only had some part of the truth. Which has caused me to coin a phrase, "That may be the truth, but it is not the whole truth." As I try to tell my story, I may be saying what I know to be the truth, but it may not be the whole truth. This story that I tell is only from my perspective, and the lives intertwined with mine may have another view if given an opportunity, to tell the truth as they saw it. It is with fear and trepidation that I press on in obedience, to speak the truth as I have experienced it.

Chapter 12

THE POWER OF FORGIVENESS

To tell my life-story, I find it impossible to share God's most significant illustrations of His grace, without exposing another person's sin. I struggle with this a great deal. How do I tell my truth without dishonoring someone in the process, whose sin will become obvious? This predicament has held me back from telling my life story in its entirety. I have husbands and parents and children who all have played an intricate part in my life. Like mine, their sin was exposed, and I face a moral dilemma to tell or not to tell. I suppose the answer to this difficulty is to get permission from those who are still alive. However, I have questions regarding my deceased parents and how I can still respect their memory. Do I keep silent? Or is telling the truth a higher law? Should I bring up someone's sin when that sin was put under the blood of Jesus? Will this telling glorify God in any way? I shall continue with my story and how my life intertwined with my father. As of this writing, I have not decided if this part of my story will ever be published. If you find yourself reading this chapter in a published book, then you know the decision I have finally made, but not without much deliberation.

I do not have many memories of my dad. I do recall that after the court's decision for my grandparents to raise me, my father was living with us too. At least for a brief period. I remember that he was a cab driver for a while, and he would take me with him until it became apparent that I was prone to car sickness. I remember he bought me a bike for my birthday that would take me a couple of years to grow taller before I could ride it sitting down. When I sat on the seat, I was unable to reach the pedals, but I learned to ride it anyway, standing up. I must have been 8 or 9 years old when my dad remarried and moved out of his parent's home.

His visits usually meant a movie, or he treated me to a hamburger and French fries or a banana split at the local soda fountain. I only remember him coming to one of my dance recitals. I remember this one time; I was so excited to see him, because he had come to the swimming pool at the park where I spent my summers, to watch me swim. I was overzealous, and in my excitement to show off to my daddy, I ran and jumped into the water without thinking, and I jumped into the deep end. Frightened half to death when I realized the water was way over my head, I kicked and flapped my wings until my head finally bobbed its way out of the water just seconds before my lungs were planning on bursting. Determined to make my daddy proud, I swam the unbelievable long trek of 10 feet from the deep water to the shallow with all the speed of an Olympic swimmer, never allowing him to know how frightened I was.

Sometimes he would take me fishing with him, which was not a favorite pastime of mine. The hours just sitting in a boat waiting for a fish to bite that would probably be taken off the hook and sent back into the water to find its family, would just drag. Sometimes I couldn't stand the waiting, so I would jump into the water from the side of the boat and go for a swim, frightening all the fish away. He never got upset with that. When I would surface from the depths of the lake, he would be sitting there in the boat with a smile across his face that said: "That's my girl," and that smile would capture my heart. I endured this fishing excursion with the forbearance because once we unloaded the boat after fishing and put the tackle and fishing gear in the trunk of the car, we headed for my father's favorite pub on the other side of the lake. This place was always the highlight of the trip for me. I sat up on the barstool and ordered my favorite kiddie cocktail and potato chips, just like a grown-up.

At the age of 14, I was fully developed, and it was around that age, my father decided he would teach me to drive the car. So, after he would spend reasonable time with his parents visiting, he would suggest we take a ride. At first, these times were fun and adventurous, and I liked the sense of power I had behind the wheel. Then at some point when we would change positions of the driver's seat, my dad, after he took control of the wheel, would drive to some secluded place and pull the car over and park it.

Those times became my father's darkest hours. Unlike the power and control I felt when I was behind the wheel, I had lost all control, reduced to infancy without a will of my own. Those unspeakable acts of betrayal that would destroy the self-worth of any child entered my psyche with memories that are still not erased. Suffering comes in many forms, but I believe one of the most difficult types of suffering and pain is the intrusion of demonic influence caused by someone else's sin. Especially when that someone is your own father! This man I idolized and loved, how could he do this to me? The trauma of these intimate acts paralyzed me and silenced me. My dad made me promise not to tell anyone, "This will be our secret," because he said, "I could go to jail, and you wouldn't want that, now would you?" I kept silent, not because I cared whether he would go to jail, although I admit that may have been part of the reason that I remained silent. I kept silent, mainly because I could not bear to hurt my grandmother. This man was her son, and even as young as I was, I somehow knew how news like this would be devastating. I also kept silent because I was too ashamed to even talk about it. I remained silent because the entrance of this type of evil is incomprehensible and unspeakable. It was wrong of me to have kept quiet. My silence may have caused great injury and violence to another innocent victim, and I pray my silence did not do that.

I responded to subsequent visits by disappearing. I would go to a friend's house in the neighborhood until I saw his car back out of the driveway and head in another direction. In time, I became an expert in denial. I put up a good front around the family whenever my father was around for family gatherings. I treated him warmly and with respect. No one would have known I had distanced myself from him after what had happened between us. He knew, however, and he did not come around much for a while after my disappearing acts. There were occasions, although they were rare when he would bring his wife and their oldest daughter, my half-sister, for a visit. His wife was not the type of woman that could warm up to another woman's child. Therefore, the relationship between my father's wife and myself was tolerable, at best.

Once I was married and had a family of my own, I always included my father in any family celebration. By this time, my father and his wife had added two more daughters to their family. My two younger half-sisters were born close to the same time as my two boys were. My father and his family were invited to all three of my children's christenings, birthday parties, confirmations, holidays, graduations, and the like. However, he always came alone if he came at all. My father was fun and likable, and although he had a dark past, he also had a side to him that was quite lovable. He was mild-mannered and easy-going. I never once heard him raise his voice to me. This was not the case, however, when he and my mother were married. I have one horrible memory of them fighting, and I saw him put a gun to his head and threaten to kill himself. I do not know how he was at home with his new family, but as a visiting father and grandfather, he seemed even-tempered.

My children enjoyed their grandfather, and I was not going to rob my children from the limited relationship they had with their grandfather. I say limited because I have only one memory of our family ever being invited by my father and his wife to visit their home. I had been there alone a few times, but even those times were rare. All encounters with my dad either took place in my home or my grandparent's house and perhaps occasionally, the home of one of my uncles or aunts. I was very careful to assure the safety of my children, and they were never allowed to be alone with him. No one was aware that I was taking these precautions because I managed to do so without being obvious.

At family gatherings, whether for Christmas or weddings, my father, for the most part, would attend them alone. On some occasions, his wife would accompany him, but their daughters would be strangely missing. I have few memories of my sisters, except when they began to mature and become young adults. It was during those years that they became included in the mix, and I did enjoy their company and their unique personalities. However, it was impossible to develop strong, healthy relationships with them due to the situation with their mother. There were some infrequent occasions where my dad and his wife would meet my husband and me for a round of golf, and then the four of us would go out to dinner afterward. I believe my father's wife enjoyed herself in spite of herself. As the years flew by, it became more and more evident to me that she had some serious emotional problems, and I always tried to treat her kindly. Sometimes this took a great deal of restraint because of the things that came out of her mouth. I think she softened slightly toward me when she learned I had become born again and was baptized in the Holy Spirit, with the gift of speaking in tongues. I had shared the Spiritual experiences I was having with both her and my dad through the years.

My dad was always looking forward to the days when he could retire and enjoy his life. He talked a great deal about the plans that he had for retirement. Well, that day never came. He had put all his hopes and dreams into his retirement years, only to discover that he was very ill. He was in and out of the hospital for a couple of years. The first time I visited him in the hospital, he looked so frail and weak. We visited for a while, and then I asked him if it would be all right with him if I would pray for him. He agreed to let me pray over him, and as I prayed, he broke down and began to cry. He began to blubber. He said that he was nothing but a "son of a #@&%*" and that was why he had to suffer. I knew what he was referring to, so I took his hand and held his hand in mine. I looked directly into his eyes and said: "Daddy, I have forgiven you. I love you, and God loves you." With those words, the dam broke, and he was able to release through his floodgate of tears, years of shame and guilt. When he gained his composure, he looked at me and said, "You have turned out to be quite the woman. I just don't know how you can forgive me."

I sat at his bedside for what seemed to be hours, talking about God. I explained to him that I had become the woman that he was now admiring because of Jesus. It was His work in me that enabled me to forgive him and to love him deeply and to love him regardless of the past between us. My dad, through his tears, voiced his concerns about whether or not God loved him, and I could tell from the things that he was saying that he did not have that blessed assurance that he was saved. Well, that was about to change. I had my Bible with me. I had in my possession many Bibles, but this one was my favorite Bible because I had my favorite scriptures underlined by yellow markers. The margins were full of hand-written notes where I had put my commentary. So, I opened it up and began to read some scriptures that

I had marked for him. After I had read several to him, I asked him if he would like to pray and ask the Lord to make His home in my father's heart just as the Lord resides in mine. I don't remember the words to the prayer that I prayed through my tears. I do remember, however, that it was a glorious day of salvation, healing, and deliverance because my father experienced forgiveness from the Lord and me that day.

As I stood up to say my goodbyes, I heard the Lord say to me, "Give your father, your Bible." I did not respond with an immediate "Yes sir," as I should have. Instead, I began to argue, "But, Lord, this is my favorite Bible, if you want my dad to have a Bible, I will rush right out and get him one. I will buy him a beautiful leather-bound Bible with gold leaf. I will get him the best Bible money can buy." The Lord continued, "Margie, I want you to give him the Bible that is in your hands." I walked back over to his bedside and said, "Here, Daddy, I want you to have this." And I handed him my Bible. It was a gift of love given in hesitation but never in regret, because the gift that my dad gave me in return is a picture that will forever be imprinted on the memory banks of my mind. It was a beautiful Kodak moment.

When I handed him my Bible, his countenance started glowing as the most joyous smile illuminated his face. I left the hospital floating on air. I left confident that the Lord was going to heal my father, there was absolutely no doubt about it, this day was just the beginning of all the gloriously wonderful things that the Lord was going to do. The following days had no signs of any miraculous healing, but I did not give up hope. I knew my Jesus had healed everyone that He came in contact with when He walked on this earth, and He was doing the same today wherever there was faith to believe. I had the faith to believe, so it was just a matter of time. Little did I know then, that this time would drag on for months and months, and his health would not improve.

My dad's condition got worse, and it was hard watching him travel those roads back and forth to the hospital. During this time, he had called and asked for me to come to him, and I did. He was so vulnerable, and it was difficult to watch him be reduced into the image of a man many years his senior. We had some long serious talks, and he told me that he was ready to meet his maker. I was confident that it was not going to happen any time soon because my God was going to heal him. Then one morning after dad had been re-admitted to the hospital again, I was awakened from sleep around 2 or 3 a.m. by a phone call from the hospital. It was dad's wife, and she indicated I had better get myself to the hospital as soon as I could because things were not good. She said that she and the girls were leaving to go home and get a little shut-eye, to clean up, and that they would return in the morning and that they would meet me at the hospital then. I quickly got dressed and headed to the hospital. It was a long drive, but during the wee hours of the morning, there was very little traffic, so it was smooth sailing. I believe it was around 4:00 a.m. when I arrived at the hospital. I went to my father's room, where he was resting peacefully in a rather comatose state. He was hooked up to a couple of machines to help him breathe and record his vitals. Even with the machine, his breathing was labored.

I found a bench out in the hall and rested there while I waited. About 5:00 a.m., his doctor came over and sat down. He asked me if I was the eldest daughter. I said that I was. He began, "I have been looking for someone in the family to talk to that is reasonable. Your father is dying. When his heart stops, we are obligated to try and revive him because he is hooked up to these machines. To try and revive him will be an assault on his body, and it will only delay the inevitable. This procedure is not something that I would want to be done to my own father," the doctor said. "I think that he should be allowed to die with some dignity." Then the doctor went on to ask, "Do you know where your father is spiritually?" This sort of question from a doctor surprised and delighted me. I assured him that my dad and I had talked at length and that he was ready to meet his maker. The doctor looked at me and said, "Good, that is something that I needed to hear." "Now," he said, "I need permission from a family member to remove the machines when his heart begins to fail, so he can have the dignity of dying in peace." Without a second of hesitation, I had to face the reality that God wasn't going to heal him and said, "You have my permission."

My sisters and their mother had returned to the hospital. My dad's wife and I were in the room with my father when the nurse came in and began to remove the machines from my dad. When his wife realized what was happening, she burst into a hysterical fit and asked the nurse under whose authority was she removing these machines from her husband. The nurse continued what she was doing and very gently said, "A member of his family." With that answer, she flashed me a look of rage and called me a murderer, and then stormed out of the room. I stayed standing next to my dad's bed and prayed. The nurse stayed too standing on the other side of his bed. Soon the nurse said to me, "It is not going to be much longer; you might want to go get his wife so that she can say her goodbyes."

I stayed just outside the door giving Laverne privacy with him as she said her goodbyes to her husband, my father. I could not help but overhear her parting remarks. She told him what a good husband and father he had been and that it was time now to go home to be with his Father. At about the same time, I heard her exclaim in an excited voice, "Virgil, what is it? What is it? What do you see?" As she was saying these things to my dad, I felt the Holy presence of the Lord. His presence was so strong that I began to weep. My tears were sweet tears of joy. I was not grieving because of my father slipping away before my eyes. No, I was feeling a strange type of joy, a knowing that my father was soon to be in the hands of a Holy God. Laverne continued, "What do you see? Do you see Jesus?" she exclaimed, and then came the silence...he was gone. When Laverne left the room, I returned to my father's bedside. I looked down at him, and although his body was still in the bed, he was not there. I looked up at the nurse, and tears were rolling down her cheeks. She looked at me and said, "That was the most beautiful thing that I have ever witnessed."

When I returned to my prayer closet, I sought the Lord for answers. "Lord," I said, "I do not understand, you have promised to heal us. I asked you to heal my dad, and I do not understand why you did not heal him when you have healed so many other people I have prayed for. Nothing is impossible with you. I really had the faith to believe for his healing, and it did not happen. Help me to understand. He was on fire for you, and we could have enjoyed some years together in the faith. Why now God, when we finally made a spiritual connection? Why, God, why?" I was interrupted by that Voice, "Margie, I had to take your father now while he was still on fire for me. I took him at the height of his love for me. If I had healed him, he would have waxed cold."

Chapter 13

HE CAME TO SET THE CAPTIVES FREE

Shortly after being baptized in the Holy Spirit, Woman's Aglow had invited a leader in the Charismatic movement, Don Basham, to speak at their monthly meeting. I went to the meeting, and I sat there listening to him spellbound. He talked about how the Lord had opened his eyes to the fact that Yes, Christians can have a demon. He learned that He and his family needed to cast out and get delivered from these evil entities. Don shared his experiences of how he and his family were delivered and set free. He spoke about how the deliverance ministry was coming back to the church where it first started. Many people were being set free. This freedom was happening through his ministry and the ministry of others who were called for this task. Little did I know, I would be one of them called. I received deliverance but also was used in a deliverance ministry. He spoke to us about how most of the demons have occupied our bodies since childhood, and although we are not possessed by them when we are a Christian, they never-the-less can influence our thinking and our behavior a great deal, keeping us in bondage.

Demons enter children when doors are open by their parents or those in authority over the child. The child can be innocent, but because that child has been abused, a passageway is created for demons to enter the child. Demons torment many righteous Christians who do not live a life of sin because somewhere in the generational bloodline, some ancestors prayed a prayer dedicating their seed to Satan. The Lord wants us free from the devil's trap. Then he said, Satan is not a gentleman, and he takes advantage of every opportunity to strike an individual, even before their birth. It just doesn't matter to Satan if his target is an innocent baby. For instance, many times, demons enter the womb because; perhaps the baby was conceived in sin. "Well," I said to myself, "that qualifies me; my parents had to get married."

Don Basham went on about how demons enter. This topic was very intriguing because I could relate. He informed us that when a child has had some type of trauma, like abandonment, sexual abuse, or even rejection, demons enter their innocent host. He said that these spirits of rejection, abandonment, and sexual abuse are just the tip of the iceberg; when they enter the body, they bring a whole family of related demons with them. Again, I said to myself, "Oh Lord, I must be full of them; I qualify on every count. I've been rejected and abandoned by my parents, and I was sexually abused." Then he went on to talk about how our sin opens the door to demonic activity in our lives, allowing demons to enter.

Many doorways open the entrance of demons. Christians open the door to demonic activity every time they knowingly or even unknowingly step into the kingdom of darkness. Christians who habitually sin open the door to demons. Christians who participate in occult practices such as astrology, hypnosis, yoga, fortune-telling, tea-leaf reading, tarot cards, ouija boards, and the like, open the door to demons. Since the sexual revolution of the 60s, Christian couples were influenced by the sexual culture of the world. More and more Christian couples are indulging in sexual intimacy outside of marriage, opening the door to various sexual and perverted demons. Extramarital affairs, drunkenness, cursing, gambling, even something as seemingly insignificant as believing a lie, opens the door for a demon to enter a Christian's body and reside there.

Yet the controversy in the Church on whether a Christian can have a demon or not continues to rage. Those opposing, are reasoning that a demon from Satan cannot live in the same body the Holy Spirit does. They use the scripture about being unequally yoked with an unbeliever as their proof text. In 2 Corinthians 6:14-17 New King James Version, the text reads as follows:

14 Do not be unequally yoked together with unbelievers. For what fellowship has righteousness with lawlessness? 15 And what accord has Christ with Belial? 16 And what agreement has the temple of God with idols? For you are the temple of the living God. As God has said: "I will dwell in them and walk among them. I will be their God, and they shall be My people." 17 Therefore "Come out from among them and be separate, says the Lord. Do not touch what is unclean, And I will receive you."

These comparisons make the point a believer is a citizen of the Kingdom of Light, and an unbeliever is from the kingdom of darkness. The believer serves Christ, while the unbeliever serves Belial. Therefore, there can be no harmony between the believer and the infidel. To take these scriptures out of context and to apply them to the ministry of deliverance is not good theology.

Our speaker concluded his message by naming these evil spirits one after another, and according to my calculation, I thought, I must have every one of them. He ended by saying that if we felt we needed deliverance that there were ministries available to us, however, many people, including himself, had done what he called self-deliverance. He said the method for that was in his book and was for sale on the book table. Once dismissed, I made a beeline for the book table and bought his book, "Can a Christian Have a Demon?"

"Oh, woe is me," I thought, as I sat there thinking this is terrible, I have to get rid of these things. I want nothing but the Holy Spirit residing in me. After dinner, I read his book from cover to cover. By the time I had finished the book, there was no doubt that I needed deliverance. I spent some time in prayer, and then one day shortly after finishing the book, when I was all alone in the house, I said to Jesus, "Come on with me, You, have work to do." I marched into my bathroom with the book in my hand and sat down on the floor next to the toilet, fully expecting the Lord to deliver me. And He did! I went into the bathroom because the author of the book that I was reading said that often, the demons come out with coughing, choking, and sometimes through purging. I wanted to be near the toilet if that was the case. I did not care how they came out, as long as they came out!

It was quite amazing. I followed the steps in the book, then I began to pray in tongues, and then soon, I began to feel the manifestation of one demon after another. They came out of me coughing or gagging, and sometimes in a burst of air from my mouth. It was so strange because they were using my breath, my voice, my tongue, and my lips, yet it was not me speaking. Having had this experience, I realize that perhaps when people say, "the devil made me do that," they are telling the truth. The devil did make them do that!

During my deliverance, the Lord opened up my ears to hear the conversation taking place between Jesus and the demons. It just blew my mind. I would hear the demon say, "No, I'm not leaving; she is mine." Then, the Lord would say. "No, she is mine, you must go." The demon would say, "But I have been here a very long time." And the Lord would say, "Yes, but now you must go." Sometimes I would hear a demon voice, sounding like a little child pleading to stay and ready to cry, when it said, "This is my home," and the Lord continued, "No, you cannot stay, you must go." Then the Lord instructed me to say the same. So, I boldly declared, "In the name of Jesus, you cannot stay, you must go." Because of the authority Jesus Christ gave me, one by one, they left my body. I was emotionally exhausted from the deliverance, but I was also in a state of awe over what I had just experienced.

When deliverance like this takes place, those vacancies must be filled with the Holy Spirit. That is very important! I was fortunate with my deliverance because the Lord was right there, teaching me every step along the way. There, of course, is no better teacher than one's own experience. People can argue with you about your theology, but they cannot argue with you about your experience. I had been a Christian for many years, maybe not a good one, but I knew the Lord Jesus Christ as my Savior. It was not until I received the power and

Baptism from the Holy Spirit to walk the walk, that real change took place in my life. However, every change that took place before my deliverance could not compare to the change that took place after my deliverance. Before deliverance, I kept going around the mountain over and over, not getting anywhere. Obstacles were in my way, and I kept having history repeat itself. It was like right before what appeared to be a breakthrough that gave me hope; things would suddenly change, and I was right back where I started, feeling hopeless again. After deliverance, I did win battles I had not succeeded before. I felt free!! My life changed for the better, giving me hope and victory!

Deliverance generally takes some time before we are completely free. An hour here, a couple of hours there, all through your life. The Bible says in Philippians 2:12, *"Work out your salvation with fear and trembling."* Deliverance causes such a violent upheaval within the soul of a person that the Lord usually does it in stages. I think we all want a "car wash." We want our deliverance to be a once and for all thing. But that is not the way it happened in my experience. It happens in many stages throughout our lifetime.

What you will discover is that certain aspects of what you thought to be your personality, was not your personality at all, it was a demon personality, and it no longer resides within you. This observation is freeing, but at the same time, it takes adjustment, as was the case with me. I was now on the road to discovering who I really was. The way that I thought about many things was so different. For instance, I was delivered from a people-pleasing demon, motivated by the approval of others. So much that almost everything that I did was to please someone else. I needed people to praise me or like me for whatever it was that I had done. It was hard for me to ever say no to anyone for anything, and I had to be the best at it that I could possibly be so that I would be recognized.

Now understand, we all need approval, and we all need to be stroked and affirmed. I am not talking about a reasonable need to be encouraged. I am talking about something entirely different. I'm talking about being driven to do more and excel. Relentlessly compelled to "one-upmanship," Even though you receive those strokes, you are never satisfied, always feeling inferior. Once I was delivered from that spirit, I was feeling pretty good about myself without the strokes from man. I felt good about myself because I belonged to the Lord, and His affirmation was enough. I could say no to someone and walk away without feeling guilty. I could stand up for myself and express how I felt about something, even if it meant I would take an opposite position on an issue without fear of rejection. I could fail and not feel like a failure. I could be wrong, admit it, and move on without a million reasons for justification. I still wanted to do the best I could but for different reasons. I was now more interested in my integrity, and I wanted to be a good witness. So, excellence was my goal; however, I lost the need to be a perfectionist. Trying to be perfect is a weighty burden to carry. Perfectionism can never be achieved, and it makes one feel worthless when it is not. Striving for excellence has an entirely different motive because it is more about attaining an excellent result for the task at hand than it is about stroking the ego. My main motivation, even today is to please God,[14] and strive to be the best I can be with the gifts that He has given me. Caring about what other people think about me has greatly diminished.

My husband did not know who this new woman was, and neither did I. I had thought the influence of these demon entities was a part of my personality, and they were not. The best part is these were things that I did not like about myself, and then to find out that they were entities influencing me, and not the real me, was liberating. It took time for me to adjust to the person that I really was meant to be all along. My deliverance I kept to myself for quite some time. Although my husband saw the change in me, he did not know it was because I had been delivered of demons. It was not until our family moved from Waukesha to Oconomowoc that I was free to share my experience with anyone. My family members were not saved, and to share this experience with them would have been untimely. The Lord introduced me to a couple in Oconomowoc, Wisconsin, who were Spirit-filled, and on fire for the Lord. They began a Church fellowship in their home, which I attended with my husband's blessing. It was there that I started my training in the deliverance ministry.

---

[14] I think it is important for me to expand on the thought of pleasing God. God, who has created me is already pleased with His workmanship. There is absolutely nothing that I can ever do that will cause Him to love me anymore than He loved me at my worst moment. So, good deeds and righteous living does not earn His love. His love is everlasting. Doing good deeds and living righteously is done out of obedience and as a love gift back to God for all that He has done for me. Each of us must examine the motivation that is behind our actions, whether it is for God or for someone else. I am motivated to please God because I love Him and how I live my life is a love gift back to the one who has given me that life.

BEYOND ALL REASON: Moving Out of Logic Into the Supernatural

My husband continued to attend a Lutheran church there in Oconomowoc, Wisconsin. We both had been attending the Lutheran church together. I had been teaching Sunday school there until it was known I was a tongue speaker. The pastor was aware of this, but once the parents of the children that I was teaching found out through a Bible Study, they no longer wanted me to teach Sunday school. Up until that point, I was praised as their teacher. I believe this happens out of ignorance.

One day, I received a telephone call from the pastor informing me that I would no longer be needed as a Sunday school teacher; and he told me why. I was very hurt and upset; nothing about me had changed; I was a tongue-speaking Christian when I joined the church. After the parents rejected my teaching, my pastor told me that I was welcome to stay. I could be a part of the congregation, but I couldn't share or teach anyone about my experience with the Baptism in the Holy Spirit. It was not part of their doctrine. Immediately, I knew that I could no longer stay and be a member of a church that wanted to stifle the Holy Spirit. What a contrast this Lutheran Church was from the Charismatic Lutheran Church that I had visited in Brookfield, Wisconsin, so many years ago. At this point, my husband was unwilling to leave the Lutheran church, so I joined him in attending services week after week. One Sunday morning, when I was sitting in the pew listening to a good sermon, it was on a subject matter preached over and over and over again. I did not need to hear it again. I was hungry for more of the meat of the word and found myself very frustrated and unsatisfied with milk and baby pabulum week after week. So, I sat there praying to the Lord. "Lord, I need something more—I do not need to hear this. I need to be somewhere where I can learn more. I know that there is so much more." It was then that I heard that still small voice say, "You would not expect your children to repeat the third-grade year after year, and neither do I." "Oh wow," I said to myself. That is exactly it…there is nothing wrong with the third grade except to be there when you should be moving on to the fourth grade. I then continued my prayer, "Please convince my husband that we need to move on." It wasn't long after that prayer that my husband encouraged me to join my friend's fellowship, knowing it was where I wanted to go to church and knowing it was Charismatic. He, however, remained in that Lutheran church until we moved out of the state.

Some years later, my husband was transferred to Illinois, and we joined a Charismatic church there. By this time, my husband had been born again and filled with the Holy Spirit himself. This fellowship moved in the power of the Holy Spirit, and it was very common for deliverance to take place at their meetings. Many were trained to use the various gifts of the Spirit that were given to them. The discerning of spirits is a gift of the Holy Spirit to distinguish the difference between the Holy Spirit in operation and the operation of evil spirits. This gift is of great importance in the deliverance ministry for identifying various demons. This gift was operative in the church that we joined at that time. So, I fit right in. I did operate with the gifts that the Lord had given me on occasion. It was here that my husband and I grew in the things of the Spirit. It was at the fellowship in Illinois that I met one of my dearest and most loyal of friends, Pat. She and I, we thought, were the most unlikely people to maintain a serious friendship. However, we have been friends now for over 30 years. We would never have chosen each other as friends because our personalities are so different. She is from one end of the spectrum, and I am from the other. It was, however, a divine appointment that the Lord set up for us. One night at our Wednesday night service, there was an announcement that the women of the fellowship were going to meet weekly on Wednesday mornings for prayer. I decided that I would go and join the women for prayer. At the first meeting, there were maybe ten women that gathered together to pray. The next meeting dwindled to perhaps a handful of ladies. Each time there was less and less that attended until Pat and me were the only ones that came for prayer. When this happened time after time, we looked at each other and began to laugh, "Do you think the Lord is trying to say something here?" Pat said as both of us sat there looking at each other. Finally, we decided it was silly to meet at the church building since it was not air-conditioned, and it was just the two of us. Pat lived just a very short distance from where we met, and so we moved the prayer meeting of two to her house where we would be more comfortable.

It was God's infinite wisdom that put us together. We have remained prayer partners and intimate friends until this day, and she is indeed my sister in the family of God. We needed each other, and God knew this. Only God knew the trials that we would face together. It was through our prayer life that we learned how our gifts of the Spirit, could complement, one another. For instance, the Lord would sometimes give Pat a word of knowledge and then give me the wisdom on how to apply or interpret that word. It was amazing. My friend Pat had a very powerful gift of the discerning of spirits; therefore, anyone with a demon in her presence was sure to be found out. Not only could she identify the demon, but because of her strong anointing for deliverance, those ugly little critters would start manifesting in her presence. They knew they were about to lose their home. Such was the case with the generational spirit of schizophrenia that was lying dormant within me, just waiting to attack sometime later. It manifested itself first with laughter and then with crying and then what I would have considered being the impossible; it took hold of my senses and laughed and cried hysterically at the same time. Pat finally had enough, and she said to the thing, "Oh shut up! You come out of her NOW!" It left me immediately, and I was exhausted, just as if I had been on the battlefield of some war. Oh, that's right, I was! A Spiritual war!

You see, my mother suffered from schizophrenia. Satan planned to destroy my life with this demon spirit, as well. Often what happens is when someone dies, the spirit or spirits that resided in that body leave and go looking for the nearest relative and enter them. I do not know what door I had opened for this to happen to me, but I'm guessing it was some lie that I believed at that time. I was so grateful it was revealed before it could take hold of me. The Lord had other plans for me, and would not allow that thing to remain hidden any longer. At other times the demons inside of Pat would manifest in my presence. Actually, in her case and mine, the Holy Spirit anointing causes them to manifest. It is because the Lord has set the appointed time for the deliverance. I do not want to take any credit because He and He alone is the deliverer. We just have to be willing to be His vessels of freedom. Well, we were both ready, so sometimes without warning, when we would meet for prayer, deliverance was on the menu. Such was the case this one time I will never forget.

Let me preface this by saying that my friend Pat has a real wit about her. Some things that come out of her mouth are hysterically funny. I thought it was a part of her personality, and even when she would mock someone, it was done in such a way that it would have me in stitches. One time when I was visiting with Pat, and her friend, the three of us decided to spend some time in prayer. Well, it wasn't long into the prayer time when Pat began to manifest a mocking spirit. I did not recognize it at first; I thought it was her except for the fact that she would not ordinarily interrupt our prayer time with such antics. This demon, using Pat's vocal cords and tongue, began to say the most outrageous things, and before long, her friend was rolling on the floor in laughter, and I had tears running down my cheeks from laughing so hard. It was at this point I heard the Holy Spirit say to me, "Margie, you need to get a hold of yourself, you are dealing with demons. You must not join in on this laughter. You need to stop it right now. I want you to deliver Pat from this mocking spirit, and I want you to cast it out from her friend as well." I had to leave the room to compose myself because what I was listening to was beyond funny.

When I returned to the room, the demons were speaking to each other. What I heard when I returned was this: "I am so glad that you came out to play with me. It's been a long time since we played together. They began to converse with one another, saying things so funny that I had a tough time restraining myself. Then I heard the Holy Spirit speak again. "I want you to silence them, and call them out," I quickly stepped to the attention to my Commander and Chief and in the authority of Jesus' name I commanded those demons to shut up and come out of their bodies and within a few minutes they were out and gone, and Satan's two victims had sobered up. These were common occurrences in those days. I never went looking for demons because I hated fighting with these powers of darkness. On the other hand, I never shied away from them either when the opportunity presented itself because Jesus gave us His authority to stamp on scorpions.

Although we had experienced some deliverance from the demon entities of Satan, our time together in prayer took us deeper. The Lord taught us that a demon will attach itself to the lies we believe unwittingly. Little by little, the Lord began to shine His light into the darkness created by the lies that we believed about ourselves or God Himself. Many of the lies are contrary to the word of God and therefore hold us in bondage. Many of these lies are lies that we have embraced since childhood. What we discovered is once the lie is broken and the truth embraced, the demon attached to that lie will lose its power, and it leaves the premises.

We were at that time on the cutting edge of the Lord, changing how the ministry of deliverance was implemented. We just listened to the Holy Spirit and did what He told us to do, and with those acts of obedience, we did great damage to the kingdom of darkness. Not we alone, but in partnership with God. With knowledge from the Lord, we were victorious time and time again. We found it is much more effective to discover the lie that the demon is attached to and replace that lie with the truth when doing deliverance. Because once the demon has lost its power, there is no struggle. The deliverance session goes smoothly. The other way of identifying the spirit and calling it out often results in a power struggle and causes the demon to manifest in ways that are exhausting to the person housing them. I must say, however, that both methods are valid, one must always follow the leading of the Holy Spirit because the most important thing is to allow the Lord to set the captive free however He sees fit. Lies of any kind keep you and perhaps your family in bondage to the Father of Lies, Satan.

I want to close this chapter with a few of my thoughts concerning the deliverance ministry. In my opinion, the deliverance ministry is the most neglected, controversial, and misunderstood ministries in the body of Christ today. For the most part, the Church has failed to educate its members on the realm of the supernatural. I believe the Church should teach about the Baptism of the Holy Spirit and deliverance, and most don't. I could not go to most mainline churches to be informed about this type of baptism or to receive the much-needed deliverance from the demons that had entered me as a child. I did not find freedom within the Church. I found my answers and freedom at a Women's Aglow meeting.

Fortunately for me, early in my walk with the Lord, I was introduced to one of the trailblazers in the deliverance ministry, Don Basham. As mentioned previously, I had purchased his book at a Woman's Aglow meeting, where he spoke on deliverance. I had no idea that he and Derek Prince would be overseers for the Fellowship that I joined years later. Derek Prince, like Don Basham, led the body of Christ in setting the captives free from demonic entities that invade and influence the soul of man. These men were my mentors.

The casting out of demons was a regular part of ministry in the early Church. Jesus' last words before He ascended into heaven after

He rose from the dead, tells us it is part of our job. Please note the Greek word for devil in the following scripture is the same word used for demons. The words of Jesus that follow are known to us as "The Great Commission."

Mark 16:16-18 16 "He who believes and is baptized will be saved; but he who does not believe will be condemned. 17 And these signs will follow those who believe: In My name they will cast out demons; they will speak with new tongues; 18 they will take up serpents; and if they drink anything deadly, it will by no means hurt them; they will lay hands on the sick, and they will recover."

It is a sad commentary on the Church that so many Christians are not equipped for the "Great Commission. "However, Pastors who are actively involved in setting the captives free, know the answer to this age-old debate. Of course, a Christian can have a demon, and of course, that Christian can be set free. The deliverance ministry is body ministry for those committed to Christ, who have repented of their sin, and have closed all doors open to the dark side. I am a witness to this truth, for I was a Spirit-Filled Christian when I was set free. Plus, I have witnessed countless Christian men, and women set free from demons.

Recently, I read an article in Charisma magazine written by John Eckhardt, addressing this very topic. He and his church members minister in deliverance, and he had this to say. The following is just a portion of the article.

"One thing that has helped us in our understanding is the realization that every person is made up of three parts: spirit, soul and body. When Jesus comes into a believer's life, He comes into that person's spirit. John 3:6 tells us clearly, "That which is born of the

Spirit *is spirit"* (NKJV). A demon cannot dwell in a Christian's spirit because that is where Jesus and the Holy Spirit dwell.

It is the other components that make up a human being—the soul (mind, will and emotions) and the body—that are the targets of demonic attack. Demons can dwell in those areas of a Christian's life. So, when we say that a Christian is demonized or possessed, we are not saying he has a demon in his spirit but in some part of his soul or body.

To illustrate this truth, the Lord reminded us of the biblical account of Jesus' going into the temple and cleansing it of thieves and moneychangers. The Greek word used for "drove out" in this account is ekballo, which means "to expel or drive out." It is the same word that is used in Mark 16:17: "In My [Jesus'] name they will cast out demons."

We know that according to the Bible God's children are the temple of the Spirit of God (see 1 Cor. 3:16). In the Old Testament the temple had three parts: the holy of holies, the holy place and the outer court. This picture is a type or representation of who we are as His temple today. The shekinah glory of God, or God's "presence," was in the holy of holies. This part of the temple represents our spirits. But when Jesus went into the temple to drive out the thieves and moneychangers, He did not go into the holy of holies. He went into the outer court, where these evildoers were carrying on their business transactions. The whole account is a picture of deliverance—of what Jesus wants to do in our temples. There may be demonic thieves in our lives that are operating in our outer courts (bodies or souls). Even though they cannot enter the holy of holies (our spirits), Jesus wants them expelled because the temple of God was never intended to be a place for thieves to operate. It is meant to be a place of worship and a place of prayer."

I agree with Pastor Eckhardt, except for his verbiage on Christians being possessed. I believe a demon can oppress a Christian rather than possess them. Everything else that Pastor Eckhardt stated, I could not have said any better. Another thing that strikes me odd is those that insist a Christian cannot have a demon have not really thought the subject of deliverance through. Deliverance is a gift to the body of Christ. We come into the Kingdom of Light often after years of operating in the kingdom of darkness. We need our temples to be swept clean. We then need those vacant places filled with the Holy Spirit. Deliverance of demons is not for the unbeliever. Why on earth would we be so negligent as to deliver an unbeliever who has no intention of becoming a Christian? Only to send them on their way and have those demons return with more of their friends and enter the unbeliever again, making him worse off than he was before? The following scripture explains this would be the case.

Luke 11:24-26 24 When an unclean spirit goes out of a man, he goes through dry places, seeking rest; and finding none, he says, 'I will return to my house from which I came.' 25 And when he comes, he finds it swept and put in order. 26 Then he goes and takes with him seven other spirits more wicked than himself, and they enter and dwell there; and the last state of that man is worse than the first."

Therefore, if the anointing to cast out demons is not for the unbeliever, then who is left? The believing Christian, of course. Jesus came to set the captives free.

Sometime in the late 80s, a young spirit filled Christian woman came to me and confessed she was having thoughts of suicide, and that she had urges to kill herself. For the sake of her privacy, I will call her Peggy. I explained to Peggy that every thought that we have is not our own. Some thoughts come from God, and some ideas come from the devil. I discerned that she had an evil spirit of suicide, and I told her so. Peggy insisted that she was a Christian and that she was taught in her church that a Christian could not have a demon. She went on with all the reasons why she could not have an evil spirit living inside her. When she was finished, I shared with her my own deliverance. I told her about the freedom that other Christians I knew had after they were freed from the demons that used their bodies as their home.

Eventually, Peggy asked if I would cast this evil demon out of her. I agreed and led her in prayer to renounce Satan and all his evil works. I instructed her that she must tell the demon it was not welcome and not wanted and that she was blood-bought by the blood of Jesus, and it must go. After this, I began to command the demon to leave; it manifested and left her. It left along with a couple of other evil spirits that manifested and gave a bit of a struggle, but finally it was gone. She was so excited. She danced around and kept saying that her pastor was wrong and that someone needed to tell him the truth.

Well, a few days went by, and there was a knock on my apartment door. When I opened the door, there stood two gentlemen dressed in a suit and tie. They introduced themselves as pastors from the Assembly of God Church and said they were Peggy's pastors. They asked if they might come in and talk with me about her. I invited them in.

They began to share with me that Peggy had come to them and insisted that she had demons and that Mrs. Kummrow had cast them out of her. She told them that the church needed to change what they teach because she was proof that a Christian can have a demon. They proceeded to tell me that the doctrine of the Assembly of God is that a Christian cannot have a demon. They went on to say how wrong I was to teach Peggy differently. They continued with their discourse on the reasons why Peggy could not possibly have had demons cast out of her. When the men were finished, I shared with them about Peggy's thoughts of suicide and her urge to kill herself. I went on to tell them exactly what had happened. How the demons manifested, and how they came out of her mouth in a burst of air. I also shared some of my own stories. They listened intently, but before they left, they asked me not to guide or teach Peggy any more concerning demons. Since they were her pastors and I believed she was free, I agreed to their request. My spirit within me was sorrowful when they left because I did not think these pastors had received anything from me. The only thing that comforted me was the fact that I had told the truth and that I had planted some seeds.

I do not recall now just how much time had gone by; my guess is around a year. The Lord was gracious enough to send me someone about a year later to tell me that the Assembly of God Church, where Peggy attended, was moving in the deliverance ministry setting people free from demons. Truth is a powerful force. Speaking the truth in love plants seeds that just might amaze you when the harvest comes in. I was amazed. I tell this story here because the truth of this message is making headway in Christendom all over the world. We are not where we should be in the American church concerning demon activity, but we are miles ahead of where we once were.

In my ministry, I witnessed a gay man finding freedom when he was delivered from demon spirits of homosexuality and perversion. These demons entered this man due to a neighbor boy molesting him as a child. The demons lay dormant until the man was influenced by the evil spirits and acted on it later in life. Once the demons were gone, so were the feelings and thoughts. Likewise, I ministered to a woman diagnosed with Dissociative Amnesia, and when the demons left, her memories returned. Another woman I knew, whose deliverance took years, was set free from Multiple Personality Disorder. Another woman was delivered from a spirit of schizophrenia. One time a demon of cancer was cast out of someone, and it came out with an accompanying foul odor that smelled like a cancer ward. Please take note I do not believe a demon causes all cancer. Discernment from the Holy Spirit is paramount in all situations.

Deliverance is part of our sanctification. Ministers of deliverance must be cautious not to rush in where angels fear to tread. I would never under any circumstances cast out demons from a Christian that I knew was involved in habitual sin. Neither would I ever move forward to deliver someone from demons unless the Lord directed me to do so. All doors to Satan's kingdom must be closed, and the individual seeking deliverance must, in my opinion, be serious about living a holy life, set apart for the Almighty. Those that are delivered must protect their deliverance by righteous living, or their final state can be worse because habitual sin invites demons to return. Unfortunately, this was the case with Peggy. Years had passed, and Peggy and I had lost touch with one another. Unfortunately, I did hear that Peggy had fallen into sexual sin with a boyfriend, and eventually, her spiritual condition declined. She found herself in worse shape than she was before her deliverance.

The Holy Spirit must always guide deliverance; otherwise, it can be dangerous for the individual. Unless the Holy Spirit fills the vacancy left by the demon, that person may find themselves in worse shape than they were before.[15] I have witnessed many people being set free, with familiar manifestations, which would be a topic for an entire book. I am convinced these evil entities convince us to do things that are against our nature and our will. Then the demon spirits condemn us for the very action they encouraged.

I have shared these few examples to make my next point. The Church, the world, and much of the medical field are, unfortunately, ignorant concerning the activity of demons. Some diagnoses have even been labeled a disease or a mental condition.

---

[15] Luke 11:24-26 "When an unclean spirit goes out of a man, he goes through dry places, seeking rest; and finding none, he says, 'I will return to my house from which I came.' "And when he comes, he finds it swept and put in order. "Then he goes and takes with him seven other spirits more wicked than himself, and they enter and dwell there; and the last state of that man is worse than the first."

My experience is many sicknesses are the manifestation of demon influence. I refrain from using the phrase "demon possession" because when demons reside within a Christian, they can only influence their behavior, not take total control of them. Demons never possess Christians because they are owned by Christ, who has bought them with His precious blood. It is the purifying blood of Jesus that sets us free from the demonic influences that may have been passed down from generation to generation or enter due to our sin. Because of the cross of Jesus Christ, we become new creations. Generational curses, our old nature, and iniquity in the bloodline are now passed away. We can be liberated. Deliverance from these evil entities is the vehicle that Jesus uses to set the captives free just as He promised.

One last and significant point I would want to leave you with is this. Deliverance is not to be feared. The Hollywood interpretation of exorcism that we see in the movies is not based on reality. We must understand that Satan is under our feet. Every evil spirit is subject to the authority that we have in Christ. If and when fear attacks, it is not coming from God. It is coming from the evil one who wants to prevent you from the victory that awaits you. Often the demon will manifest in antics like causing you to fall asleep, to be anxious, angry or fearful all to delay or cancel the ministry of deliverance. So, my advice to anyone seeking deliverance, is press through no matter how uncomfortable it may seem at first. These feelings will go away. The key to victory is to trust and surrender to the deliverer, Jesus. Jesus came to set the captives free. It is our responsibility to guard and protect our freedom by living righteously once He has delivered us.

BEYOND ALL REASON: Moving Out of Logic Into the Supernatural

Chapter 14

THE POWER OF A VOW

I had no idea how powerful the bondage of a vow could be until I tried to break the vow that I had made long before my born again experience. I made a vow when I was 23 years old, and at the age of 38, when I turned my life over to the Lord, I fully expected to keep the vow that I had made until my dying day. It wasn't long after my initial experience with God that I learned that ungodly vows just like ungodly soul ties need to be broken because they hold you in bondage to the plan of the evil one for your life. I was determined I was going to live my life in obedience to God no matter what it might cost me. From the start, my walk with the Lord was based on the truth in every area, but one. I had made a vow not to tell. I had vowed I would go to my grave with this secret. When I made the vow at the age of 23, I was sure that I was protecting the people that I loved with my silence. I was wrong. I was not protecting them at all. I was doing just the opposite; I was opening the door to Satan in their lives by an unspoken lie in operation. Satan is the father of lies, and my vow was based on a lie; therefore, it was an open door for him to walk through and mess with my family and me.

Once I understood this principle, I was determined I would tell all, knowing that the truth would set everyone free. I was much more concerned with the truth being out in the open than I was with what this confession might cost me. I went about making plans in my mind on how I was going to tell my husband. Tonight, when we get into bed together, I will tell him that I need to talk to him about something. However, when the lights were turned out, and we were in bed together, my thoughts began to swirl around. Oh, no, I can't tell him here with the kids in their bedrooms next to ours. What if he gets outraged and begins to shout, they will hear us fighting, and who knows what he will say. No, I will tell him when we are alone someplace, maybe out to dinner. He would have kept his voice down in a public place. One plan after another would replace the previous method; until I decided we needed to take a trip, and I would tell him then. He would have time to cool off before it was time to return home to the children. So off to Florida, we went, and in my mind, I had the conversation that I would have with my husband rehearsed a hundred different ways. I decided that I would get it over with immediately and let the "fall-out" land right away, so we would have time to clean it up before it was time to return to Wisconsin. I remember I planned to engage in this conversation on the second day after both of us had a good night's sleep. That night I sat in the bed of our hotel room and began to talk and talk and talk, except I could not bring myself to bring up the subject that had brought us to Florida in the first place. I opened my mouth to udder words that were tied and bound with heavy twine to my voice box. No amount of effort would release those words from their bound state. JUST SAY IT, I told myself, and I would open my mouth, and it was as if I was struck dumb. Well, that mute spirit stayed with me the entire vacation. I never told him then, and I never told him for many years. Although I tried many times, I found it to be an impossible task. I hated myself for what I considered a lack of courage.

Day after day, I beat myself up because I was such a liar and a deceiver, and I prayed and prayed the Lord would make some way for me to come clean. It just never happened, and although I hated myself for this weakness, I learned to live with it. What I did not understand at the time was that breaking an ungodly vow is entering into spiritual warfare. Satan does not want that vow broken, and he will play with your mind, bind up your words, and bring you into a state of condemnation. Once it was revealed that Satan was the one who I was fighting with, I devised a plan that surprisingly worked.

Unfortunately, it was years after the first time I tried to tell my husband about the vow that I had made. We had moved from Wisconsin to Illinois and had joined a Charismatic fellowship in South Holland, Illinois. My husband Bill and I had been at this time, meeting regularly for house church on Sunday evenings in the house of our pastor and his wife. Our church met on Wednesday evenings for worship and a sermon. Sunday mornings were devoted to the children of the congregation, and Sunday nights, the adult members of the congregation broke up into small groups in various homes of the members of the congregation. These small groups created an atmosphere of trust and intimacy where individual ministry and deliverance could take place. It allowed the members of the body to operate in the gifts of the spirit for each one's anointing. We supported each other and prayed for one another. It was a place designed for our growth and operated out of the idea that each joint of Christ's body supplies something. I felt comfortable in this setting, and I did not perceive there was anyone in this house-church that would judge me. Frankly, even if there was someone judgmental, I did not care. I wanted to be free. I was willing to hang out my dirty laundry for everyone to see. As a group, we had confessed our sins and weaknesses with one another because we wanted to change; we wanted to grow in Christ. So, I devised my plan. I decided that on a night that my husband would not be available to come to house-church with me, that I would go alone and tell everyone the trouble that I was having with breaking this vow I had made as a young woman. I figured that if everyone in my house church knew my story, then I would be forced to tell my husband. Plus, I truly needed the prayer support from my group that I knew I would have for me to be able to do this. I had failed so miserably so many times before, and I was not going to fail again.

When the night finally came that I was alone in house-church, I had no problem telling my story and the vow that I had made. That was because the vow only involved keeping this secret from my husband. My words were not bound up; they were quite fluent. My tongue was moving as rapidly as my heartbeat. I could tell my secret apparently to anyone but Bill. I explained that I had tried many times to tell my husband what I had just told the group, but the words that I needed to speak to him would choke me. I was informed that the power of that vow caused the bondage. I needed to break that vow. I was led in a prayer confessing my sin for making an ungodly vow in the first place. We also asked for God's forgiveness and that God our Father would break the power of that vow, and release me from it and from the hold that Satan had on me to keep this lie in operation which prevented me from telling the truth. Since the path leading to the truth was cleared from its hindrances, I was sent home to tell my husband the truth.

I burst through the door of our home with the truth dripping from my lips. "What are you doing home so early," he asked me? "I was sent home because I have something, I need to tell you. TRACEY IS NOT YOUR DAUGHTER! She was conceived during the time I had that affair," I blurted out with ease. His face drained, and then for what seemed like an eternity, he just looked at me. Finally, when he spoke, he said, "I have always been suspicious of that." My husband was aware of the affair that I had had in the early years of our marriage. He had forgiven me, and we never discussed it again. I was tormented for years over something that he knew deep down in his heart anyway. I felt like the weight of the world had just been lifted from me now that everything was out in the open. Then because I wanted the truth to be made known to Tracey and our two sons, I said to him, "You know we must tell Tracey the truth too. She has a right to know." Without a minute's worth of hesitation, I heard my husband say very firmly, "NOT EVEN OVER MY DEAD BODY! She is not to know!" With that, the discussion was over.

In the days that followed, I began to analyze the situation, and I concluded that spiritually, the only thing that had changed was the fact that I was free from the tormentors. We still had a secret in our family, and I was wise enough to know that this gave strength to the powers of darkness in our lives. So, I began to intercede. The Lord requires us to walk in truth, and He will intervene where I am unable to do so. My confession freed me, yes, but it also showed me that my husband was not the least bit surprised about the identity of our daughter. His statements also exposed to me that he was not interested in counting the cost of walking in the truth. I had to ask myself why? I was the one with all the risks. It was my sin that was going to be exposed to Tracey and her brothers. I was the one that they could very well end up hating for forcing this lie upon them. I could lose everything, yet I was willing to take that risk and trust God with it, and my husband was not. Why?

After several months of prayer on the subject, I decided I would bring it up again. I did, and this time I asked my husband, "What are your reasons for not wanting to tell her the truth?" He could not explain to me his reasoning. He pretty much just repeated our previous conversation, saying that she would not be told as long as he was alive. I asked him why he felt that way, was he afraid of losing her? His reaction made no sense to me because he had done nothing wrong. I blurted out, "I am the one at risk of losing her, not you!" Getting nowhere, I left the outcome in the hands of the Lord, because now we had another inner vow in operation, his. This vow was going to take some spiritual warfare to break, and I would not go against my husband's wishes. So, I prayed, and I prayed some more, never dreaming that the Lord would answer my prayers in such a dramatic way.

Chapter 15

CODE BLUE

When the doctor made a determination to call a code blue, I was unaware of how crowded the room had become in radiology after the doctor had summoned the staff for help. I had come to the hospital because I had discovered a lump in my right breast. It had to be removed, and the surgeon needed to know the exact location of the lump. A surprising event happened in the morning of my scheduled surgery.

When the nurse wheeled me to Radiology, I'm sure those technicians had no idea identifying the lump's location would cause such a stir. The radiologist inserted a very long needle into my right breast. I am assuming it was at that point the doctor had summoned for more help. The room was buzzing with doctors and nurses bumping elbows, and carts were rolled in with electrical equipment. I was unaware of all the commotion because I too, had been summoned. I found myself in the most peaceful of all places, Heaven. I was in the presence of the Lord. I was happier than I had ever been in my life.

There are no words adequate to describe the love and acceptance that I felt. It was just awesome. I was surrounded by what I perceived to be the golden cherubim. However, I could not say for sure. The bodies of these beautiful beings looked to me as if they were pure gold. They were brilliant and shiny and very tall. So tall, that I could not make out their faces because they towered far above my head. They encircled me, and I was not permitted to leave this circle.

The Lord and I had what seemed like a long conversation. Our question and answer session did not include speaking words. I had many questions to ask Him, but all I had to do was send Him my thoughts, and He would send the answer back in thoughts as well. I remember asking Jesus the most important question that there could be to ask the creator of the universe. He chuckled and said He would be more than happy to answer. I waited with great anticipation for the answer because I had waited my entire life to have the answer to this question. When the answer came, I remember feeling a tremendous amount of relief; at last, I knew the answer. It brought me such peace to have what I thought was the question of the ages answered.

Then just as I was thinking that I was really going to like being in Heaven, and I was also thinking about how happy I was to be there, He said it was time for me to go back. I began to beg Him to let me stay. I remember pleading, "please, please don't send me back." I had no thought of, nor did I have any concern for anyone that I had left behind. Everything and everyone that I loved and cared about paled in comparison to the Place and Person that I was with. "Oh, please don't send me back," I begged again. He said, "You cannot stay; you have work to do."

Within a second, it seemed I was re-entering my body. As my spirit man entered my body, I became very much aware that I was entering pain. I experienced for just a split-second, excruciating physical pain as well as emotional pain. This burden of pain had been completely gone while I was in the presence of PURE LOVE. The experience of being out of my body is difficult to explain. I was free from all pain. Also, free from all negative impulses and darkness. I was free from all the weight that the cares of this world had put upon me. It was not until I re-entered my body that I became so acutely aware of just how oppressive and burdensome the cares of this world are. Each of us carries so much more weight than we realize.

As I began to gain consciousness, I was aware that a team of doctors and nurses encircled me as I lay on the floor of the radiology room in the hospital. I was assaulted with the reality that I had just traveled from the superlative heights of eternity to the debasement of a cold tile floor. My head felt like an elephant was sitting on it. All the pressure from the weight of the elephant had located itself in my eye sockets. As I arose from the dead, the doctor was greeted by an outraged woman. "WHAT DID YOU DO TO ME?" I shouted at the doctor. I was angry with Jesus for sending me back to purgatory, and I took it out on the doctor.

The doctor began to apologize, saying that he was sorry. As it turned out, the needle inserted into my breast to identify the location of the lump was inserted too far, and the needle went into my heart. He said that they had tried everything to get me back and that they were unsuccessful, so he tried the last thing that he could think of. He put both of his thumbs into both of my eye sockets and began to apply pressure. Well, that answered the question of why it felt as if an elephant had sat on my head. The doctor thought that I was angry with him for causing me so much pain in his effort to bring me back to life. However, the truth was, as I said, I was angry with Jesus for sending me back and also furious with the doctor for even trying to revive me. That is why I sat up and said: "WHAT DID YOU DO TO ME?"

It had nothing to do with him sticking his thumbs into the crevices of my brain; or eye sockets. It had everything to do with the most excruciating awareness that I was now experiencing. I had an acute separation from the desire of my heart, and I was desperately homesick for HIM, and the peaceful environment that I had experienced while I was with HIM. I still am.

Once I was cognizant, they began to roll me down the hall to the surgeon's theater. My first thoughts were, I do not believe this! I just died, went to Heaven and back again, and they are acting as if this is an every-day occurrence, "let's get on with the show" attitude. Then I thought to myself, well after all, what do I have to lose, maybe they will make another mistake, and Jesus will let me stay this time.

My surgery went well, and the lump in my breast turned out to be benign, as I knew it would. This radiology procedure may have stopped my heart, but tests showed there was no damage at all to my heart. The Lord is a miracle-working God. The Lord said I had work to do, and that He had deposited information inside me that I would need for my end-time ministry. I have no memory of the many questions that I asked. Nor do I remember any of the answers. No wonder He was willing to answer that ever so important question. That question I asked seemed to be some secret to the whole universe. He replied with a chuckle, knowing that once I returned, I would have no recollection of the question or the answer. He was so right; the subject and His favored answer are no longer relevant. The only thing worth remembering is HIM ALONE!

It would be days later that I would learn just how busy the Lord was answering my prayers while I spent time with him in his dimension.

BEYOND ALL REASON: Moving Out of Logic Into the Supernatural

BEYOND ALL REASON: Moving Out of Logic Into the Supernatural

Chapter 16

MY PEOPLE DIE FROM LACK OF KNOWLEDGE

As I lay on my sofa, recuperating, my thoughts replayed my awesome visit to Heaven and my conversation with Jesus. I was dismissed from the hospital to recover at home from breast surgery. This surgery was not the first breast surgery that I had to go through, but it most certainly was the most interesting spiritually. My mind wandered in time to the first breast surgery and how grateful I was that I had found the lump in time. My husband was in the shower, and I was in bed reading when I rolled over on my right side. As I rolled over, my left hand ended up under my right breast, where to my horror, I felt a rather large lump. "Oh, my God!" I exclaimed as my husband entered our bedroom. "I have a huge lump in my breast."

As I lay on the examining table, my mind was already swimming in many directions. My doctor found an additional lump in my left breast as well. When my doctor gave me a pelvic examination, my mind was reeling as she said to me, "I hate to tell you this, but the lumps in your breasts are the least of your worries. You have a tumor in your uterus as big as a grapefruit. I need to schedule surgery immediately." I had to have a hysterectomy and two lumpectomies at the age of 40. I thought for sure that my life was over. Scripture tells us that sexual sin is the only sin against one's own body.

1 Corinthians 6:18   Flee sexual immorality. Every sin that a man does is outside the body, **but he who commits sexual immorality sins against his own body.**

I was expecting something eventually to show up on my body because of the consequences of my sin. One cannot escape the reaping and sowing process. It is biblical and can be found in Galatians 6:7:

7 Do not be deceived, God is not mocked; for whatever a man sows, that he will also reap.

I figured that this was the price that I was going to pay for the life that I lived before Christ. I knew that I had done this to myself after all, was it not my sexual organs being invaded by the big C? I was sure of it. Frightened and scared, I went on a shopping spree and bought some beautiful clothes. I was going to look fantastic while I waited to die. Fortunately for me, God had other plans. In His grace, He had allowed me to discover the lump in my breast to get me to the doctor. It was at the doctor's office that a more serious problem was discovered before it developed into cancer. The tumor in my breast turned out to be benign. Upon examination, after the hysterectomy, the tumor cells were in the last stages before forming into cancer cells. I was so grateful, because discovering the lump in my breast may have saved my life. God works in mysterious ways.

The Lord told me that I had work to do when I was with him in Heaven, so I knew that this last lump in my breast would be benign. Lying on my couch, day after day, I had time to reflect upon all that had taken place. My trip to Heaven was continually on my mind. What could it all mean anyway? The only conclusion that I could reach was that I serve an awesome God. He had revealed Himself to me in so many wonderful ways. I sure did not understand why, because I felt like I had let Him down miserably so many times. Yet, He was always there for me. Often, he had to pick me up and rescue me, even from myself. I laid on my couch for days, and I felt something was wrong. It should not be taking me this long to recuperate. After all, this was not major surgery this time; it was just a small incision into my breast to remove the lump. But then there was that needle that was inserted into my heart that caused my lights to go out, and the blue lights to come rushing into Radiology. Yes, something was wrong. I was still so weak. I felt like I was fading and getting weaker and weaker each day instead of getting stronger.

Concerned, I called my friend Pat for prayer because of her strong gift of the word of knowledge from the Holy Spirit. She agreed to go into prayer for me. When she called back, she asked me whether or not anyone attending me at the hospital, had long black hair. "Yes," I said. "There was an oriental woman with long jet-black hair that hung down to the middle of her back. She was the nurse that inserted the needle into my breast that caused all the trouble." "Well," Pat said. "All I know is the Lord gave me a vision of this woman, and I think it has something to do with that needle. You need to pray and find out from God what this is all about."

After we hung up the phone, that is just what I did. "Father," I prayed, "What is going on? Why am I getting weaker every day, and why did you give Pat this vision of my nurse? It wasn't long after the prayer that I heard my favorite voice say: "You need to ask Me to forgive you." I shook my head, very puzzled. I was not in any sin that I was aware of. I wondered what He could be talking about? So, I asked, "What did I do that needs forgiveness?" "You allowed them to insert that needle into your body," came His answer. Confused and not understanding how this was something that needed forgiveness, I continued to question God. "Why is this a sin?" I asked Him. He replied, "Because this was nothing more than an ancient practice of acupuncture disguised as a medical practice." "But Lord," I said, "I did not know." "Yes, I know, have I not said that my people die from lack of knowledge," was His answer. Then He went on to say, "When that needle was inserted into you that woman prayed over you for evil spirits to enter you, and they did due to your ignorance. Now, you need to ask me for forgiveness, and I will deliver you from these demons that are making you so weak." I was dumbfounded, but who was I to argue with infinite wisdom? I did as I was instructed. Once I confessed the sin that I was now aware of, the Lord did what He had promised to do. One by one, I felt the demon entities leave my body. Within minutes my strength returned to me, and I got up off of my sick-bed feeling fantastic and refreshed. I then headed to the kitchen to surprise my husband with a nice home-cooked meal. This meal was something that he had not had all week. While waiting for things to simmer on the stove, I picked up the phone and called Pat. "You'll never guess what happened?" I said when she answered the phone. I continued on with the story of a new discovery and my miraculous recovery.

I was very much aware that acupuncture was an open door to demon activity. I had been taught this by many teachers in the deliverance ministry. As past President of Women's Aglow, teaching that acupuncture was an open door to demons was something that the organization taught regularly. The leaders of my church in Wisconsin taught this, including Derek Prince, who was an overseer of our church. I was not ignorant of this fact. I was ignorant about the fact that this particular medical procedure performed on me in the hospital was indeed related to acupuncture.

Before I quote from Prince's book, "They Shall Expel Demons," I will clarify something important. If you have entered into this ancient practice out of ignorance, the Lord is faithful to forgive, and he will deliver you just as He did me. Many people I know in Christian circles do not understand the origin of this practice. It is occult in nature, and yet they claim they have found acupuncture to be helpful. However, my question is, how long has it been helpful? Also, have there been any mysterious problems with poor health in other areas since the acupuncture treatment? Satan is a liar and a deceiver, and this is just one of the many ways that he finds to deceive the people of God and cause destruction in their lives. Maybe not initially, but this demon activity will affect you eventually in your body. Acupuncture may have immediate results of relief, because if it didn't, how could Satan get you to believe in it? Later, however, other even more serious health problems will arise. My concern today is that there are not enough voices heralding the vices of Satan, and acupuncture is just one of them. Since I have had my own experience and have been taught by the Lord concerning this practice, I will not only share with you my experience. I will as well warn you of its dangers.

The Christian deliverance expert and Bible teacher Derek Prince wrote in the book that I quoted, "They Shall Expel Demons," and this is what he said. "Another occult practice that opens the door to demons is acupuncture. Some physicians and other medical personnel today justify its use on the ground that 'it works!' But an analysis of its occult background reveals acupuncture will never ultimately promote the well-being of those who submit to it." Prince cited the following warning in the book, from a Chinese doctor who said this: "About eight years ago, at a retreat in Singapore, God spoke to me about the dangers of acupuncture and its link to the occult, especially its inseparable origin with traditional Chinese medicine. I immediately renounced my practice of acupuncture -- a skill I learned in Hong Kong and practiced successfully for five years. "As soon as I came back home, I announced to my startled staff of doctors, nurses, and patients that acupuncture is dangerous and that I had renounced it and would not practice it anymore. I gathered all my machines, needles, books, diploma, and charts and made a great bonfire of them publicly. The total cost of these items was about $15,000—but the blessings after that were priceless, because, my wife, who had suffered from chronic migraine and had acupuncture done by me many times before, was immediately healed without medicine or prayer. My unexplained fear of darkness immediately vanished. My medical practice, instead of suffering a loss, received a double-fold increase in blessings. About three years ago, we saw a very unusual case during a healing rally in Kuching, East Malaysia. A Christian lady came forward for prayer regarding her rheumatism. As soon as we started, the Lord gave a word of knowledge that she had submitted herself to acupuncture treatment in the past. She confirmed it, but each time she tried to renounce it, she was thrown onto the floor, screaming in severe pain."

"We realized that she was being tormented by demons that had gained entry to her body through acupuncture. After we took authority over the demons and cast them out in the Name of the Lord Jesus Christ, she was delivered and healed. She then told us that each time she had tried to renounce acupuncture, invisible needles began to pierce her over the parts of her body, where she had previously submitted herself for treatment. Let me end by relating a tragic case. The Christian brother who taught me acupuncture, suffered from severe depression and committed suicide under mysterious circumstances. The world does not know the whole truth, because he had everything in life, but I think I know: He came under a curse and paid for it with his life."[16]

These stories and many others have been documented concerning this deceptive practice of acupuncture. Having been in the deliverance ministry myself, I can attest to these kinds of things happening to those who have unwittingly opened the door to demon activity. Sometimes these demons come in with acupuncture only to hide for a while until just the right moment in time to do their damage. All of us need to be grateful that our Lord is merciful and kind and willing to forgive our involvement in the occult. However, our ignorance is of no excuse, just as He told me, "My people die from lack

---

[16] *"They Shall Expel Demons,"* Derek Prince, page 136

of knowledge." Even so, if we are willing to confess our sin, He is faithful to forgive.

May the following prayer be a blessing of release from any demon activity caused by the practice of acupuncture in your life.

My Father and my God, I confess before you that I have received in my body the needles of acupuncture. I now see acupuncture as an evil deception of Satan, and I renounce all the practices of Satan, including this practice of acupuncture. All sin is missing the mark, and I have missed the mark concerning acupuncture; therefore, I confess it as sin and ask for your forgiveness. I ask for your hand to touch me for the deliverance of all demons that entered my body through the door I opened by allowing the practice of acupuncture. I also ask that your Holy Spirit will fill every empty space their evacuation has caused. In your merciful kindness and with your balm of Gilead, Jesus Christ, I ask for your healing virtue to be released in my life. Please bring the supernatural healing power that only your Holy Spirit can manifest in my life because of the shed blood of Jesus Christ. I Thank You, and I Praise You for all that You Will do for me, which I cannot do for myself. Amen.

Chapter 17

GOD WORKS IN MYSTERIOUS WAYS

My husband was delighted when he returned home after work. He saw; that I was up and about and prepared a nice meal for us to enjoy together. He had been waiting to talk to me. He wanted me to know what happened to him at the hospital when they called a "code blue." He was waiting until I felt better, and from the looks of things, I had miraculously recovered from the time he left in the morning until the time he arrived home that night. We rehashed the events of my hospital stay. He was sitting out in the hospital hall when they called a "code blue" on me. After we talked about that day, he said to me, "Tracey must be told the truth!" I could not believe my ears! We had argued about this often. Even though I disagreed with him, I always submitted to my husband's wishes and would not have told Tracey the Truth without his consent. Instead, I went into prayer and petitioned the Lord to change his mind; if telling Tracey, the truth was indeed the Lord's will. "What are you saying, and why have you changed your mind?" I inquired. He said that when they called a "code blue," and all the commotion was going on, he was fearful that something horrible was happening to me. It occurred to him that if something terrible happens, like for instance, if I were to die, and he had to tell Tracey, she would probably not believe him. He said that the only person that she would likely believe would be her mother, and because of that, it was up to me to tell her.

The Lord had been busy; answering my prayers the day that I was in the hospital and having an out-of-body experience with Jesus in Heaven. It became clear to me that this experience was two-fold. Not only was the Lord depositing information into my mind for the end times, but He was also working on changing my husband's mind. It took a near-death experience to break the stronghold in Bill's mind. Is it not true the Lord works in mysterious ways?

Since we were planning a trip back to Wisconsin for Easter, I decided I would tell Tracey at that time. I was so scared I would lose her, but I knew that this was something that needed to be done. I was sure now that it was the will of the Lord to tell her the truth since it had become pretty obvious that God had taken some very extreme measures to get my husband's attention and change his mind. Since my born again experience, so many years prior, it had become crucial to me to be truthful about everything, even to my own hurt. I did not want to give the "father of lies" any satisfaction, nor did I want any doors of deception open that would give Satan legal right to do his dirty work with me, or more importantly, my family. Plus, my integrity had become very important to me. I was no longer the woman that would lie to protect herself. I planned to tell my daughter the truth about her conception. I also planned on telling her brothers that their mother had been unfaithful to their father. This discussion would not be easy.

When we arrived in Wisconsin that Easter morning, I immediately took my daughter to her bedroom and told her that I needed to talk to her about something. She was so scared I was going to tell her something like I was dying. Anything else would have been better than what she was thinking. When I spilled my guts, she looked at me and said, "That's it? That's all? Thank God, I thought you were going to tell me that you were dying." Because of my recent breast surgery, she thought that perhaps I had not told her the full truth about the lump in my breast and that it was worse than what I originally told her. My husband, who had some crazy idea in his head that once she knew the truth, would want nothing to do with him, and he was waiting outside the door, fearing her reaction.

Tracey darted for the door to tell him all was well and that she loved him more than ever for raising her as his own. This blasé response to what I considered devastating news was superficial. Tracey, like her mother, often has a delayed reaction to her emotional responses. When her brothers arrived, and I sat each one of them down separately to make my confession to them, Tracey took flight. She ran out of the house and hid from all of us. My youngest son, who is the closest to her in age, went after her. By this time, she was crying. The reality of what she heard was starting to sink in. Her whole identity had been a lie. She began to manifest shame, and it broke my heart because she was the innocent one. I was the one who should bear the shame, not her. No one sins alone. Sin by its very nature is destructive, and when the consequences of our own sin bring its destructive arm into our own life to wreak havoc, we can bear up under those consequences because we realize we have done this to ourselves. It is an entirely different matter when we watch the pain that our sinful behavior has inflicted on those we love and are dear to our hearts, like our own family. I had to watch the pain that this betrayal inflicted not only upon my husband and daughter but upon my two sons as well.

Given the fact that telling the truth could cause great devastation, one might feel the need to ask, then why tell them? Wouldn't it be better to keep the secret? Isn't confessing your sin to God enough? The answer to those questions is quite complicated. There are several reasons why telling the truth is the way of the cross. Every sin that you or I have ever committed was paid for at the cross. The blood sacrifice of Jesus paid the price for all past sins, and any sins committed in the future. The price that Jesus paid for our sin is immeasurable, and he paid it willingly in obedience to his father's plan of salvation. Although sin was erased by Jesus' blood that was shed at the cross and forgiveness from our Father in Heaven is always available to any repentant sinner, there still remains the consequences of sin that reaches far and wide, much like the butterfly effect. What scientists call the "butterfly effect" is a matter of physics that proves the flapping of butterfly wings on the East coast sets into motion a reaction that could produce a hurricane in the Pacific sometime later.[17] Likewise, the consequences of sin began with just a little flapping of the wings when I was only twenty-two, yet it caused a hurricane when I grew older.

---

[17] "*American Scientist*" - https://www.americanscientist.org/article/understanding-the-butterfly-effect

Had it not been for the divine intervention of Jesus on the timeline of my life, that hurricane may have developed into a tsunami.

One of the requirements of being a disciple of Jesus is to pick up our cross and follow Him. In other words, just as the cross of Jesus Christ costs Him, His life, so will the cross I carry, cost me my life. You see, I have been bought and paid for by the blood of Jesus, my life is no longer my own. I belong to God now. Therefore, if I belong to Him and have become a member of His household, then there are household rules that I must follow. God gave me this awesome gift of eternal life with Him, which is the ultimate expression of how much He loves me. I have because of free will, a choice to follow the household rules, or a decision to disobey them. I do not obey them because I have to; I obey them because I want to. I want to because it is my way to demonstrate to God that I love him. It also communicates I trust Him, especially when He requires something of me that my natural mind rejects as unreasonable.

As followers of Christ, we are to be imitators of Christ. Since Jesus is the personification of truth, then as an imitator of His nature, I too want to be known as a truthful person. Each one of us is an imitator of someone. Before Christ, I was an imitator of Satan. The Bible tells us that Satan is the "Father of lies." Therefore, whenever I lied, I was imitating Satan, becoming a liar and a deceiver just like him. I didn't know that I was imitating Satan because when we walk in darkness, we are blind to the truth. However, when I crossed over from darkness into the glorious light of the Kingdom of God, I could see the truth. When we walk in the light, we have life. When I crossed over from darkness into the light is when my life really began. That is when my identity changed; I chose to be a "seeker of truth." And I've been walking in my new identity since then. The lies that I told were all for self-preservation — one lie on top of the other to protect the original lie of having an affair and birthing a child out of wedlock. I had woven a web of deception with the lies I told, to protect myself and the identity of my daughter. Even after I became a born again believer, I was under the impression that this secret of mine could remain between God and me, and it would not be necessary to tell anyone about it. It was the working of the Holy Spirit that began to change my mind. For it is His job to lead us into all truth. The scriptures themselves began to convict me, especially the scriptures that Jesus quoted first about abiding in Him; when he said, that when we abide in Him, *"you shall know the truth, and the truth shall make you free."* [18] He also quoted this: *"There is nothing covered that will not be revealed and nothing hidden that will not be known."*[19] I just reasoned it would be much better if I exposed myself than to wait and be exposed by the mighty hand of God. I knew that this is what He required of me, so I decided it would be wise to cooperate with Him.

In addition to being convicted by the scriptures that I had not been honest with my family, I began to see that there is a natural law in operation that the Bible calls the reaping and sowing process. As said previously, the Bible tells us that "what so ever you sow you shall also reap." It also says that "the measure you measure with will be the same

---

[18] John 8:32

[19] Matthew: 10:26

measure things will be measured back to you." What that told me was that I had sown deception; therefore, in some way, I would definitely be deceived in the future. I did not want the measure of deception to get any bigger since it would come back on me. I had lied to my family, and therefore others would be lying to me. Conversely, on a more positive note, those things that are sown, like truth, for instance, will reap a harvest of truth. I began to realize that for every action, there is either a positive or negative reaction in the sowing and reaping process. The world says it another way, "What goes around, comes around." Einstein called it cause and effect, which modern physicists have expanded into what they call the "string theory."[20] As I was growing in the things of the Spirit, the Lord began to teach me about doors that we open to the evil one that allows him to come into our lives to deceive us. One of Satan's greatest tools against the truth is to propagate a lie and then cause us to believe that lie is the truth. When we believe his lies, it puts us in bondage to him. For the battle with Satan begins in our mind. The lie that I had believed was that I was protecting Tracey emotionally by keeping this secret to myself. It took an act of God for me to discover that this lie was actually harming my daughter because it gave Satan entrance into her life. My daughter was walking far off from the Lord when she became very ill with systemic Candida and took a leave of absence from her job. I sought the Lord for her healing at that time, and the answer to my prayers began a chain reaction of events, otherwise known as string theory. This brought the entire family to the moment of truth that took place on that Easter Sunday

---

[20] *"String Theory for Dummies"* www.dummies.com

morning when I told her the truth about her identity. At the time of my daughter's illness, my relationship with the Lord had grown, and He had taught me how to pray more effectively. He taught me to seek Him for the key to answered prayer.

Scripture tells us that we have not because we ask not, and even when we do ask, we ask amiss.[21] What I discovered is we will often ask for the wrong thing. Even when it seems like the right thing or a good thing to pray, we could be praying for something entirely wrong. Using this situation of my daughter's illness as an example, I will explain to you what I mean. The logical thing to pray when someone is ill would be for that person to get healed. This prayer I did do because I know it is the Heavenly father's will to heal His children. However, with the delay of the healing, I began to ask why? Not just why the Lord was not healing her, but I also began to pray for the Lord to show me any hindrances that there might be that was preventing her healing. I had also asked my prayer partner Pat to be praying for Tracey with me. It took some time before the answer came, and it came by way of a word of knowledge that the Lord had given to Pat. She called me one morning and said, while in prayer, the Lord gave her the words "birth certificate." She said I don't know what this means except that the Lord is drawing attention to Tracey's birth certificate, so pray about it. So, I went into prayer and inquired of the Lord what significance Tracey's birth certificate had to do with her illness. The Lord spoke to me at last

---

[21] James 4:2-3

and said, "Go get her birth certificate. So, I did. Then He said, "What do you see?" I looked it over, and I didn't see anything unusual.

Then the Lord spoke again and said, "Her birth certificate is a lie. It is a door open to having Satan in her life. Close the door, and she will be healed." How do I do that? I inquired. He said, "Change the name of the father." "Do I need to do this legally?" I asked. "No, just change the birth certificate in front of you," He said. Without hesitation, I grabbed a pen and tried to do as I was instructed. I say tried because just as I was about to cross off my husband's name and write the name of Tracey's birth father, my right arm began to shake uncontrollably. My entire body was trembling, but my right arm and especially my right hand that held the pen was shaking so hard it made it impossible to write. This reaction I immediately recognized as spiritual warfare, which told me that if Satan and his demons were working this hard to keep me from changing this document, then surely changing it would break their stronghold over my daughter. Although it was a struggle, I managed to steady my right hand and wrist with my left and break the lie by writing the name of my daughter's biological father on the birth certificate in front of me. Once that was done, the shaking stopped. Miraculously, within days, my daughter was completely healed, and she returned to work with more energy than ever. I was obedient to what the Lord asked me to do, and He was faithful to do what He said He would do. As unbelievable as it seems, the breaking of this lie led to my daughter's healing and her salvation, and the miraculous Baptism of the Holy Spirit. This obedient act of changing the deception on the birth certificate birthed her Spiritual life. It was the beginning of a "string" of events that exposed lies and darkness. All the lies and darkness were replaced with truth and the Light of Christ.

Let me string those precious jewels of the Lord's divine intervention, together for you. 1. The revelation of Tracey's birth certificate as the key to breakthrough, given to us by my prayer partner Pat, through a word of knowledge 2. The revelation that there was a lie on the birth certificate. 3. The obedient act of changing the name to Tracey's biological father on her birth certificate. 4. The breaking of the vow that I made never to tell my secret, through prayer at the fellowship home church meeting. 5. Confessing the truth to my husband, who said she was not to be told the truth. 6. The discovery of a third tumor in my breast. 7. The visit to Radiology and my near-death experience; resulting in a "code blue" emergency that changed the mind of my husband. 8. Confessing the Truth of Tracey's identity to her on Easter Sunday morning.

This string led to Tracey having a strong curiosity about the word of God, and she was constantly on the phone calling me from Wisconsin with questions about God and the Bible. After a while, we decided to bring her to Illinois, where we could spend quality time together as I ministered to her and answered her thousands of questions. Jesus revealed Himself to her in glorious ways that led to her salvation and Baptism in the Holy Spirit. When she returned to Wisconsin, she returned speaking and singing in tongues. My daughter learned first-hand that the truth will set you free.

John 8: 31-32, 31 Then Jesus said to those Jews who believed Him, "If you abide in My word, you are My disciples indeed. 32 And you shall know the truth, and the truth shall make you free."

I learned that "Spiritual" things must be spiritually discerned. I learned that Satan is a legalist, and as long as this lie prevailed, Satan had a legal right to my daughter. I learned that the cost of keeping a secret is far greater than the price of telling the truth. I learned the depth of what it means to be a "true worshiper." To be a true worshiper, one must be free from all lies and all deception, regardless of what it might cost. Hiding the truth is much more costly.

John 4:23, 23 "But the hour is coming, and now is, when the true worshipers will worship the Father in spirit and truth; for the Father is seeking such to worship Him."

I am telling this "string of events" with my daughter Tracey's permission. Both of us want to tell our story to convey to you what we have learned in the hope that these principles and revelations may bring light into many lives. If in the telling, others will be set free, the unveiling will be well worth it.

BEYOND ALL REASON: Moving Out of Logic Into the Supernatural

Chapter 18

PROVISION FOR THE VISION

Truth has a way of wreaking havoc when it surfaces, especially when the truth begins to expose the lies that one believes to be the truth. My entire life was based on lies, beginning in my mother's womb, and I was determined lies and deception were not going to follow me to the tomb. I began to pray and seek the Lord even more fervently, to uncover all deception where ever it might be found. I wanted truth at all cost! I still do! Jesus Christ is the TRUTH! Be careful what you pray, because the results may be life-changing and traumatic. I have experienced what Jesus meant when He said, *"Do not think that I came to bring peace on earth. I did not come to bring peace but a sword."*[22] When Jesus began to swing His sword of truth even more in my life, it was not without casualties. The fallout was devastating to every member of my family. I cannot divulge the details of this fallout, because it is not my story to tell. I am however grateful, that the Lord

---

[22] Matthew 10:34

swung His sword of truth, and is still swinging it because eternity is at stake. I can, however, continue with the rest of my story.

When the phone call came, I had no idea that my life was about to make a dramatic change once again. I thought that when I heard Madeline's voice on the other end of the line that she was calling to set up a time for us to meet for lunch, or perhaps she was inviting me for dinner at her home. She had done this many times since I had returned to Wisconsin. No, instead, she had called to inform me of the plans she and her husband Walter were making for their future.

"Marjorie," she began, "Walter and I have been praying and seeking the Lord about ministry and how He would have us serve Him. After much prayer, we believe the Lord wants us to move to Israel and to serve Him there. We are selling everything and making plans to move. In preparation for our ministry and for the move to Israel, we believe we are first to move to Dallas and attend Christ for the Nations. I just wanted you to know, but that is not the only reason for the call. Walter was awakened in the night by the Holy Spirit to pray for you. The Lord has something for you too, Marjorie, and He wants you to pray and seek His face to find out what it is." As Madeline was saying all these things to me, the Lord was speaking to my heart as well. To Madeline's surprise, I replied, "Madeline I do not need to pray about this, I know what the Lord is saying. I am supposed to join you and Walter and go with you to Christ for the Nations." "YES, she said, all excited. "That's it!"

I hung up the phone thinking, WOW, this is some surprise! How thrilling it was to think that God wanted me to go to school for training in the ministry. My heart desired to be in ministry, but I never expressed this to anyone except God. I really did not ever expect it to happen. I did not have faith for it to happen. I knew, however, that this was a divine appointment, and this day was going to change my life again. Although I was very excited about the prospect of being in ministry, I had some genuine concerns. Those concerns were financial. I had exactly $400.00 in my bank account. I knew that it would not take me very far. So, I sat down on my sofa to have a long talk with my Father. "Father," I prayed, "I know beyond a shadow of a doubt that you have called me to go with Madeline and her husband to Christ for the Nations. What I don't know is how in the world am I going to pay for the move, the tuition, and my living expenses?" With that question posed to the Lord, I waited for His answer. When the answer came, it took all the faith that I could muster up, to be obedient to what the Lord was telling me to do.

The Lord had said to empty my bank account and sow the money, expecting a harvest. I was to send it to Christ for the Nations to help pay someone's tuition. Oh, I knew about the principle of sowing and reaping, i.e., "What so ever you sow, you shall also reap." I had sown into many fields of ministry, and I had experienced the reward of the harvest. However, I had never emptied my bank account to do it before. This action was a measure of faith that I had not operated in. I quickly sat down and wrote out a check for $400.00 to Christ for the Nations with a note I was planning on enrolling, and this check was seed faith to help pay someone's tuition. I addressed an envelope and mailed it before I was tempted to change my mind. Satan was already bombarding me with thoughts in my mind about all the "what ifs."

What if there is an emergency? What if the car breaks down? What if this and what if that? I was not going to let fear rule my thinking. God had said to do this…therefore it was a done deal. I went about making plans, not knowing how everything was going to turn out. I told my children about my plan to leave for Dallas, I filled out the application for admittance to Christ for the Nations and mailed it in. I gave my notice at work, and I began packing the few things that I intended to take along with me.

One of the things that I have noticed in my life is so many of God's suddenlies begins with a phone call. This time when I answered the phone, my soon to be ex-husband was on the other end of the line. It had only been a short time since the doorbell rang, and the sheriff had served me with the divorce papers. We rarely spoke to one another anymore, so I was a bit surprised to hear his voice after I said, "Hello." He began the conversation by saying that the boys had told him that I was planning on going to a missionary school in Dallas. I told him this was true. He then went on to say that he had some books and things of mine I might want before I left for Dallas. He then asked if it would be OK with me if he dropped them off sometime soon. I agreed, and we set a date.

When my husband arrived, he arrived with two boxes of books and some miscellaneous items. He carried the boxes in, sat them down, but he never sat down himself. So, we both stood for a while as we talked. It was a bit uncomfortable; since it had been some time since we had been together. He seemed a little nervous; I know that I was as well. We engaged in some small talk. He wanted to know what my plans were and when I planned on leaving. He then asked me the thousand-dollar question. "How do you plan on paying for all of this?" He knew my financial situation because I had asked him for money so that I could buy new tires for my car, and he had refused to help. He also knew that I did not even have the funds needed for my attorney.

What had happened was this: He said he wanted to make this divorce as amicable as possible and suggested that we use the same attorney and that he would pay for it. Since I didn't have the money for an attorney of my own, I agreed. An appointment was set, and I met with Bill and his attorney, whose office was in Illinois. During the consultation, I did not like the way things were going. I did not think that what was being proposed was to my best interest. So, I left and told him I was going to get my own attorney. The problem was that I did not know how I was going to pay an attorney.

My prayer partner, Pat, had recommended an attorney that she knew, so I set up an appointment with him. I had hoped he would accept his fee being paid once I had my settlement. However, my attorney said that he did not do business this way and that he would need a retainer of $1,700.00. Not only would he need the $1,700.00, but he would also need it that very same day. The reason for that was because of my procrastination. I had delayed responding to these divorce papers. I suppose I was in denial and wished they would go away. I left my attorney's office in a panic, what was I to do? So, I called my friends Pat and Jerry and told them the predicament that I found myself in. Jerry, without the slightest hesitation, said to me, "You come right over, and I will write you a check for that amount." When I arrived at their home, Jerry met me with a strange look on his face. "Marj," he said, "I do not know how to tell you this, but after we hung up the phone, the Lord spoke to me and told me that I was not to give you this money. He said that you needed to ask your husband for it." I said, "What? Are you sure because this man wouldn't even give me money for tires when I needed them?" I could not imagine how, in the world, I would convince Bill that he should pay for my attorney. Trusting Jerry and because I had no other alternative, I went to their phone and called my husband. This is how the conversation went:

"Bill, I just left my attorney's office. He needs $1,700.00 by the end of the day to respond to the court in time. Because you want this divorce, I think you should pay for my attorney fees."

He said, "What? Are you crazy? I offered you my attorney so you wouldn't have to pay any fees!"

I said, "Yes, I know, but I did not think you guys were fair."

He continued, "Now let me get this straight. You want me to pay for your attorney so that you can get more money out of me?"

I agreed and said, "Yes, that's about it!"

Confused, he said, "Well, I don't know, I need to talk to my attorney about this."

Determined, I said, "OK, but I need to get back to my attorney's office before 5 o'clock, and it is already 3'o'clock."

He said, "Give me a few minutes, and I will call you back."

I said, "OK, bye."

He replied, "Bye."

Ten or fifteen minutes went by, and the phone rang. I answered since we were expecting it to be Bill, calling back. "Hello"

"I can't reach my attorney. Where do you want to meet? I will have the check ready for you."

I think the only person more surprised than me was the man writing out the check to give to my attorney so that my attorney could get more money out of him. I began to laugh because if anything was ever "beyond all reason," this was it!

Moving forward, In my living room was the same man standing in front of me, asking how I thought that I was going to pay for this schooling. We both knew it would be months before the divorce would be settled. I would have money then, but I needed it now. Registration would be in just a few short weeks. I answered him just as truthfully as I could. I did not know where it would come from. I told him that I just knew that the Lord would provide for me somehow, in some way. With that answer, my then-husband reached into his pocket and pulled out his wallet, opened it, and pulled out a check. Handing it to me, he said, "Well, maybe this will help." Yes, indeed, it would help; it was a check written out for fifteen thousand dollars. I was speechless!

One of the most important lessons that I have learned in this walk with the Lord is that the Lord expects obedience from us. The scriptures say blessings follow obedience. One of the biggest hindrances that we have, and it keeps us from being obedient is our own logic. When we try to reason out the solution to the problem, we will invariably talk ourselves right out of doing what the Spirit has said to do. Why? Because it does not make any sense to our minds. It does not make logical sense to ask someone who is divorcing you to pay for the attorney that will try to get as much money from him as possible. It does not make sense to give the little bit of money that you have and give it away, thinking that if you do that, more money will be on its way. Reason is an enemy of faith. Reason says, "When the money is provided, then I will move forward." The Spirit of God says, "Move forward, and then the provision will come." Reason says, "Save your money until you can afford to do the thing." The Spirit of God says, "Give away your money to provide for someone else's need, and I will provide for your need. I have learned that if "the voice" that guides me doesn't make much sense, then it is probably God; His voice encourages faith.

The voice of reason generally follows the voice of God, imparting all sorts of fear. The voice of reason attacks me all the time in this walk with God. My goal, however, is not to let fear rule my decision-making. I do not want to miss the exciting ways that the Lord provides when I am obedient to His leading. Another thing that I have learned is more often than not; the provision comes from those that are closest to you. However, I will be sharing in another chapter of how provision came from a very unexpected source.

My act of obedience to leave Wisconsin and to enroll in school at Christ for the Nations turned out to be one of the all-time highlights of my life. I had a small little apartment right on campus. It was a real privilege to be in that environment for the time I was there. Every day began and ended with a worship service. Some of the best contemporary Christian music heard today was birthed at CFTN. Thinking that I would eventually move to Israel, I majored in my minor, which was Jewish studies. I was fortunate enough to have the brilliant Dr. Jeffery Seif, as my professor, who challenged me toward excellence. I met a lot of wonderful people while I was there, and made some terrific friends.

One of my classes at CFTN was in the creative arts department. We participated in creating artistic ways of presenting the gospel through drama, song, worship dance, and various pageantry. I had spent my youth and teenage years at the dance studio. After marriage, however, I had put my love for the dance on the shelf. The beauty of expression in worship dance ignited the desire to dance again. I, therefore, auditioned for the dance team at CFTN but was rejected. Truthfully, I was rusty and auditioned with little thought and time spent in rehearsing the dance presentation. Instead, I joined the Tambourine Team, which turned out to be a real blessing, because dance was incorporated into the routines of the tambourine patterns.

One of the highlights of my stay in Dallas was the connection the Lord made for me outside the campus of CFTN. I met a woman who pioneered the worship dance movement in Dallas, and she asked me to join her dance team, SALT. Through her encouragement and instructions, the skills that were dormant within me surfaced. I had the privilege of dancing with her and the Salt Team on various stages across the metroplex. One of my fondest memories is when we graced the stage in May for "A Night to Remember Israel."

I learned another valuable lesson that will hopefully help you as well. I learned that the Proverbs 18:16 scripture that says: *16 A man's gift makes room for him, and brings him before great men,* can also be referring to a person's giftings and talents. Although the above scripture is speaking about a monetary gift, the gifts and talents given to us by the Almighty have intrinsic value. They likewise open doors of opportunity and bring us before great people. I was rejected by the CFTN dance team, which in retrospect, turned out to be a blessing. If I was accepted, I never would have had the opportunity to dance with the SALT team. The Lord is the One who makes room for you and your gifts.

After the first semester, the friends that I had come to Dallas with, decided that they were not going to enroll in another semester. They were anxious to begin their ministry in Israel, and so they left the school to do just that. The invitation was to join them with their move. However, I did not believe that was what the Lord was calling me to do at the time. The Lord had other plans for me, and the revelation of that plan would be shown to me later as the pages were turned. I would be going to Israel, but not for another year. The trip that I was to take was preceded by a prophetic vision I had forgotten all about.

Sometime before the breakup of my marriage, I was alone in my living room, worshiping and praying, and after a great deal of time in prayer, the Lord gave me a vision. It was the first real open vision I had ever had. When I say "real open vision," what I mean by that is, it was the first time I was looking at something in real-time that was not actually there. In the past, I had many visions that I call thought visions.

BEYOND ALL REASON: Moving Out of Logic Into the Supernatural

That is to say that in my mind's eye, I had thoughts that had provoked pictures in my mind about something that the Lord was trying to tell me, and I could envision what I perceived the Lord to be saying. This particular vision was not like that. This vision was like a movie screen placed in front of me, and on it was a film playing. As I watched, a beautiful scene was unfolding before me of an inviting shoreline. It was as if the camera was shooting the view from somewhere in the heavens. Then little by little, it zoomed in closer to the earth as if you were in an airplane about to land.

    I saw the most beautiful blue sea and sandy beach as the foaming waves were lapping at the shoreline. Then the scene began to change as it seemed to be traveling inland, and I saw much greenery, and this time it zoomed down on what looked like a resort with wooden Adirondack lawn chairs painted white and all lined up in a neat row. There were beautiful flowers everywhere and tables with umbrellas to protect one from the sun's rays. The sun was shining, and the skies were clear and a brilliant blue. Then just like that, it was over, except for the large letters rolling down the screen, much like when you see movie credits appear. The letters spelled out the name of a country— ISRAEL.

    At the time of the vision, I felt like the Lord was saying that I was going to Israel. This thought was something that was a desire of my heart; however, I felt if that were to happen, it would take a huge miracle to change my husband's mind because he had no desire whatsoever to take a trip to Israel. This vision occurred long before I knew that divorce was on the horizon. So, I just kept the vision and my desire to go to Israel on the back burner, thinking that if this was the Lord's will, eventually some way, somehow, it would happen. Little did I know, at the time of the vision, that my entire world was about to change. However, the Lord knew that I would soon be going through some of my darkest hours, and I believe He gave me the vision to hold on to so that I would have some hope for the future. However, given the pain and the upheaval that happens to one's life when divorce invades your household, I really never gave the vision much thought. It wasn't until sometime later, when I was enrolled at Christ for the Nations, that the vision came back to my mind, and the incredible accuracy of the vision became a reality.

As a student at Christ for the Nations, I was aware that every year, there was a group of students, supervised by Dr. Weis that went to Israel on a missionary trip. I decided that I would join the group and would be going with them during my second year at the school. The trip was planned for three weeks, and we were planning on leaving by the middle of May. Because my funds were running low by this time, I sold my diamonds at a diamond exchange in Dallas to help pay for the trip. Norma, a friend who had graduated from Christ for the Nations the previous year, was now living in Jerusalem. She was now the only person that I knew in Israel because Madeline and her husband Walter moved back to the states.

I wrote Norma a letter to tell her that I was going to be in Israel for two weeks in May and one week in June. She wrote back and told me that, unfortunately, she would not be in Israel during the time I would be there. She said that she had plans to be in the States at that time, raising money to support her ministry for another year in Israel, and continue her work in Jerusalem. I was very disappointed that I would not connect with her when I would be there.

Finally, May had arrived, and so had the day that I boarded the plane destined for Israel. As our plane was approaching the airport in Tel Aviv, I looked out the window and had one of those "déjà vu" moments. Below me was the most beautiful blue sea. The Mediterranean shore, with its sandy beach, was exactly like the one that I had seen in my vision. I had all but forgotten about the vision. There it was unfolding as a repeat performance in living technicolor. It was as if the Lord was saying to me, "See, I told you that one day you would be here in Israel." The Lord had many surprises for me in His land of "milk and honey." This was just the beginning.

From Tel Aviv, we took a bus to Jerusalem and lodged at a kosher hotel, which was very interesting. It was there that I learned that in a kosher kitchen, I must use a separate spoon to stir the cream in my coffee. From Jerusalem, we took side trips as we toured the land. We also had the opportunity to stay at a kibbutz just outside of Bethlehem for a few days. When the time came to go to Galilee, I was most excited because I was anxious to visit the location where Jesus spent so much of His time. As we traveled north headed toward Galilee, I could not help noticing how much greener the countryside was. It was lush green, just like I had seen in the vision. Upon arrival at the hotel, I got off the bus with some friends. We decided to look around at the grounds that we would be staying for the next few days. We circled to the back of the hotel anxious to see Lake Gennesaret, better known as the Sea of

Galilee, for the hotel was centrally located on beautiful frontage close to the shore of the sea. As I approached the coast, I could not believe my eyes. Lined up all in a row were the white wooden Adirondack lawn chairs I had seen in my vision. Decorating the patio were the colorful and beautiful flowers along with the tables and their umbrellas. The scene had everything in it, just like I had seen before in the vision. The Lord had shown me a glimpse of my future that day as I prayed alone in my living room. I had gone through some very dark hours and had reached some shallow valleys since the day of the vision. I was very much aware that I had reached the other side of the mountain, and the warmth of the Son was shining brightly upon me, giving me a future and a hope., as I stood there in the reality of a vision fulfilled, praising the Lord God of Israel, who does all things well. Who am I? I thought to myself that God should be mindful of me? I'm just an ordinary woman, serving an extraordinary God!

We toured the land and took in all the pertinent sights, and the time had slipped away so quickly. The Missionary group that I came to Israel with was scheduled to return to the states within a few days when I heard "the voice" say to me, "When everyone returns to the States, I want you to stay here." Wow, I thought, now wait a moment, I don't know anyone in Israel, I am running out of money, and I have no place to stay. I would be a woman all alone in Israel; this cannot be a good idea. How in the world am I going to do this? What I heard was the voice of logic and reason, convincing myself that I had not heard from God. "Lord, I said, I am willing to stay if this is what you want me to do. I am not going to stay unless you provide a place for me to stay," and I left it at that. The following Saturday evening, we ministered down on Ben Yehuda Street. The city of Jerusalem comes alive on Saturday evening after Shabbat. The shops are open, and people mingle at the sidewalk cafes. The streets are busy with crowds everywhere. There is such a sense of community when Israelis gather at the village square after their day of rest. It was on Ben Yehuda Street that the Lord taught me how to witness to a Jew. It is not kosher to be a visitor in Israel to evangelize. This is not permitted. However, if someone approaches you with questions, you are permitted to answer as long as there is no pressure to proselytize. Therefore, I had to be very careful as to what I was going to say to the Jewish gentleman that approached me and got right in my face.

The students that I was with were singing and dancing in the streets to Messianic music, and it was obvious that we were all Christians. Suddenly this disgruntled man walks over to me and rather loudly says, in an angry voice, "I DO NOT BELIEVE YESHUA IS THE MESSIAH!" I responded by saying, "Well, sir, I do." He then began to rant and rave, saying things like, "This one is Messiah, and that one over there is Messiah, people think everyone is Messiah. Your Jesus is not the Messiah." I answered him by saying, "I did not come to Israel to convince you that Yeshua (Jesus) is the Messiah, although I do believe Him to be the Messiah of Israel because I have experienced Him. No, I came to Israel to let you and your people know that there are Christians in the United States that support and love Israel."

The entire conversation with this man took place within a crowd of people that surrounded us. Then from out of nowhere, appeared another man, who walked up to the first man I was engaged in conversation with and pointed his figure right into the man's face, shaking it, and said, "You must listen to this woman!" and he disappeared. I believe, to this day, the second man was an angel. Who does that? While all this was going on, the Lord was having a conversation with me as well. The Lord said, "Ask him if he is a praying man." I turned to the man and asked, "Are you a praying man?" He rather indignantly answered, "Well, of course, I am!" The Lord then said, "Now ask him, have you ever asked God if Yeshua is the Messiah?" I repeated the question just exactly as the Lord had said it, and you would have thought I had hauled off and soccer punched this Jew in the stomach. He just stood there staring at me for the longest time. His countenance changed, his shoulders slumped, and he said in a very meek voice, "No, I have not, but I will." With that statement, he turned and sheepishly walked away.

This meeting with the man, I believe, was a divine appointment. The Lord orchestrated it for one of His own. I know that one day, we will meet again within the pearly gates of Heaven. For there is no doubt in my mind that God the Father revealed His Son, Yeshua, to this Jewish gentleman when he asked the question that holds the key to his eternal destiny. This encounter taught me that the very best way to evangelize the Jews is to ask them to ask Father God who the Messiah of Israel is. The Lord is the Savior, and He will reveal Himself to those who ask.

Our group wanted to seize the moments left by sharing the love of Christ on the streets of Jerusalem while we still had the chance. I returned and joined those who were singing and dancing in the street.

Off in the distance, I could hear someone calling my name. I looked around and didn't see anyone that I knew, so at first, I thought there must be another Marjorie in the crowd. At last, I saw her; it was Norma, my friend. Her trip to the States had been postponed until Tuesday. She said that the Lord had instructed her to come down to the square and look for me because He wanted her to give me the keys to her apartment for the summer, while she was back in the States. I was astounded!

What a wonderful blessing the Lord had provided for me. With a provision like this, I knew that I had nothing more to fear for the remainder of the time I would stay in Israel. Since the Lord had provided me with an apartment for the summer, I knew that He would provide everything else that would be needed, so my fears all melted away.

BEYOND ALL REASON: Moving Out of Logic Into the Supernatural

Chapter 19

HEAVEN'S CONNECTIONS

I informed Dr. Weis that I would not be returning with the rest of the group when they left on Wednesday. I learned then that several other students had also decided to stay on to explore Israel on their own. They, however, had decided to return to Tel Aviv. I opted not to join them since my provision was in Jerusalem. I gave one of the students, Norma's phone number and address in case of an emergency, her name was Judy. On Tuesday, I managed to somehow to find the apartment without any trouble. Surely there must have been an invisible hand directing the way. Living among the people is a far cry from touring.

While touring, we stayed in some elegant hotels that had excellent food. None of the hotels were as modern and luxurious as those that we find in America; however, they were nice. It was more or less a culture shock when I unpacked at Norma's apartment to settle in. I felt like I had stepped back in time into the 40s. The tiny refrigerator could only hold the food needed for a day or two. The washing machine was one of those kinds with the rollers to squeeze the water out, and no one in my building had a dryer. The bathroom plumbing was antiquated.

All in all, the apartment stirred up a lot of nostalgia for me, because the appliances in Norma's apartment reminded me of the appliances that we had during my childhood. One day I took the bus outside of the city to where a new mall had recently opened up. While I was there, I went into an appliance store and discovered why no one had new appliances. The cost would have been at least triple the price paid in the States. The cost of living is very expensive, it seemed to me, except for the food at the open-air market.

The apartment was centrally located, so, for the most part, I could walk to most everything. I could walk to the Wailing Wall, the grocery store, the old city, the Jewish and Christian quarters, and the open-air market. The food markets were beautiful. Fresh fruits and vegetables of every variety imaginable were displayed at very reasonable prices. Because of the limited room in the refrigerator, a trip to the open-air market was a trip that I made every few days. One day after I had been in the apartment just a few days, there was a knock on the door. When I opened the door, there stood a young woman with two suitcases. She introduced herself as a missionary from Romania.

I knew of this woman from a previous conversation with Norma that she might be visiting and had an open invitation to stay. She said to me, "Frequently, when I am in Jerusalem, I stay with Norma, but I knew that she was going to be back in the States this time when I arrived. So, I decided to stay with some other friends that I have here in Jerusalem. However, the Lord spoke to me and told me to come to

Norma's anyway. So here I am!" We laughed, and I invited her in and told her that she was welcome to stay as long as I was there. She was an amazing young woman who, when she heard the voice of the Lord and His direction, she just did whatever the Lord told her to do. She informed me about the time some friends of hers were leaving for Romania, and they invited her to come with them. She wanted to go, but there was no time to get a passport for her. The Lord had instructed her to pack her suitcase with Bibles and smuggle them in. She asked the Lord how she was to do this without a passport. He instructed her just to trust him and go through customs with her friends. She told me that she was really nervous, but she followed her instructions from the Lord. To her great amazement, as she went through customs, no one asked her for her passport, and no one opened her suitcase. She said it was as if no one saw her at all. Likewise, on the plane, it was as if she wasn't there. I love to hear stories like this one; it builds my faith to believe for even more supernatural happenings in my own life.

    I was so grateful that the Lord had sent this young woman to me because she turned out to be such a blessing. She was very familiar with Jerusalem, and she showed me all around. She had many friends in the city, and we had invitations to the homes of Jewish believers in the city for a Bible study. We were even invited to an Israeli birthday party one evening. The Lord had planned a surprise for me at the birthday party. One of the guests was a woman that I had met at a Messianic home fellowship in Milwaukee, Wisconsin. We were both astonished we should meet again in Jerusalem of all places. Only God can accomplish such a feat. It was very sobering to be invited into the homes of these Jewish people because I became much aware of the fact that they live under a constant threat of war. In each house or apartment, one room was devoted to the storage of water and food and gas masks. They always have to be prepared.

After a couple of weeks, my new missionary friend had to leave. I was sorry to see her go but grateful to have made her acquaintance. Shortly after she left, I received a phone call from Tel Aviv. It was from Judy. She and the students with her had invited me to come to Tel Aviv. They had met a gentleman that they wanted me to meet. We set a date, and she agreed to pick me up. When I arrived in Tel Aviv, and the car turned into the driveway of the man I was yet to meet, I noticed the driveway was lined with old rusty missiles. I learned later that the missiles were gathered from the six-day war, placed on the property as a memorial to the Lord for His divine intervention and victory.

After parking the car, I stood outside, anticipating who lived in this huge home. Who was this man I would soon meet? We walked to the door and rang the bell. I was introduced to a very eccentric man by the name of Aaron Levy when I passed through the entry door. Aaron invited us to stay with him and his wife, Helen, for the weekend. Aaron was a Jewish believer in Yeshua. While I was there, I learned that Aaron was a modern-day Jewish prophet. He had an altar to the Lord built in his home that we were not allowed to get near. This sacred place was where Aaron worshiped the Lord while waiting for the Lord to meet and speak with him. According to Aaron, this is where the Lord met with him and gave him the strategy for the six-day war. He asked to meet with the government powers that be and gave them the strategy that was given to him by the Holy Spirit. As we know, Israel won that war against all the odds. Aaron Levy's notoriety, of his prophetic accuracy, reached the United States, and he appeared on the Johnny Carson show. He showed me articles and pictures relating to this time in his life, even showing me a newspaper clipping of him and Johnny Carson together. Upon questioning Aaron on how he became a believer, he related the following story.

As a young boy in Romania, he lived with his mother in an orthodox home after his father died. His grandfather, who they lived with, was a Rabbi. Aaron told me that as a very young boy, he asked his mother what he was to do when he had questions that only a father could answer. His mother told Aaron that he had a Heavenly Father and that whenever he had questions, he should go to his room, get on his knees, and ask God for the answers. This routine became Aaron's practice. He would go before God, ask his question, and wait for an answer. The Lord, he said, always answered him. He thought that this communication with God was normal and really didn't think much about it.

Then the time came when Aaron became the age when it was time for his Bar Mitzvah. He told me that they were an impoverished family, but because of this special occasion, he was told to go to the shoemaker for a new pair of shoes. When he arrived at the shoemaker, the shoemaker asked Aaron what occasion it was that he gets a new pair of shoes. Aaron told the shoemaker that it was his Bar Mitzvah. With that answer, the shoemaker said to Aaron, "I see; now you are a man! Aaron, since you have become a man, I have something to show you. Come with me, please." He took Aaron to the back of his shop, where he opened a Bible to Isaiah Chapter 53. Aaron, he said, "It is time I tell you about the man in this chapter. He is the Messiah of Israel." The shoemaker instructed Aaron who Yeshua was, and sent him on his way. When Aaron got home, he went to his room to get his Bible, and he opened it to Isaiah 53 and took the Bible to his grandfather and asked, "Grandfather, who is this man?" This question made his grandfather very angry, and in a loud voice, he told Aaron that he was never to mention this man again in his house. Upset and confused, Aaron went to his room and got down on his knees and opened his Bible to the section of Isaiah that he was forbidden to talk about, pointed his finger at chapter 53, and asked his Heavenly Father, "Who is this man?" The voice from Heaven that he had become familiar with answered him. "This is my Son; He is your Messiah."

From that point on, he became a believer that the Messiah of Israel had come in the person of Yeshua HaMashia (Jesus the Christ). He kept this to himself until the day of his wedding. As was the custom in his family, his wife was chosen by the family. She was promised to him since he was a child. Aaron said that after the wedding, when he and his wife were alone, and before the marriage was consummated, he desired to tell his bride the truth. He wanted to tell her about Yeshua so that they could start their marriage right. Aaron told his new bride the whole story, and when he finished, his bride said to him. "Aaron, if this is the way that you believe, then I shall believe this way too."

The Lord called Aaron and his wife to Israel to spread the truth of the gospel in the land. They believed that they were the first Messianic believers in Israel. Boldly, they shared the "good news" to whoever would listen. Therefore, their lives were threatened, and attempts were made to burn down their home. They were greatly persecuted for the sake of the gospel. Israel is a challenging place to be when you are a Jew, and you believe Yeshua is the Messiah. The orthodox Jews believe you are no longer Jewish and that you have departed from the faith.

While we were in Aaron's home, we had the great honor and privilege to sit under his teaching for three days. We were guests in Aaron's house, and therefore we adhered to his agenda while we were there. He made the schedule, and we followed it. We arose very early for breakfast. After breakfast, we sat around the table for Bible study, then lunch was served, and we had another Bible Study after we ate. A couple of hours in the afternoon, we were free to take a nap or relax. One day we used the time to shop for groceries for dinner. After dinner, we were free to do as we pleased. We preferred to sit at Aaron's feet and hear his encounters with the risen Lord.

The Lord used Aaron prophetically all over Israel. He taught us how he made a distinction between Aaron Levy, the Prophet, and Aaron Levy, the friend. When he had a "prophetic word of the Lord" to deliver, Aaron said he would very boldly march into the home or office of the person. Since he was operating in the office and the anointing of a Prophet, he would speak of nothing else except the word of the Lord that was meant for them, and then abruptly leave. He would then turn around and return to them and announce, "This time I come as your friend." With this method, there was no misunderstanding; everyone knew when it was Aaron speaking from the Lord or speaking as a friend. One evening, Aaron invited us to go with him to a political meeting right there in Tele Viv. We were about to witness a demonstration of how Aaron Levy made a distinction between Aaron, the Prophet, and Aaron, the friend. We arrived, parked the car, approached the doorway of where the meeting was being held. As Aaron was about to go inside, he turned to me, who was right behind him, and said, "You wait right here until I come for you." After ten minutes or so, Aaron returned to us after giving someone inside a prophetic word from the Lord. He stepped outside with us, and said, "OK, follow me," and we all went in and found a seat. It was apparent that this time, he entered as a friend, for he went around the room shaking hands and greeting those he came in contact with.

Helen, Aaron's wife, shared with us women that Aaron was a difficult man to live with because he had no outside interests outside of God. All-day, every day, it was always about God and advancing the Kingdom. There was little money for anything else. She said, "Once when they were invited to a wedding, she told Aaron that she wanted a new dress to wear to the wedding. His response was that she already had a dress. She said, "So guess what I did? I took the draperies down, and I made myself a new dress out of them." We all had a good laugh with her after she shared how she got a new dress for the wedding.

Aaron has since gone home to be with the Lord. Having been in the presence of this great man of God was indeed one of the wonderful memories that I have of my trip to Israel. The Lord opened many doors for me while I was in Israel; the entrance to Aaron Levy's home was only one of them.

BEYOND ALL REASON: Moving Out of Logic Into the Supernatural

These awesome experiences I wanted to share with you because it is loud and clear that all over the world, the Lord does speak to his people. He spoke to me to stay in Israel, He talked to Norma to give me the keys to her apartment, and He spoke to my missionary friend to smuggle Bibles into Romania. He spoke to Aaron to believe that the man in Isaiah 53 is the Savior of the world and his Messiah. God wants to have this kind of relationship with everyone. Unfortunately, not everyone wants to have this type of relationship with Him. If you are yearning to hear His voice and experience His love, just humble yourself; get down on your knees and do what Aaron did. He will speak to you if you will only ask Him to. My suggestion, though, is to ask questions you do not have the answers to and keep on asking until you hear the answers.

BEYOND ALL REASON: Moving Out of Logic Into the Supernatural

Chapter 20

MORE ADVENTURES WITH THE LORD

The Divine Therapist

Returning to Dallas to resume life on the campus of Christ for the Nations was difficult because Israel had felt like home to me, and for that reason, I did not want to leave. However, it wasn't long until the reality of Israel, some seventy-one hundred miles away, had to be faced as an actuality. My memories of Israel began to fade, but never to be forgotten. It was hard to believe that only one semester was between me and graduation. The time had gone by so swiftly. Yet, there had been so many incredible adventures that were packed into that relatively short amount of time. With only one more semester to go, one could not help but wonder what new experiences I would find ahead.

Little did I know when the phone rang in my little apartment at Christ for the Nations, that a new adventure by the Lord was planned. Upon answering the phone, I found it was a friend of my daughter's that I had taken under my wing. For the sake of protecting her identity, I am going to be calling her Sally. Sally called me Mom because of the close relationship that we had. When I answered the phone, I heard her say, "Mom, its Sally, and I am flying into Dallas Fort Worth, and I was wondering if it would be alright if I come and spend a few days with you." I asked her what was bringing her to Texas, and she said she was checking herself into a hospital in Fort Worth after she spent some time with me. Sally was born again, on fire, a believer, and was filled with the Holy Spirit and spoke in tongues. She was checking herself into a Christian clinic to deal with some past issues hindering her walk with the Lord. This clinic had an exceptional reputation for dealing with emotional problems of the past that hindered an individual from moving forward. I was proud of her for making this decision.

We spent several days together, and since she had come to see me over the Thanksgiving holiday, the two of us were invited to spend Thanksgiving with Cheryl, a friend of mine I had met at CFTN. The following Monday, I drove from Dallas to Fort Worth and dropped Sally off at the hospital. Before we parted, Sally asked me if I would come and visit her in the hospital while she was there. I assured her that I would. The day that I returned to visit with Sally is a day that I will never forget. I parked the car, went up the elevator to the floor that she was on. I went to the reception desk to inquire what room number she was in and found my way to her room. After our Hellos, Sally asked me if I would join her in group therapy that was just about to start. She said that family and guests were welcomed to join in, so I sat in with her on the session. When it was over, we returned to her room. We exchanged small talk when we got back to the room. Then Sally told me that she had a roommate that she wanted me to meet. "Mom," she said, "I told her all about you." My roommate wants the Baptism in the Holy Spirit, and I told her that you would pray for her. You will won't you?" She asked. I nodded my head in the affirmative, and with that, Sally went flying down the hall to fetch her roommate.

In a flash, Sally brought her roommate back to the room. She introduced me, and without a one-second delay, Sally wanted me to pray for her new friend. Before I prayed with her, I explained what to expect and took her to the appropriate scriptures, so she would have some understanding as to what she should be anticipating. Then I prayed that the Holy Spirit would overpower her and come and fill her with Himself. Nothing happened at first, so I told her to raise her hands and to begin to praise the Lord and even sing to the Lord, which she did. It wasn't long when out of her mouth came a beautiful new language, and she began to sing to the Lord in her new prayer language as tears of joy rolled down her cheeks. Sally and I were rejoicing with her. Then suddenly Sally ran out of the room and ran down the hall again. Sally went to all the women's rooms announcing, "My Mom is here praying for the Holy Spirit. Anyone that wants the Baptism in the Holy Spirit and to speak in tongues come to my room." Before I knew what was happening, there was a room full of women wanting prayer for it. I did not have time to explain everything like I thought that I should because once the women filled the room, the Holy Spirit fell upon them. They came with such expectancy, that once they were through the door, they had their hands in the air and were praising God. This event was a move of God, and I had nothing to do with it except being there. I did pray, but it would not have mattered because the Lord met those ladies right where they were in such need of Him.

Before I could even finish praying, they were all filled with the Spirit of God; it seemed to me at once. I was listening to all sorts of different tongues. Some were praying in their new language, and some were singing. Many of the girls overpowered by the Holy Spirit were slain in the Spirit. I asked Sally to help me because I was unable to catch these bodies by myself as the Holy Spirit was taking them to the floor. Those that neither one of us were able to catch, just floated to the floor like a feather. The floor was full of bodies, and those left standing were praising the Lord. Sally's door was left open, and the noise of the praise and worship made its way to the men's rooms. Following the sound, their curiosity led them to where all the commotion was. All these men were now standing and observing at Sally's door. The rules did not allow any men to enter the women's rooms, so they were crowded together around the entry. The next thing that happened was a nurse on the floor came into the room and said to me, "Will you please take this down the hall and into a room large enough that the men can join you?" I was not about to argue, so I asked the nurse where to go, and she led the way as I followed her down the hall. Everyone that was in Sally's room and the men that stood outside the room followed the nurse and me down the hall and into the room that she recommended we should use to continue. Well, continue, we did!

We had one exuberant Holy Ghost revival. Now it was the men's turn. Jesus showed up big time that day. The Holy Spirit just took over. He met everyone's needs. All I had to do was ask, "Do you want the Holy Spirit?" After I asked that question, the power of God would come upon those men. Big and burly, as some were, down they went under the sweet anointing of the Holy One. It was just as if they were floating on air. The deep voices of these male recipients joining the women as they all spoke or sang in tongues, was beautiful music to my ears. There were men and women together in the room, crying, laughing, praying, singing, and bodies out on the floor, under the influence of the Holy Spirit. It was a sight to behold. Many of the men and women were in casual attire, sweats, and the like. Some were in PJs and robes. This place was, after all, a hospital and the greatest pajama party I was ever invited to. I shook my head in amazement and reminded myself that the Lord was using me as His conduit on this day; in this hospital, on this floor where all these precious people came for emotional therapy. Although they had just come from group therapy, nothing could compare to the therapy happening in their precious souls. Jesus poured the new wine of His Holy Spirit into their wounded hearts. In all my years I have never witnessed such genuine joy and rejoicing as what occurred on that day. There was a rather large window in this room, and the draperies were open. I did glance out into the hall every so often, while all this was going on. There in the hallway were some of the nurses on the floor, taking it all in. They were standing there watching, probably in amazement, because the Great Physician had shown up on their watch. This revival of the brokenhearted was planned and orchestrated by the Lord. His Glory was revealed to the entire ward of that hospital. No one dared to interrupt what the Holy Spirit was doing with these patients.

BEYOND ALL REASON: Moving Out of Logic Into the Supernatural

It had been around fifteen years after my own experience of being filled with the Holy Spirit when this very unusual encounter with the Holy Spirit occurred. I had been ministering under the anointing of the Holy Spirit for some time, believing that nothing was impossible with Him. When laying hands on people, I had seen them get healed, even to the point of watching legs lengthened, death bed recovery, emotional breakthrough, and I had prayed with various people the Lord would fill with His Holy Spirit. The Lord even used me in deliverance many times. In fact, the young woman, Sally, that I am telling you about, previously had a spirit of suicide cast out of her. She was set free from the torment that came from the harassment of that evil spirit. Everything that I had personally witnessed in ministry paled by comparison to what took place at the hospital that day. I had been the witness to many remarkable miracles. Still, this particular encounter with the personhood of the Holy Spirit stands out as one of the most awesome events that I ever have had the privilege of being a part of in ministry.

I had an opportunity to speak with one of the men patients before I left the hospital. I introduced myself to him, and he told me that he was a pastor and was in the hospital because of a nervous breakdown due to the pressures of the ministry, "Until today," he said, "I was going to give up the ministry. I have been drifting from God because of some of the things happening in the Church. I was ready to give it all up. Then, you came today, and the Holy Spirit visited us." I told him that I had very little to do with what had happened there that day. He then went on to tell me what had been happening behind the scenes that I was unaware of. He said, "I was in my room praying, and

I could hear all the beautiful praise and worship. As I listened, I could tell people were singing in tongues. I asked the Lord what is that, and where is it coming from? The Lord spoke to me and said, "Go, and open your door, and you go find them, and join them, I want you to get in on this." So, I opened the door and followed the sound of the worship down the hall to one of the women's rooms. I stood outside in the doorway and asked the Lord how I could get in on it if I were not allowed to go inside a woman's room. By now, other men were rushing down the hall and joined me at the entry to the room. I had just asked the Lord how I could join you guys when the nurse came and moved everyone out of the room and into the room where the rest of us men could join you!" Both of us were so excited about what the Lord had done! We sat and talked about it for a while. Then he went on to say, "I was sitting here thanking the Lord for all that He did today. I know that I will never be the same. I also know that I have been called to the ministry. After today, I am pumped now to step back into that call."

When everything had calmed down, and it was time for me to leave, one of the nurses that was watching this visitation of the Holy Spirit, joined me as I waited for the elevator. Once we were on the elevator and doors closed in front of us, the nurse turned to me and said, "I need to tell you something, it is not the policy of this hospital for you to come and pray with the patients like you did today." She then gave me a great big smile and stepped off the elevator and went her way. My heart was so full as I walked to my car, so fired up that I wanted to take the "Holy Spirit, the One who broke the policy," with me and go visit every mental hospital in the Dallas Fort Worth area. Returning to the campus and my apartment was bittersweet after such a powerful time under the anointing. Everything seemed mundane by comparison.

Called to Ministry

Every semester I had taken more credits than what was necessary to graduate, and this semester was no different. I was determined to take advantage of the fantastic opportunity that I was given. It did nevertheless require my undivided attention to study. Especially my classes to learn Hebrew required much of my time and devotion. This last semester I found to be much more stressful because, on top of a full schedule, I needed to also report to a part-time job I had found to help me financially. Since I had gone through the gift of $15,000.00 for tuition, living expenses, and the trip to Israel, I needed a source for income, for the monthly alimony I was receiving was not enough. Because of this added responsibility, I had very little spare time left for myself.

One day, during downtime, I heard about an ordination ceremony rehearsal being held in the auditorium. I was curious about who would be ordained and how the services were conducted, so I walked over to the hall on campus to watch. Very few people were there outside of the students on stage rehearsing and including some faculty members who were directing the students. Therefore, I walked down to the front row and sat down to observe. Not everyone who attends Christ for the Nations is ordained. Only the students who believe they are called by God and have had that call confirmed by faculty members are accepted to proceed with the ordination process. Each student is highly scrutinized and interviewed before the school ordains them. Most of the students that attend CFTN leave the school with diplomas of Theology but are not ordained for full-time ministry. I had met many students that had incredible amounts of integrity and single-mindedness about advancing the Kingdom of God and serving the King on a full-time basis. I came to the auditorium to see if any of those that I knew were going to be ordained.

A faculty member was speaking to the students and marking off a spot on stage where they should stand when their name was called. Then they were instructed to take their places and do a run-through. The student called by name would then walk to the spot marked before exiting the stage. Nothing unusual about this procedure, however, I became undone. With the calling of the first name, my eyes began to tear up. Then with each consecutive name called, the tears started to flow until I was crying almost uncontrollably.

Embarrassed and very puzzled why I was so emotional, I got up from my seat and left the auditorium to return to my apartment. Still crying when I put the key in my door, I opened the door, shut the door behind me, and in between sobs, I cried out to the Lord. "What is wrong with me? Why am I behaving in such a manner?" "Because," He said to me, "I am calling you to be ordained." Now I know that it is ridiculous to question or to argue with the Lord, but I did. "What? "I can't be ordained; I am a woman, and a divorced woman at that. It's against my theology," "Well then," came the voice that I looked to for guidance, "You do not know the scriptures. It may not be your theology, but it certainly is mine. Search the scriptures." "Christ for the Nations will never ordain a divorced woman," I said as if I were in a position to know more about this than God. I resolved that indeed, God was calling me to be ordained. I just did not really believe it would happen here at Christ for the Nations, not with such scrutiny that each candidate had to go through. So, more out of obedience than out of faith, I put my application in and went to the necessary group meetings, fully expecting to be turned down. We were told that the faculty would be praying about each candidate and that everyone would be called for an interview. Having done everything required of me, I went about my business knowing that I would be turned down, but I was happy with myself that I had been obedient and had at least gone through the motions. In the mean-time, life went on as usual until there was a little more than a month to go before graduation. December was going to be a busy month. There were finals to prepare for and preparations to be made for graduation. Then the festivities for Christmas sandwiched in a week before crossing the stage at graduation. I had shopping to do and list a mile long to complete before that final day that I would be saying goodbye to the campus and to so many friends that would be returning to their homelands.

I had not heard a word from the ordination committee, and time was running out. When speaking with a couple of other friends who were being ordained, they had shared with me that they had their interview some time ago already. This talk convinced me that I was right all along, I was a divorced woman, and in the eyes of the authorities at Christ for the Nations that would disqualify me. Therefore, no one had called me for an interview, and they should have by now. Not wanting to face the rejection, I just let it go for a couple of weeks. Then not knowing, began to wear on me, so finally, with only a few days left before graduation, I picked up the phone and called the professor in charge to inquire why no one had called me. When he answered the phone, I said: "Hello, this is Marjorie Kummrow, I put my application in for ordination months ago, and I was told someone would be calling me for an interview, and no one has." He said, "Oh Marjorie, I am so sorry," (at this point I thought to myself, OK here it comes) He went on to say: "I am so sorry that no one called you. That was an oversight on my part. You see, when the faculty began to pray about you as we do for each student, the Lord spoke to us, and He told us that you were to be ordained. So, we did not see the need for an interview. I'm sorry that no one called you to tell you." Awestruck, I stood holding the phone in my hand long after he had hung up. The divine hand of the Lord was leading me into waters, that according to me, was way over my head. I did not have much faith in the call upon my life to include "ordination." Guess what? It was about to happen anyway.

Graduation day came and went, and the Ordination Service followed. As I walked across the stage when my name was called, I felt such humility to be given such an honor and privilege; to be called by the Almighty to serve Him in such a capacity. I was prayed over and received prophetic words from the Dean of Women and some of my professors. This blessing was a tradition at CFTN. When Dr. Jeffery Seif, the professor for all my Jewish studies, prayed over me, he also invited me to work with him at the church, where he was the pastor in DeSoto. Texas. I accepted and worked under Dr. Seif's leadership for a year before returning to Wisconsin. It was an excellent opportunity for me to learn even more about the Jewish roots of the faith, as Dr.

Seif taught his congregation from a Hebraic perspective. My contribution to his congregation was that I was a Deacon, and I used my gifts and talents to enhance the Creative Arts for the church.

On the church property was a house that the staff graciously offered to friends of mine, Bret and Laura Tye, who were active in the church. They, in turn, offered to share their home with me. I have such fond memories of our time together. Eventually, though, it became apparent it was time to return to the Midwest. The church had grown, and the house was now needed to house the Sunday School children. I had been looking for a job to provide more income. For the first time, I was not hired for any jobs I applied for. I did not have enough income to provide housing for myself, and the Lord was not providing it supernaturally. So, I had no choice but to move back home. Sometimes the circumstances in our lives are the signposts directing the way. Therefore, I began making all the preparations for the long drive north.

Chapter 21

A TASTE OF GLORY

I had called my friend and prayer partner, Pat, and invited myself to stay with her until I got myself back on my feet again. I knew that I would be welcome in her home because that is the type of relationship we have. Actually, we are more like sisters than just good friends. I know that I can count on her anytime to have my back. As I headed north in my little Chevy Beretta with a U-haul trailer following from behind, I began to reminisce about the glorious times Pat, and I had in prayer through the years. We had some awesome times with the Lord. One time, long before this particular phenomenon was sweeping through Charismatic circles, we were in prayer, and what had later become known as "holy laughter" hit us. We laughed and laughed until our sides ached. For hours, we were out of control with laughter. We did not understand why or what the Lord was doing with us. It was much later that reports of "holy laughter" began circulating the Christian news media. We learned from others that just as the Lord brought emotional healing through crying, He was at this time in our lives, bringing emotional healing through laughter. [23] It certainly is much more fun to laugh yourself "whole," than to cry.

Both Pat and I entered Christianity, expecting the supernatural and divine hand of God to lead us, to heal us, and to provide for us. So, when we got together for prayer, we expected God to show up and anticipated His supernatural hand would be present with us. Such was the case when Pat had invited several of our friends to join us one evening for prayer. Previous to that invitation, we had been at our Wednesday night fellowship meeting, and Ian Andrews was the guest speaker. He had a Word from the Lord that the night was to be devoted to spinal/skeletal healings except for one person who was going deaf. That one person just happened to be Nicole, Pat's daughter. Nicole knew that the word was for her when Ian asked who was going deaf. She was healed that night, and to this day, according to Nicole, she has bionic hearing! The first person to sit in the chair for skeletal healings that night was Pat's husband, Jerry. His leg was lengthened, and he received a new disc in his spine. Ian had asked Jerry which way he wanted it to be when he went to pray for his legs. Should they pray for his leg to lengthen or to shorten? Being a rather short individual, he chose to be taller. About a week later, Pat had dinner guests, and during dinner, her friend asked her to pray that both of his legs would be equal in length. Pat said that she almost fainted with such a request. She was not, after all, Ian Andrews, but she proceeded to imitate what Ian did

---

[23] There is a decisive difference between "holy laughter" that comes from the Holy Spirit and the laughter that comes from Satan through the influence of a "mocking evil demon". One must exercise the gift of the "discerning of spirits" to tell the difference.

and stood over her friend and said, speaking to his leg, "I command you to lengthen in the name of Jesus." They all watched the leg grow in great amazement.

After a phone call to me about what had happened at dinner, Pat and I were off and running. Since the Lord was in the mood for lengthening legs, and we knew that He is no respecter of persons, we just assumed whoever wanted a touch from Him would get it. We invited whoever was interested in joining us for a night of "leg-lengthening or shortening." We fully expected the Lord to do the same with anyone in the house that needed it that night, just as He had done previously. So, we instructed everyone to take their shoes off and sit in a chair with extended legs. We would then check to see if one leg might be longer than the other. To our delight, several candidates needed their legs lengthened by the Lord. We prayed and asked the Lord to lengthen the shorter leg to match the other. He did! Right before our eyes, we watched the leg move as it lined up with the other leg on our first patient. This event was to the amazement of everyone in the room who was watching. I can still hear the ooh's and the ahh's from everyone's excitement. The next volunteer couldn't wait to be next. It then occurred to us that we should ask whether the individual we were praying for wanted to be taller or shorter because someone might want one leg shortened instead of the short one lengthened. Regardless of the request, the Lord was willing. Everyone who needed the miracle of leg-lengthening or shortening was met by the supernatural hand of God that evening. It was exciting to be in partnership with the Healer!

BEYOND ALL REASON: Moving Out of Logic Into the Supernatural

Unfortunately, and sad to say, we have lost many of our freedoms. Today it is possible that we would be arrested for practicing medicine without a license, as have some pastors that I have read about. Never-the-less, I will take my chances with that risk. I would never withhold an opportunity to pray for someone's healing. I am not the healer; Jesus is. I am a person of prayer. God does the healing! It is just plain stupid to think that someone who is ministering healing through one of the gifts of the Holy Spirit; is practicing medicine without a license. It would not surprise me that in the future, we will need a "physician's license" to pray for healing and a "commodity license" for the next supernatural event that I am about to share.

Pat and I had a friend who belonged to a little church on the south side of Chicago, and she was reporting to us that during the services there, one of the Lord's supernatural invasions into the natural occurred. During their meetings, "gold dust" began to appear, not wanting to be left out of anything that the Lord was doing, we prayed for the gold dust too. We were just like children, asking daddy to do the same for us. Low and behold, the Lord answered our prayers. In our excitement, the manifestation of little gold sparkly flecks appeared on our hands. As time marched on, I found gold sparkles on my face, hands, and arms. It wasn't long after that I noticed silver and gold flecks showing up in makeup at the cosmetic counters across the land. Isn't it just like Satan to have His counterfeit gold dust, even though it is a forgery?

Speaking of "gold dust" brings to remembrance, something that happened during a church service here in Glendale, Arizona, where I reside now. One Sunday morning, the Lord decided to have an awesome display of His Glory. It began to rain, or should I say, it began to pour, "gold dust" in the middle of the service. It was quite a shower. The pastor had to stop the service because there was such a commotion. Everyone came running to where it was raining gold. It was raining so much "gold dust" that even the people sitting next to the person God was raining on, got covered with it. Therefore, I was covered with this "gold dust" because sitting next to me was my daughter, who was the recipient. Above Tracey, coming from what looked like the ceiling, was an open portal surrounding the chair where my daughter sat. She had gold dust in her hair, all over her clothes, in her opened bible, and on her shoes. There was so much that when she got home, she dusted off her clothes and gathered up the "gold dust" and put it in a little glass vial to keep for a keepsake. After a few months, the "gold dust" turned into oil. What an awesome privilege it is to walk in the Glory of God Almighty!

    I realize we just took a little detour on the "gold dust trail," but I couldn't resist. The "gold dust" that showered my daughter was unlike anything I have experienced before, or after for that matter. When the Lord manifested gold for Pat and me, it was just a few little sprinkles compared to the down-pour that hit Tracey that Sunday morning. As I said previously, my son Bill called to tell me that He was attending a Charismatic church where the gifts of the Holy Spirit were in operation, and he received a gold tooth. This type of manifestation was not unusual in Charismatic circles at the time. Reports of this nature were broadcast all around the world. Signs and wonders were following those that believed. I could not help but wonder as I traveled north, what new adventures the Lord had in store for me.

I was so relieved when, at last, I saw the welcomed exit sign to I-294. I was now in familiar territory. I'd be at Pat's in less than an hour. This drive would have been my third cross-country trip, but this was the first time I ever drove with something behind me piggyback style. At first, I was very concerned, but after a few hours on the road, I began to relax. It just never ceases to amaze me about all the things that the Lord has brought me through. You see, when my husband and I separated, I did not even know how to fill the gas tank of my car. Since then, I have not only learned to pump gas for myself, I have flown to the other side of the world, stayed in Israel alone, and made three cross-country trips driving alone. The Lord has continuously encouraged me to do the things that are fearful to me. Fear has no hold on me when I do it anyway.

It really is amazing how quickly fear leaves when I have determined this. 1.) I am not alone; the Lord is with me. 2.) Regardless of how fearful I feel, I am going to do it anyway. I have had to come to these resolutions after failing a few times, and allowing reason and its counterpart, "fear" to overtake me. The only exception is when the Holy Spirit cautions or forbids me to proceed. Fear, I have found, is a liar!

I lived with Pat and her two daughters for a little bit over a year. A year of survival. We worked our butts off at a near-by mall for minimum wage. We worked long hours at Christmas time, with little money left over for fun. Because we had each other, we found ourselves laughing at our situation more often than not. Alone, we would have cried!

The Lord Will Make A Way

Earlier, I shared how your gift will make room for you. Well, that is exactly what happened after I lived with Pat for a while — the gifts and talents God imparted made a place for me. I had taken my tambourine with me to a church in the area that was having a conference with other local churches in attendance. During the worship, with a tambourine in hand, I joined the other dancers in the aisles as we worshiped the Lord together. From that experience came an invitation to teach dance at the same little South Chicago church, where we learned of the "gold dust." I spent a season there with a team of lovely women who loved worshiping the Lord through dance movement. We interpreted a dance to Sandy Patti's "We Shall Behold Him." When it was presented to the congregation, it turned out to be a powerful anointed dance. Besides the dancers, on opposite sides of the stage were two women dressed as angels. They were instructed to bow to Jesus with the dancers at a certain point. Everything went well, and all of us felt the presence of the Lord as His Glory descended on the dance team as we worshiped the King.

In the front row was a small child, the daughter of one of the angel actresses on the stage. After the dance, her mother joined her, and she turned to her mother and said, "Mommy, why didn't you bow when the angel bowed down? Her mother answered by saying, "But honey, I did bow when the other angel bowed." Her daughter said, "No, mommy, not that angel...I mean, when that GREAT BIG ANGEL

BOWED DOWN with the dancers. You did not bow down with him!" The Lord had opened the eyes of a little child to reveal to us that we had an angelic visitation that joined us while we danced to "We Shall Behold Him." We shall behold HIM! When this story was relayed to me, I understood why I had been so teary-eyed the morning of the presentation.

After I had lived with Pat for a year or so, I received a phone call from a friend. This friend I had led to the Lord when I lived in Wisconsin. Jeanne was one of my "sellers" when I was selling real estate. She lived in my neighborhood, and we became good friends after she received the Lord. She attended the same fellowship as I did for a while. I had not been in contact with her for several years. When I heard her voice on the other end of the line, I asked her, "How in the world did you ever find me?"

"Well," she said, "It wasn't easy." She explained that she had been trying to locate me for some time. One day when she was in prayer, the Lord spoke to her and told her to find me and send me some money. Now that she had found me, she wanted to know where to send the check. When I hung up the phone, I just stood there in wonderment. The Lord was motivating someone that I had not heard from for years. You just never know where the blessings of the Lord will come from. I had been thinking about finding a place of my own and starting a ministry, but I did not know how I was going to proceed with the limited funds that I had in my possession. When the check for $5,000.00 arrived, my heart stopped! Wow, this would make it possible to do all that was in my heart. The Lord was prompting me to move forward, and HE was providing the means to do so. I was ever so grateful to the Lord and to Jeanne, who was obedient to the voice of the Lord. His ways are far above our understanding.

Life in Old Town

I moved from South Holland, Illinois, to Old Town Chicago. My son Bill, who lived in Chicago at that time, made me aware of a new apartment project provided for 55 and older at affordable prices. I answered their ad, qualified for an apartment, signed a lease for an apartment on the 17th floor with beautiful views overlooking the city. It was especially breathtaking at night with the city lights dancing with activity.

I moved my meager belongings in, excited with anticipation as to what was next on the Lord's calendar. I spent quite a bit of time in prayer and waited and waited for direction from the Lord. He was silent, and I was not used to that. I found a little charismatic Methodist Church just outside of Chicago in Oak Park that I attended. After a time, the denomination was looking for pastors they wanted to place in rural areas. I took courses and filled out paperwork as a candidate, but then the entire thing fell apart. This little charismatic congregation split with the Methodist denomination over a dispute concerning the gifts of the Holy Spirit. I was not privileged to the details, but I would never be happy pastoring a church where the gifts of the Spirit were stifled. Once again, I experienced how our gift will make room for us. When I attended the services at the Oak Park church, I stayed in the back of the church with my tambourine and worship garlands. During worship, I would express myself through the movement of body language as I worshiped and praised the Lord through the dance. One Sunday morning, when I arrived, the Pastor invited me to come forward to the front of the church, where a platform was constructed for worship dance. I was awestruck! This move of God felt like a promotion to me. I was brought from the back of the church to the front. It didn't matter to me that I was behind the congregation. I wasn't dancing for them to see me. I was dancing before the Lord, and He made room for my gift upfront and on center stage.

In addition to attending the Oak Park Church, the church next to my apartment building used the recreation area in our building to have a weekly Bible Study. I participated in that Bible Study. This area was empty most of the time, so I took advantage of the times when nothing was planned and used this place to practice and create new dance movements to interpret my favorite worship music. The Bible Study introduced me to other people in the building that had an interest in spiritual things and the Word of God. It was here that I met one of my neighbors who was planning a wedding. She had seen me dance and had asked me to dance at her wedding. I was honored and accepted her request. What I did not know is where the wedding was going to be held. I had thought perhaps she was getting married at the little church next to us. When the day came for rehearsal, the future bride gave me the address and the time to meet her there. When I arrived at the address, to my surprise, in front of me stood a towering cathedral of magnificent beauty. If these walls could talk, what an astounding history would be told. I felt honored and humbled at the same time to be making a statement of adoration through the dance to the King of Kings in this setting. Only God can open such incredible doors for His children. Who am I that God should choose to favor? I'm just a simple handmaiden, saved by grace!

Around ten years before the worship dance was birthed within me, and while I was still in Wisconsin, our fellowship invited an evangelist from England, Jim Partington, to minister to our group. During his time with us, he prophesied over me, saying that the Lord was going to put me on a stage and make a spectacle of me. At the time this word was given, making a spectacle of me did not sound like a very good thing. Although the word spectacle can have a negative connotation, it can also have a positive meaning. After looking the word up in the dictionary, I discovered it also could mean: "Something that can be seen or viewed, especially something of a remarkable or impressive nature, or a public performance or display, especially one on a large or lavish scale." I pondered this word and kept it in my heart for a decade. Then one day after dancing on a stage or two, a light bulb went off in my head. Indeed, the Lord had put me on a stage and made a spectacle of me! Almost every time I did the worship dance "Language of the Soul," I thought about how the Lord just made a spectacle of me once again.

A New Resident at the Old Folks Home

Here I was with all this education and no outlet, so I decided since there was such insufficient knowledge in the body of Christ about our Jewish roots, that I could introduce pastors to some useful materials. I began selling books written about the scriptures from a Hebrew perspective to pastors all over the country. Blessing these men and women with these materials, and hearing the excitement of their response after reading the books was very fulfilling. The problem was that by the time I paid for the materials and the long-distance phone calls, the small profit was not enough to live on even with the alimony I was receiving.

My daughter Tracey was having some devastating personal issues during this time I lived in Old Town Chicago, and the only solution was for her to move in with me. I knew it would be OK with management for her to stay for a while as a guest. However, I did not see this as the solution for the long haul, even though the Lord was providing miraculously for both of us . Living in an "Old Folks" home, as Tracey called it, was quite a challenge for her. There were no people her age to socialize with; her social life with people around her age was reduced to zero. Yet, she made the most of it and was very outgoing with the residents. I could still see this lifestyle in Chicago was causing discontent for her. Depression had set in and was affecting her physically. I was also concerned for her in other ways as well.

For one thing, she couldn't live in the "Old Folks" home indefinitely. As young as she was, she would not qualify for residency. She would be asked to leave eventually. Or so I thought. However, when I approached management and explained the situation, they made an exception to their rules. This exception was one of those obvious times, where the hand of God's favor was made known to Tracey. Her time with me on Maple Avenue, was a season when my daughter found herself in the "valley of uncertainty." I wanted more for her, and she needed an atmosphere that exhibited life.

One morning when I was in prayer, I heard the Lord very clearly say to me. "I want you to get your daughter a puppy." My first reaction was not good. I could not imagine having a puppy on the 17th floor, and besides, I did not want the responsibility of a puppy, nor the cost that comes with a dog. There would be vet's, bills, and food. I was using my reasoning powers and not trusting the Lord, and that had to stop. "Lord," I said, "I do not have the money to purchase a puppy for Tracey. He replied, "I know. What I want you to do is go to the pet store down the block and tell them that the Lord has sent you. Tell them that I, the Lord, want them to give your daughter a puppy." What? I did not even know that there was a pet store down the block. What I did know was that the Lord had the answer in helping Tracey's sadness. I kept thinking to myself, how am I going to do this task without people thinking I am some whacked-out nut case?

Before I made a fool of myself, I inquired with the management of my apartment complex about getting a puppy for my daughter, who lives with me on the 17th floor. Dogs were allowed in the building, but only at the lower level. I thought for sure that they would say no because of these rules, and that would be my way out. Yes! But no, that was not the case! They said due to the circumstances, they would allow Tracey to have a puppy. I was shocked! I walked away thinking that God had prepared the way, and I better be obedient. So, I headed to the pet store, not caring what they thought of me and my request.

It was December, so I got dressed warm and cozy for my winter walk to the pet store. I did not tell Tracey what I was up to. I arrived with my heart beating profusely in my chest. I approached the counter where the clerk was and said, "Hello, my name is Marjorie, and what I am about to tell you may seem a little strange to you, but this morning while I was in prayer, I heard the voice of the Holy Spirit say, I want you to go to the pet store down the block and tell them that I sent you. The Holy Spirit then said I need to tell you that the Lord wants you to give my daughter a puppy." The gentleman stood there, staring at me for a good long time without saying a word. Then when he finally spoke, he said, "Wait just a minute," and disappeared behind a curtain hanging over a doorway to the back. Shortly, the owner returned and asked me to repeat what I had told the clerk. I did, and the owner looked at me and said, "You know the strangest things have been happening to me ever since I allowed a Bible Study group to use the back room for Bible Study once a week. Let me think about this a minute, and he left by way of the curtain. Next thing I knew, someone was returning with a little male dachshund named Rudy. They told me that Rudy could not find a home because nobody wanted him. Some had tried but always returned him. My daughter could have Rudy. I knew the type of dog Tracey desired through conversations with her. She wanted a young female puppy she could train early and hypoallergenic, so she didn't shed all over. There are about 20 breeds like that, and the pet store did have some. Rudy was an older male puppy and not the breed for her at all.

Now there is a lesson here that we will get into more later, but when giving an offering to the Lord, or when God has chosen you to be a vessel for blessing, you should always give your very best. I bundled Rudy up and headed home to my daughter. I was disappointed because I just knew this was not a fit. This dog lifted his leg and peed on everything marking his territory, had inappropriate male behavior, and was extremely high-strung. There was something seriously wrong with this dog, and just as I had suspected, it was not a good fit. Plus, Rudy shed. Tracey was delighted with the idea of having a puppy. She really tried to love Rudy, but she also had an allergic reaction to him. It was clear Rudy was not meant to be hers. After a day or two, I returned to the pet store with tears in my eyes, and with Rudy. "Unfortunately," I said, "Rudy is not working out," and told them why. The clerk took Rudy from my arms, laughing that nobody wanted Rudy. How sad that they would laugh. Here I am heartbroken and in tears, and they are laughing. I was then told to bring Tracey in, so she could pick from two or three other dogs that they were willing to give her.

In the mean-time, Tracey began to get concerned because of the dog allergy she developed through the years. She noticed some reaction for the short period we had Rudy. So, she inquired of the Lord concerning her allergy to dogs. The last thing she wanted was to get a dog that would make her sick. The Lord revealed to her the reason she had allergies in the first place was due to the anger she still harbored against her brother for giving her dog, Jake, away when we moved. We were moving from our home to a duplex, and my husband had said we could not take our dogs with us. Tracey's brother gave little Jake to his girlfriend without ever asking Tracey if it was alright. Then the Lord told Tracey that she needed to forgive her brother for what he did. My daughter took care of business, and verbally spoke words of forgiveness into the atmosphere. Then the Lord told her to write it down on a piece of paper like a contract and to sign and date it. So, she immediately typed up a document with all the pertinent information, the date of the transaction, what angered her, the fact that she offered her brother forgiveness, and sealed it with her signature. This document is a perfect example of being beyond all reason. This action, by the way, is a legal transaction that takes place in the Courts of Heaven, that silences the accuser and shuts the door to Satan's ability to inflict and harass us because of unforgiveness. To test the results, Tracey and I went to visit a friend of mine whose Chinese Pug just had a litter of pups. Most people with dog allergies only have them with dogs that shed. Tracey got down on the floor with these puppies and had played to her heart's content. She was covered with dog hair from head to foot. Yet, there were no symptoms of allergies. We were praising the Lord that she was free. Unforgiveness is a spiritual weapon that keeps us in bondage, of one kind or another.

    Knowing that she didn't need to worry about dog allergies any longer, Tracey was ready to head to the pet store. I introduced her, and by now, everyone that worked at the pet store knew the reason she was there. We were taken to a room on the side where they brought her a couple of dogs, including a Mexican hairless terrier that looked like a rat with no fur. Again, there was no connection made as my daughter tried to play with these dogs. These dogs were unhappy to see her and were not playful, and these were the only dogs offered to her. They missed their opportunity for a blessing. They wouldn't consider other dogs that Tracey desired, even though they were in the same price range. We left the pet store disappointed, but God was not finished! Help was on its way!

It was around Christmastime, and Tracey had received $500.00 from her grandmother. She heard from the Lord to go back to the pet store and get her puppy but not to spend any more than $250.00. She caught her eye on a little Shih Tzu puppy, which has been her favorite dog since a child. They are a hypoallergenic breed. The price was $500.00, and she could have done her own thing and paid for it, but she was told a certain amount from the Lord. She had to be obedient. She sadly walked away from that puppy. Then the pet store brought out puppies in her price range, but they didn't bond with her, and there wasn't that connection. The dogs she desired were for more money than she was told to spend. Just as we were about to leave, someone came through the door holding a cardboard box with a fluffy cute puppy in it. The puppy was put in a crate among the other crates of puppies for sale. It was a little Lhasa Apso Poodle mix (Lhasa-poo), and Tracey begins to "ooh and ahh." There was no mistake; a connection was made with both Tracey and the puppy. The female puppy was brought out for Tracey to play with, and they bonded instantly. They said that this puppy, they could not give away because she was worth $250.00. I thought to myself, "So were the Mexican Hairless and other dogs like Rudy that were shown to her with inappropriate behavior problems that they wanted to give to her free. They were for $250.00." It didn't matter now. Tracey heard the $250.00 figure loud and clear. This young puppy was the perfect fit. She was also a female and included both mixes of Lhasa Apso and Poodle, which are hypoallergenic breeds that don't shed. Tracey received her heart's desire for being obedient and immediately purchased her puppy, and we headed home.

Unfortunately, to them, it was beyond reason to give her this puppy that was the same price. What made sense to them was to give away any one of the dogs that they had a hard time selling. What they did not realize, in my opinion, is if they had given Tracey the dog she fell in love with, the Lord would have blessed the store owner by multiplying the seed he planted by 30 or even 100-fold. Had the store owner been obedient in giving his best, his reward would be the Lord's best. I have always felt sad for the pet store owner that he missed it. This is a perfect example of the Lord's willingness to bless both Tracey and the store owner, but the human-will got in the way. His greatest problem is working with the "Will" of those He has created.

Thrilled with her new puppy, Tracey decided she wanted the Lord to name her since He had arranged everything, so she asked Him what He would like to call the new puppy. His answer to her was "Sarah." Disappointed in the name, Tracey said, "Lord? That doesn't sound like a dog's name, but more like a child's name. I would name my little girl Sarah, but I really don't like that name for my dog." She heard that still soft, gentle voice say, "OK, then, how about Sadie?" "Yes!" she said, "I like Sadie!" The Lord then told Tracey to look up the meaning of Sadie. Wanting to know what the name Sadie meant since the Lord chose it, she went to a name book to discover the meaning. When she found the name Sadie, rather than giving a meaning, it said: "See Sarah"!! The Lord has such a great sense of humor! We had a good laugh over God having a little fun with Tracey. It was apparent that God was after a meaning of the name, just like how important the meaning of names was in the Bible. Sarah, and Sadie, by the way, means Princess.

This story has a happy ending for Rudy too. The pet store informed us that a little girl fell in love with Rudy, and he found a new permanent home. Sadie, Tracey's little Princess, brought much life to the "Old Folks" home until Tracey was back on her feet and moved to Arizona to begin a new life there. Our little Sadie was a Godsend for sure and brought Tracey back to life.

Then It Happened Again!

I needed to supplement my income, so I answered an ad in the paper for a telemarketer at a mortgage company walking distance from my apartment. I got the job and spent my evenings convincing people to refinance their mortgages. It did not take me long to figure out that I could be a mortgage broker and make a lot more money. I approached my boss, and he was in total agreement. In fact, he said he was waiting for me to draw that conclusion. I went through a brief training and was given leads to pursue. I began making lots more money, but I was unhappy. When I wasn't working, I was praying, "Lord, why has nothing opened up in ministry? Why am I here? Why? Why? What do you want me to do?" I would have done anything that the Lord asked me to do. I would have gone anywhere the Lord asked me to go. I had learned a very expensive lesson from not trusting the Lord with a trip I had planned with the friend I met at CFTN and lived with while working at the Church Dr. Seif was pastoring. Bret and I had made plans to go to India on a mission trip. I had paid for my flight ticket, and the only thing holding me back was "reason." I began to reason, what about this, and what about that? I let the fear of impending circumstances, that never materialized, keep me from an adventure with God. After paying for an airfare ticket I never used, I was determined not to allow reason to get in the way again. Not trusting God with all my "what if's" was a regret that could not be fixed. This was a new day, and I was serious when I told the Lord that I would do whatever HE wanted me to do and that I would go where ever HE wanted me to go. Yet, the Lord was silent, and I did not like it one bit.

I was not looking for a man in my life to be fulfilled. I was focused on the Kingdom. I did not want to get married again. I wanted to be free to come and go as the Lord directed me with no strings attached. Married women have responsibilities that are tied to their husbands, and that's the way it should be when you are in partnership with someone else. I was really enjoying the single life and walking with the Lord. I wasn't praying for material things. I had lived a life of material blessings and found they did not satisfy. I wasn't praying for financial help; I was making a decent living. I was praying for my destiny in the Kingdom of God, and could not understand why I seemed to be at a standstill. Life had been one glorious adventure after another until I moved back to the Midwest. I began to question whether or not I had made a mistake. But, no, looking back, there were too many signposts along the way guiding me. I just needed to be patient and hang on a little longer, I told myself. The Lord had called me, He had equipped me, and He will direct my path.

Time seemed to drag on and on. I walked to work and back again every day. The office that I worked in was right on Michigan Ave. My apartment was on Maple Street, maybe four blocks away. During the nice weather, I would pass the quaint sidewalk cafes on my way to work and again on my way home. It was always the same scene, with different faces. This one day I was so tired of the same old routine, that during my lunch break, I crossed the street, walked the underground tunnel to the beach, sat down on a bench looking out over Lake Michigan. I sat there alone, praying, pleading with the Lord to speak to me, and begging Him to give me some direction. I heard nothing. Disappointed, I returned to work, and the rest of the day seemed to drag by ever so slowly. Finally, it was time to leave, and I just wanted to get home where I could have a good cry. I could tell my emotions had been building up for a couple of days now. Maybe if I had a good cry, I would feel better.

I walked into my building, said hello to the regulars that sat in the lobby talking about all their aches and pains, went and got my mail, waited for the elevator, pushed the button to the 17th floor, exited alone when the elevator doors opened on my floor. I turned the corner, and at the other end of the long hallway, I saw a rather distinguished-looking gentleman dressed in a black suit, locking the door at the apartment that was kitty-corner from mine. It had been vacant. It looks like I have a new neighbor, I thought to myself. THEN IT HAPPENED AGAIN! The same VOICE that had thundered in my car, so many years ago, loudly, thundered again. I could not believe what I heard. "THAT MAN IS YOUR HUSBAND!"

BEYOND ALL REASON: Moving Out of Logic Into the Supernatural

Chapter 22

THE COST OF GLORY

The stories you have just read ends with the Lord introducing me to my husband. He moved to Arizona, and I followed later, and in time we were married. It would require the writing of another book to share the rest of my testimony. The God of Glory continues to amaze me as He reveals Himself to me and requires me to obey Him when it is beyond all reason. Writing this book is an example of doing something beyond all reason. I wrote it because the Lord asked me to do so. Reason tells me that since I am not a well-known public figure, no publishing house would want to publish it. My sphere of influence is minimal, and therefore I thought even self-publishing this book will not reach many. Available on Amazon are two books I have previously written that receive little attention. Yet, I was determined not to let reason talk me out of being obedient to what the Lord had asked me to do, and that is writing the book you have in your hand. Time will tell what the Lord has precisely in store for this book, or who will benefit from it regardless of the Lord's goal; I know what my motivation has been. As I have mentioned in the previous chapters, besides my aim to be obedient, I have shared my encounters with the risen King to encourage you to press into the supernatural realm where the impossible becomes possible. I hope my experiences will help build your faith to believe and trust the Lord for a miraculous rendezvous of glory for yourself. I would be remiss if I didn't tell you that there is a cost to be paid for the privilege of walking in the Glory of the Lord, as I have. The price is the complete surrender to the will of the Lord in every area of our lives. Fortunately, that cost does not need to be paid all at once. Gradually we become living sacrifices as we submit to His bidding. Walking in the glory realm will put a demand upon your life that will challenge your commitment to a Holy God. If you are willing to do what it takes, I guarantee, you will never be the same. Although the sacrifices I have endured have had a hefty price attached to them, the many ways Heaven has rewarded me was worth it.

There is much more available to each of us in the glory realm than we have experienced. I called this last chapter, "A Taste of the Glory," because I have only tasted a bit of the Lord's Glory. Perhaps, I have tasted much more than some, and yet I know that I have tasted much less than others. Other people have experienced much more than I have. Ruth Heflin comes to mind. She has changed her residence from earth to Heaven, but while she was here, she wrote about the "Glory." One of her books was titled GLORY. She defines the "glory realm" as the realm of eternity. With experience, we can recognize the manifestation of the presence of the Lord in our midst, for He is Glory.[24]

Ruth's experiences, and many others like her, cause me to press in for an even greater measure of the "glory realm." In Ruth Heflin's meetings, she tells of the glory being manifested as a cloud descending and rising from the floor to cover her until the people could no longer see her. She said that sometimes the glory comes down in dewdrops, golden drops of rain or as gold dust, like I have experienced. There are other times when a pillar of fire or gray or yellow smoke would show up at her meetings. Ruth teaches that unity in Praise and Worship creates the environment for the manifestation of the glory realm. We must dedicate our lives to the Lord, and praise and worship should be our lifestyle. When it is, the Lord loves to reveal His Glory to us. I have found in my life, five key disciplines that invite Jesus to reveal Himself in various ways. If you incorporate these five mandatory skills into your life, amazing things are bound to happen.

Five Keys Needed to Experience God's Glory

1. The study of His Word is paramount. Setting time aside every day for the study of the Bible is a must. Reading the word is always a good practice, and just three chapters a day and five chapters on Sunday will get you through the Bible in one year. The study of the word, however, is better, and it increases your knowledge of the text.

---

[24] *"Glory,"* Ruth Heflin, page 125

Timothy, says we are to study to be approved.[25] Today we have the internet, and many useful study tools are available for free. There are many ways to study the Bible. We can study chapter by chapter, study by topic, or do a study on one particular word. The entire Bible is a revelation of Jesus, so our study habits will increase our knowledge of our Lord. The diligent study of the Bible will cost you your valuable time.

2. Obedience is next. As we study the Word of God, we must conform our thinking to the living word and obey it, even when it hurts to do so. As we imitate Christ and obey His Word, we will find ourselves separated from the world and the ways of the world. This will result in the loss of friendships and often even family members. Our refusal to sin with them, as we have in the past, will create a chasmic distance. Losing relationships is a cost to be paid to walk in His Glory!

3. Worship. Becoming a worshiper in Spirit and Truth is essential. Jesus told us that the Comforter is the Spirit of Truth and it would be His job to lead us into all Truth.[26] Therefore, I believe in order to worship in Spirit and in Truth, we must receive the gift of the Comforter. Becoming a worshiper is a high call to touch the heart of God. It brings us into His presence where we are changed. The cost of true worship is great, for we must invest much of our time to this

---

[25] 2nd Timothy 2:1

[26] John 15:26 But when the Helper comes, whom I shall send to you from the Father, the Spirit of truth who proceeds from the Father, He will testify of Me.

endeavor. Worshiping once a week at church is not enough. Cultivating personal worship at the throne of the most-high means giving up other things that require our time. As we change in His presence during worship, it will cost us our opinions, our philosophies, and often our dreams. The exchange is the honor of walking in His Glory!

4. Prayer. Pursuing and submitting to God through prayer is foundational. Devoting one's life to prayer is costly because it means giving up large blocks of time in your day or having the Lord wake you in the middle of the night to pray at length. Prayer is a two-way street. We make our petitions known to God, and He makes His requests known to us. Prayer is the place of intimacy with our Savior. Prayer is where we learn to hear the voice of the Lord. Prayer is where we are tested for our obedience to His Rhema word. His request for some obedient act may be very costly. However, to be disobedient could be even more detrimental. A call to pray may require an hour, a day, a week, or a month or more of your time. Commitment to an assignment to pray may require isolation and solitude for days on end. The trade-off is the extraordinary walk with Jesus as He shares His secrets with you and teaches you to bathe in His Glory!

5. Finances. Submitting to this final discipline may be one of the most difficult. It is allowing the Lord to have complete control of our finances. We must learn to release our money to the Lord. This method pleases and enables Him to do whatever he wants to do with our funds. Our giving must be sacrificial. This sacrifice means being

obedient to His direction when He says to give away more than what you might have been thinking. As mentioned in a previous chapter, I emptied my bank account trusting the Lord to provide. You may be asked to do the same. Trusting the Lord with our finances also means obeying when He says not to give anything, which happens as well. Trusting the Lord with our finances goes beyond tithing and offerings. Our thinking must change. We submit all that we have monetarily to His care. Sacrificial giving is allowing God to open doors to the Glory realm that would not be open otherwise.

Implementing these five keys in your life will launch you on a journey into the supernatural realm. The Lord desires to reveal Himself and all His Glory to us. However, not all will see, not all will hear. Only those that have eyes to see and ears to hear will recognize the Lord of Glory when His presence is manifested. All of us live way below the heights that are available to us in the Glory Realm. The Lord's desire is we press into Him to discover all that He has for us.

Let me close the pages of this book with a prayer.

Father God,

I thank and praise you for every person that has read this book. I ask that You will reveal Yourself to each one in some Glorious way. Bring my readers closer to You and shine Your Light into their lives, scattering all darkness. Provide for everyone in supernatural ways that will thrill and delight them. Rescue those bound by logic and reason to trust You for those things You require that are "Beyond All Reason." In the precious name of Jesus, I pray these things. Amen

I desire to experience even "more" of Jesus, and my prayer is that you will want the same. May the weight of His Glory confront, change, and charge you for higher living in Him.

Rev. Marjorie Kummrow

ABOUT THE AUTHOR

Rev. Marjorie Kummrow is the founder of Sweet Manna Ministries committed to educating Christians concerning their Jewish roots. She graduated and was ordained at Christ for the Nations Bible School, where she made Jewish studies her emphasis.

After graduation, she spent a summer in Israel educating herself and ministering to the Jewish people there. Upon returning from Israel, she worked under the leadership of Dr. Jeffrey Seif, who mentored her in Jewish studies at CFTN and DeSoto Community Church in Texas. Rev. Marjorie's education, study in Israel, and scholarly mentors were the rich foundation to launch her Jewish Roots Ministry.

Rev. Marjorie has also been honored by a second ordination in Phoenix, Arizona, under the umbrella of Rev. Barbara DiGilio of Mayim Hayim Ministries. She is currently active under this International teaching ministry exploring the Word of God from a Hebraic perspective. In addition, Rev. Marjorie was asked to be on the teaching staff at GateView Ministries by founder, Dr. Pamala Smith, of Chandler Arizona.

Rev. Marjorie is also the author of *Jesus & Hanukkah*, *What Does Jesus Say About Homosexuality*, and *The Hand of the Lord*. Rev. Marjorie has three children and is presently residing in Glendale Arizona.

BEYOND ALL REASON: Moving Out of Logic Into the Supernatural

BEYOND ALL REASON: Moving Out of Logic Into the Supernatural

www.ingramcontent.com/pod-product-compliance
Lightning Source LLC
Chambersburg PA
CBHW071233290426
44108CB00013B/1399